SHAN HACKETT

by the same author

Suez: The Double War

SHAN HACKETT

THE PURSUIT OF EXACTITUDE

by

ROY FULLICK

LEO COOPER

First published in Great Britain in 2003, reprinted in this format in 2009
Pen & Sword Military
An imprint of
Pen & Sword Books Ltd
47 Church Street
Barnsley
South Yorkshire
S70 2AS

Copyright © Roy Fullick, 2003, 2009

ISBN 978 184415 896 6

The right of Roy Fullick to be identified as Author of this work has been asserted
by him in accordance with the Copyright, Designs and Patents Act 1988.

A CIP catalogue record for this book is
available from the British Library

Printed and bound in England
By CPI

Pen & Sword Books Ltd incorporates the Imprints of Pen & Sword Aviation,
Pen & Sword Family History, Pen & Sword Maritime, Pen & Sword Military,
Wharncliffe Local History,
Pen & Sword Select, Pen & Sword Military Classics, Leo Cooper, Remember
When, Seaforth Publishing and Frontline Publishing

For a complete list of Pen & Sword titles please contact
PEN & SWORD BOOKS LIMITED
47 Church Street, Barnsley, South Yorkshire, S70 2AS, England
E-mail: enquiries@pen-and-sword.co.uk
Website: www.pen-and-sword.co.uk

CONTENTS

Acknowledgments   vii

Introduction   xi

Chapter One
     Antecedents, Australia and the American Connection   1

Chapter Two
     Academe and the Army   14

Chapter Three
     Arabs and Others   30

Chapter Four
     Past Alamein to Airborne   47

Chapter Five
     Airborne to Arnhem   63

Chapter Six
     To the Market Garden   75

Chapter Seven
     The End of 4 Parachute Brigade   99

Chapter Eight
     The Stranger   124

Chapter Nine
    Across the Rivers   153

Chapter Ten
    Down to Earth   164

Chapter Eleven
    The Years of Progression   171

Chapter Twelve
    The Academic   194

Epilogue
    Statement of Account   215

Bibliography   223

Index   225

ACKNOWLEDGMENTS

The first debt of gratitude that must be freely acknowledged is to the subject of this book himself. Shan Hackett's apparent inability to discard or destroy any piece of paper, however trivial its nature might seem, that bore on his life and times and his meticulous assembly of a great mass of material into a comprehensive archive, have provided endless opportunities for tangential and illuminating glimpses into Shan's attitudes and philosophies

The examination of so much primary source material would have been a task daunting to the point of discouragement had it not been for the whole-hearted support and encouragement given by Lady Hackett and her two daughters, Elizabeth and Bridget (Hope). Their willingness to draw unreservedly on vivid recollections of life in the Hackett household and, particularly in Bridget's case, her unfailing abilities in converting a tentative enquiry into the production of just the right collection of documents and photographs, considerably eased the task of attempting to draw a rounded picture of a fascinating man. I am particularly grateful to them as well as to Rex Hackett, the meticulous genealogist of the family, to Sebastian Hope, a grandson and to Isabel Drummond, a cousin.

Other documentary material in the Liddell Hart Centre for Military Archives and elsewhere within King's College, London, was made freely available and I acknowledge fully the help given and patience shown by their staffs to a biographer not always certain of his requirements. The same was true at the Imperial War Museum, whose series of compact discs of interviews with Shan Hackett on his military career was especially valuable in supplementing the printed word with added dimensions of personality and immediacy. The RUSI, the British Army Museum, the Records and Historical Department of the Foreign and Commonwealth Office, Caroline Dalton, the Librarian of New College, Oxford, the Librarian of the Royal Military College of Science at Shrivenham and the Offices of the Home Headquarters of the Queen's

Own Royal Hussars were invariably supportive. Special mention must be made of the Public Record Office at Kew, where the ability of the staff to guide the visitor through an incalculable labyrinth defies credibility.

I am particularly appreciative of the help of those many individuals who had known and worked in peace and war with Shan Hackett during his lifetime. Hearing their strong and highly personal accounts made powerful testimony to the influence he must have had, and continued to have, on their own lives. It would be impossible to list in full all those who spoke so freely and, almost always, so movingly of one they had felt as much a colleague and friend as a commander or superior. Of the other survivors of 4th Parachute Brigade at the Battle of Oosterbeek who related their experiences mention must be made of Geoffrey Powell and John Waddy, both company commanders of 156 Parachute Battalion during the action and both lucid chroniclers of the battle, and of Jasper Booty, the Staff Captain. The contribution of Dr Adrian Groeneweg, director of the Airborne Forces Museum in Arnhem, was of particular value to me. His encyclopaedic knowledge of the battle and of the battlefield brought events vividly to life during a tour that must have followed every footstep taken by Shan Hackett during those few days in 1944 and could hardly have been better condusted by the subject himself. From the Dutch civilians who had direct recollection of the events that had enhulfed their townships I must single out Gerard and Roger Unger, whose Sunday walk as young children with their father was interrupted by the arrival out of the skies of 1st Airborne Division.

Of the later military career, the contributions of the late Field Marshal Lord Carver and of Generals Hugh Beach, Ted Burgess and John Strawson deserve special recognition. I have also been much aided in that portion of his life that Shan spent as Principal of King's College by Doctor Helen Hudson, Miss Mollie Butcher and David Foskett, QC and a graduate of KCL, as well as by Patricia Methven, Chief Librarian of the Liddell Hart Centre and by Kate O'Brien, the Archives Services Manager of King's College London.

Doctor Michael Collins-Persse, past editor of the Corian, (the journal of Geelong Grammar School) and Roger Day, the School's London correspondent, were essential in describing Shan's schooldays and in the depiction of the contributions made by Shan's father, Sir John Winthrop Hackett, to the development of Western Australia.

To my publisher, Brigadier Henry Wilson and my unflappable editor, Tom Hartman, I owe especial thanks for their unfailing guidance and support given at what must have occasionally been unwelcome times in their very busy lives. And finally, (where she would wish to be), to my wife Gay for her characteristic and invariable forbearance throughout it all.

Roy Fullick
London / Gloucestershire / Arnhem / Oosterbeek
2003

INTRODUCTION

The impression, which tended to be an abiding one, made by Shan Hackett was that one was in the presence of the quintessential English gentleman, born and brought up in the Shires. There were those who spent years in his company without ever varying from that estimation and who would not and could not believe it when told that the true story might be otherwise. Small in stature, ruddy in his complexion, with a neat military moustache and always impeccably dressed, whether in uniform as the cavalry officer and the general, in the subfusc of the university college principal or the tweeds of the countryman in his Cotswold mill house ('he would not even come down to breakfast without wearing a tie', as his widow recounted), he radiated a persona that defied any classification other than the one that was obvious to every observer. People found themselves astonished to learn that someone, incontestably a gentleman in every proper sense of that word, was in fact an Australian of Irish descent and Norman ancestry, whose father had emigrated from his native country in his late twenties and who himself had first set foot in England at the age of nineteen to enter university. It may be supposed that his native accent, together with any obvious manifestations of an Antipodean upbringing, became submerged at New College, although Lady Hackett, who was to meet her future husband for the first time some years after he had come down from university and taken his place in his regiment, felt aware of his Australian nature from the very beginning. She, however, had the advantage of a first observation through European rather than English eyes. Be all this as it may, none of it in the slightest way diminished his underlying qualities and personality, of which his exercise during a long and brilliant career of achievement in many fields was to establish him deeply in the respect and affection not only of those who served with him but also of a great number to whom he came only by report and reputation.

It is perhaps by his qualities as a soldier and in particular by his association of his name with the Battle of Arnhem that he first became known to the general public. The times in which he grew up were favourable to a warlike development and brought out in him what had so well been laid down during his formative years in his native country; a competitive sporting instinct, a quick and thoughtful mind with a deep love of scholarship and learning, a strong sense of history and of the lessons that may be drawn from it and, underpinning the whole, a love of language, its roots and origins and the influences that have shaped it into what for him was an exquisite tool in the framework of mankind, the English tongue. He could be fierce with those who used it carelessly and thoughtlessly and would not hesitate to rebuke and to correct, as he would one who showed a lack of respect and proper treatment for the horse on which he was mounted or the mechanisms of whatever task there was to hand. He was to set this down in his *Who's Who* entry, where the encapsulating phrase reads ' The pursuit of exactitude, which some call pedantry'.

He also had the gift of great courage, amply and frequently manifested by his bravery under fire. As an example, his rescue at Arnhem from almost certain death of an officer who would survive to become a post-war Chancellor of the Exchequer had all the hallmarks of a rapid assessment of the situation and instant and effective action that only someone who had no regard for their own safety could have carried out. Shan was one of those rare beings to whom General Wavell's comforting words, which sustained so many lesser mortals during the war, which were always to remember that the enemy was just as frightened as oneself, would have been regarded as an interesting observation of no immediate value. Because he was aware what a finely balanced affair a battle could be, he knew that those who could hang on beyond the point at which the other side had had enough would carry the day. He made much use of his great ability to inspire those around him for whom he was responsible and to raise and maintain their morale so that they were still fighting at the time the enemy had reached his breaking point. The dictum of another great general, Napoleon, that the moral is to the physical as three to one, is one with which Shan would have been in perfect agreement.

The circumstances of war often lead to rapid promotion, particularly on the battlefield, where the disappearance of superior officers may be sudden, unexpected and brutal. Shan's advancement was unusual by the circumstances of the times in that he was given command of a fighting brigade without ever having commanded his regiment, making the leap in command terms over what is normally regarded as the key appointment, one aspired to by every regimental officer and for some the limit of their military ambitions. He did, it is true, hold the rank of lieutenant-colonel for a while before taking on the task of raising and training his parachute brigade, but it was as a staff officer at GHQ Middle East, over-seeing raiding forces.

His brigadier's appointment no doubt was owed to the reputation he had built up first in the Syrian campaign against the Vichy French and then later against the Afrika Korps and the Italians in the Western Desert. It is in some ways curious that someone whose reputation had been made in the conditions of mobile warfare on horse as well as in armoured vehicles should have been given command of troops whose mobility was limited to the capabilities of the marching man. His quali-ties of leadership, his tactical skills and his evident quality as a fighting man would have been the considerations that led him to the command of the elite troops they were amply to prove themselves to be when they found themselves in action.

There is no doubt that the desert war suited Shan's temperament to an even greater extent than had service in peace and war with his cavalry squadron of the Transjordanian Frontier Force. He relished the concept of a war without hate where it was possible to appreciate the qualities of the enemy without in any way diminishing belief in one's own side. The absence in great part of a victimized civilian population, the camaraderie of the commonwealth desert army, the ability to fight in battle without the abandonment of civilized values and common humanity, were the factors that in his mind raised the desert campaigns to levels not found in other theatres of war and unlikely to exist again anywhere in modern warfare. He might well have heard and would have appreciated the true story of the Green Jacket colonel who, moved to reprimand a private rifleman for throwing away an empty bully-beef tin, could say to him without irony that he was always to leave a clean desert.

Shan's sense of common decency and of shared Christian values come through again most strongly during the period that followed his serious wound in the Arnhem battle, the successful medical operation followed by being spirited away from the hospital and German captivity by the Resistance and then by the long hard winter in hiding in the care of a courageous Dutch family. The unassuming self-sacrifice of these ordi-nary yet exceptional people, in danger of the most savage reprisals were their charge to be discovered, made a profound impression on him that was to last, along with an overwhelming sense of gratitude, undiminished to the end of his life.

Shan's postwar career was one of advancement, up to but without quite achieving the highest rank in his profession. The tag of being too clever by half can be a damning one in English public life; Shan never took pains to conceal the depth and breadth of his scholarship and what a minister was later to describe as 'gratuitous acts of intellectual superiority' could, and did, grate on colleagues whether superior or subordinate. The fact is that he was a highly educated and well-read man, a fluent and prolific writer, proficient in several languages other than his own, with a beautiful speaking voice and able to speak extempore in fully-formed paragraphs and completely conscious in his own mind of his possession of all those gifts. In reality the great majority of his relationships both personal and professional were harmonious, productive and were recollected in warmth on both sides, although it was still a source of discomfort to be the object of his displeasure.

His memorial service at St Martin-in-the-Fields in November 1997 gave solid evidence of the place he held in the hearts of those who had known him. Among the great assembly of luminaries in the church were substantial numbers of more ordinary people who would not necessarily have been close to him, junior NCOs and private soldiers from units under his command, ex-students from King's College London, who had travelled at their own expense, some considerable distances, to show their feelings for a commander in whom they had felt able to place their trust.

Shan's pace barely slackened in his later years. Whether writing, lecturing, counselling and giving advice and help, keeping his sixteen acres of the Cotswolds productive in the company of his beloved family, or fishing with Margaret, a devoted and much-loved companion to the end of his days, he did not go gentle in that good night.

This, then, is the story of Shan Hackett, a remarkable soldier, academic and human being.

RFF
London, 2003

Chapter One

ANTECEDENTS, AUSTRALIA AND THE AMERICAN CONNECTION

The history of the Hackett family is intertwined with that of Ireland from the time of the Norman invasion of the country in 1170, one William Haket forming part of the expeditionary force that sailed in August of that year under Richard "Strongbow" de Clare, Earl of Pembroke. It may be inferred that the Hakets were Normans who, following the success of William of Normandy, the first King William of England, at Hastings in 1066, had taken part in the occupation and colonization of the south western part of Wales, this being the base from which the invasion of Ireland was launched and which is known to this day as 'Little England beyond Wales'.

As in England and in Wales after their Norman occupations, the victorious in Ireland were rewarded with greater or lesser grants of land, with feudal rights over the indigenous peoples of the territory. The Hakets [the unreliability of early spelling and the uncertainties of the development of patronymics being what it is, the present-day "Hackett" will be used from here on to refer to all descendants of the original invader] were given lands on the eastern side of what is now the County of Tipperary, in and around the towns of Fethard and Rathmacarthy.

The first directly traceable ancestor is a Sir John Hackett, Knight, of Rathmacarthy, who is believed to have lived around the year 1300. He had two sons whose names have not been recorded and of whom the younger inherited the Fethard properties, becoming the head of the branch that led to our Sir John Hackett. The tomb of Edmund Hackett, which recorded his 'pious death' together with that of his wife Anne on 27 July 1508, was certainly still to be found in the church at Fethard up to the outbreak of the first World War but it is not certain that it has

1

survived the changes that followed during the remainder of the twentieth century.

The family, as pre-Cromwellian Irish landed gentry, played its part in the twists and turns of their country's history. There were bishops and archbishops bearing their name in the early Catholic church. They lived through and came to terms with the Reformation and a Sir Thomas Hackett was Lord Mayor of Dublin in 1688, the year of the Glorious Revolution in England and of considerable turmoil in Ireland.

Through marriage over the centuries, they established connections with the Pakenham-Walshes and the Winthrops, the ancestors of the latter family being prominent in the young American colonies, father and son becoming respectively Governors of Massachusetts and of Connecticut and whose descendants remain influential in the United States and particularly New England to this day. The Winthrop connection was established by Shan Hackett's great-grandfather, a serving officer of the 8th Light Dragoons, the regiment which as the 8th King's Royal Irish Hussars, as it had become, he, Shan, was in turn to join and to serve in with great distinction.

John Winthrop Hackett, Shan's father, was born in 1847, one of the eight children of the Reverend John Winthrop Hackett, rector of St James's Church at Bray, County Wicklow, and his wife Jane, who came from the distinguished family of Monck-Mason. He was the third-born and the eldest boy of three sons and five daughters, one of the girls, Jane, being John's twin. All three boys had distinguished academic careers and, additionally, John seems to have been a good athlete, have a fine speaking voice and be fond of speech-making. To his father's disappointment, he decided not to go into the Church, although both his brothers were to, Thomas, the younger, succeeding his father at St James's and Henry becoming Dean of Waterford.

John Winthrop gained his BA at Trinity College, Dublin, in 1871 and was called to the English and Irish Bars in 1874. Despite his athletic prowess, he seems not to have been an altogether fit man and was prone to catch cold easily. The death of John's twin-sister from tuberculosis at the age of fourteen may also have given cause for concern about his health. A great friend, Alexander Leeper, had already made one visit to Australia and had been most impressed with the potential of the young country. Leeper had decided to return to Australia and proposed to John Hackett that they should go together to the new land, where two intelligent young men might make successful careers for themselves as well, perhaps, as their fortunes. There was an extra incentive for Leeper, who was of a delicate state of health, in the likelihood that the climate of Australia would prove more beneficial to him than the rain and low-lying mist and fog of his native country. This consideration was put to John Winthrop as well and Leeper's enthusiastic persuasion and the picture he drew from his recent and direct experience soon removed any doubts that John Winthrop might have held. The family were persuaded of the soundness of the proposal and accordingly, in 1875, at the age of twenty-eight, JWH set sail with Alexander Leeper in the sailing ship *Hampshire* for the other side of the world. They went first to Sydney, where John Winthrop was called to the Australian Bar but here he found the weather, although vastly different from that of Ireland, still not entirely favourable to his health. The following year he moved south to Melbourne, where he was appointed sub-Warden of Trinity College at the University and lectured in Law, Political Economy and English. The academic life was not sufficient to satisfy this determined and ambitious man and he began to think seriously that his future might lie in the developing territories some two thousand miles away on the far side of Australia. With the matter of his health never far from his mind, he might well have been influenced in his deliberations by talk of the cooling breeze, known as the Fremantle doctor, that blew in from the sea with unvarying regularity each afternoon. Whatever weight this carried, in 1882, at the age of thirty-five, John Winthrop made the decision that his future lay in Western Australia, where he next went and where he was to build a remarkable career and accumulate considerable wealth as a newspaper publisher. He had the great good fortune to be befriended soon after he arrived there by the Reverend Charles Harper, who offered John Winthrop a position as sub-editor on the West Australian newspaper of which the Harper family were the proprietors. Western Australia was, at the time of John Winthrop's arrival in 1882, in an accelerating stage of development. The British Government began to take a serious interest in the territory in 1826 when it became concerned about French colonial ambitions in the area. A programme of colonization was put in train and, as elsewhere on the sub-continent, soldiers and transported convicts formed the nucleus of the first communities. Surveying began and proposals were made for settlements to be established in the region of the Swan River. These efforts made a faltering start; labour was in too short supply to work the vast tracts of land open to development and so until 1868 the workforce continued to be augmented by the transportation of convicts. Despite the mineral and agricultural possibilities of the territory, the population of the whole of Western Australia at the time of John Winthrop's arrival was not much over 40,000 and it was not until immigration was stimulated by, in particular, the discovery of gold that numbers started to increase sharply so that by 1910, the year of Shan's birth, they had reached 275,000.

The economic development that sustained this population growth was to provide the perfect backdrop for the intelligent, shrewd and ambitious John Winthrop. He quickly perceived, as many others before and since, that one sure way to power and influence in a young territory of enormous potential was through the press. From his first appointment in 1882 as a sub-editor of the *West Australian*, his progress was rapid, becoming a partner in 1883 and editor in 1887. By 1912 he was the sole proprietor of both that paper and of the *Western Mail* and had become an extremely rich man. This success was not achieved without serious differences with his original benefactor. The first arose when the Reverend Harper's second son, Prescott, a Rhodes scholar, returned to Perth from Oxford and John Winthrop was instrumental in denying the young man the partnership in the newspaper that his family felt was his natural right.

John Winthrop chose his alliances skilfully. Early on in Perth he became a close friend of a man of his own age, John Forrest, the able and ambitious son of penniless immigrants, who had explored much of Western Australia as its Surveyor-General. Much of Forrest's growing wealth derived from the gold discoveries that his own survey work had helped to reveal and when his attention turned to politics he found a willing and powerful ally in the newspaperman. Between them, they led the drive towards self-government for the territory, which was achieved in 1890, with Forrest as the first premier of Western Australia. From there their energies were directed toward the greater goal of Commonwealth status for Australia; both went on to become members of the national convention that in the years 1897–98 drew up the commonwealth constitution. It was said of the two of them that it was Hackett who had the subtle brain and Forrest the commanding will. John Forrest was later the first native-born Australian to be raised to the peerage while John Winthrop, after two unsuccessful attempts to enter the Commonwealth Parliament in the Liberal interest, confined himself more to his own power-base at the western end of the continent and remained a member of the Legislative Council (upper house) of Western Australia for twenty-six years. He was knighted in 1911.

During all this active and productive time John Winthrop remained a bachelor and his half-century came and went. He seems to have been a good employer and was the first in Australia to introduce the eight-hour working day. He used the power of his newspapers to further the causes of economic development, of the federation of Australia and, again ahead of his time, female suffrage. What he lacked was a wife and a family that might inherit his energies and abilities and make their own contribution to his adopted country.

4

Another prominent family of Western Australia was that of Drake-Brockman, whose head, like John Forrest before him, had been the Surveyor-General of the territory. When Frederick Drake-Brockman, nine years younger than John Winthrop, found himself in 1905 the intended father-in-law of the older man, it was a situation by no means to his liking. His daughter Deborah being only seventeen at the time the proposal was made, his resistance was fierce and determined and was buttressed by the Harpers, for many years close friends of the Drake-Brockmans and equally disapproving. The Harpers' opposition was the second instance of difficult relations between them and John Winthrop. Although Deborah's mother had herself been only twenty at the time of her marriage, the age difference with her husband was merely three years and not the almost forty years seniority which John Winthrop was proposing to bring with him. Here again his choice was shrewd. Deborah Drake-Brockman was a remarkable daughter of a remarkable mother, Grace (Bussell) Drake-Brockman, who had been born into one of the earliest pioneer families of Western Australia and who in 1829 created the settlement of Busselton. When she was sixteen, Grace was riding with a young native servant along the beach near her home when they saw a sailing vessel, the *Georgette*, in difficulties and being driven ashore in heavy surf. Without hesitation, the two rode into the water and were successful in conducting the whole of the ship's company to safety on dry land. This brave action earned her the gold medal of the Royal Humane Society and the gift of a watch and chain from the British Government and she was known for the rest of her life as the 'Grace Darling of Australia'. Her daughter Deborah lacked none of the determination of her mother. As far as she was concerned, John Winthrop would become her husband, whatever her parents' view might be and however strong their opposition. They were married in 1905, in the Busselton church built by her grandfather with his own hands and where the weddings of both her mother and her grandmother had taken place.

The ceremony was described in the contemporary newspaper report as quiet. There is the inference that invitations to the ceremony and the reception that followed (held not in the bride's home but at the Esplanade Hotel) had been restricted to relations and close friends. Certainly Sir John Forrest, the bridegroom's close political and business ally, was, for whatever reason, not able to attend and a fulsome message of good wishes from him was read out by John Winthrop during his reply to the toast of the bride and groom.

Whatever the misgivings might have been of the bride's parents and however potentially damaging the very considerable age difference between the partners might have been to the achievement of a successful

5

and fruitful marriage, the auguries for any future offspring were good. From the mother's side would come qualities of proven ancestral courage, great determination and strength of will and a preparedness to flout convention and overturn received wisdom. This she had demonstrated not only in overcoming opposition to her marriage to an older man but earlier, in her formal education, which had been conducted in a boys' school. From the father would come the benefits of a highly educated brain, a deductive mind, sound political and commercial judgment and an unbroken track record of success along his chosen path through life. As would have been usual in any newly-married couple at the time, children were not long in arriving. By the time Shan was born in 1910, three sisters had preceded him, Verna, Patricia and Joanna. The arrival of a boy after a sequence of three girls was greeted, according to family lore, 'with such joy that the church bells were rung'. Whether this literally happened is not recorded. In 1913 another sister Debbie, the final member of the family and almost certainly conceived in the hope of producing a brother for Shan, was born when her father was sixty-six years of age.

Shan was not yet six when his father died, acknowledged as having been a great contributor and benefactor to the State of Western Australia. He played principal parts in the foundation of the University of Western Australia, in the building of Perth Cathedral, in the setting up of Perth Zoo and even in the planting of cherry trees to beautify the city. The greater part of his large fortune was left not to his family but went to support those institutions he had helped to found and become established. His only son never expressed the slightest resentment at his father's action but approved strongly of wealth accumulated in Western Australia being returned to it to help the advance and development of the State. Shan was later to say that he was happy not to have been left great sums as that might have encouraged him to lead an idle life.

The Australian society into which Shan was born, while modelling itself to a large extent on the late-Victorian and Edwardian society of the United Kingdom and particularly on the dominant English part of it, nevertheless had very much its own conception of the ways in which the new country would develop. In a number of these John Winthrop played a leading role as a believer in universal suffrage, in strong State and Federal structures backed by sound constitutions and in the continued economic development of his own Western Australia. The way of life of the successful was on the opulent side of comfortable; they built large mansions for what were invariably large families, continuing right up until 1914, as in England, to assume that a supply of servants to maintain and to run these great establishments would be as constant as the

6

rising and setting of the sun. So, too, a family of a size able to carry on the development of the seemingly limitless potential of the country, while maintaining and increasing its own wealth and standing was the norm. In the expression of the time, parents were expected to produce 'a quiver-full'. Shan had four sisters, but, as we know, no brothers, while his mother was one of seven Drake-Brockman children, of whom four were boys. As an expression of the responsibility they bore towards the privileged situation they had been born into, children were expected to excel, both academically and physically, and the circumstances to support these aims progressively came about. Schools with very high teaching standards were set up and flourished, while the climate and large family properties encouraged an active outdoor life.

Australian society very much took its example from England as the mother-country and modelled its life styles as closely as possible upon English practices. The recent origins of Australian family fortunes, their almost invariably humble beginnings and the absence from society of previous generations of aristocracy and squirearchy whose manners had to be aped and aspired to, meant that children tended to grow up with the same high ambitions as their fathers and grandfathers and to bring equal levels of energy and drive in achieving them. An indolent class of sons of nouveau-riche parents, anxious to be seen as gentlemen rather than as hard-working sons of successful men, seems not to have taken root in the new land of Australia.

If geography and circumstance helped protect Australian society from the risks of contagion from some aspects of English decadence, it did not diminish its admiration for the facts of imperial power and imperial achievement. Around the turn of the century, as the long Victorian age was replaced by the Edwardian, the British Empire was at its height, its dominion over a great part of the globe apparently unchallengeable, its rule, at least in its own eyes, enlightened and progressive, its industrial might only just beginning to be overtaken by others. The bright focus of this great power, the source from which it all appeared to spring, was the Imperial Court and it was on this Court that the wealthy and aspiring Australian family turned a fascinated attention. When knighthoods, baronetcies and peerages began to be bestowed on prominent and important Australians, there were some individuals who staunchly refused to be considered for them on the principle that such things did not belong in a new country, in control of its own affairs and making brisk progress towards developing its own strong political structures. It was, however, rare to find a mother whose dearest wish was not to see her daughters presented at Court and taking part in a London season, whatever the expense of the enterprise and the tedium of the long sea voyage that had to be undertaken to achieve it. There was also, more often than not, the discomfort of being regarded as coarse colonials by certain of the English society in whose company they might find themselves during the adventure of their English season. A contemporary account speaks both of the welcoming smile on the lovely but lacquered face of Queen Alexandra and of the boredom on the face of King Edward the Seventh as the line of young ladies moved forward to their presentation, a boredom relieved only by the arrival before him of a particularly striking or beautiful example of womanhood.

The effect of the snubs and boorish behaviour, of which many Australians were the victims, was to build in them a desire to compete and to show the Motherland of what the young country was capable. Lineage, long tradition and established social customs they might be without, but what they did have were great physical and material resources and the determination to exploit them, in sport as well as in commerce. The Hacketts were, perhaps, less susceptible than some others to the risk of slight. John Winthrop's long Irish lineage was documented and unchallengeable, while his wife's family, the Drake-Brockmans, could without question be described as belonging firmly in the upper classes of Australian society.

Shan's mother was presented at Court in 1910, the year of Shan's birth, when she must already have been pregnant with her only son. There was a return to London during the following year, when John Winthrop was invested with his knighthood. Shan was born into a confident and successful family, certain of its place in the establishment, with the father exercising great and enlightened influence at the heart of the developing constitutional scene and the mother, dynamic, enquiring, entrepreneurial and still, as a mother of four children, only twenty-three years old and with a great deal left to achieve during what was to be a long lifetime. It must have been with justifiable optimism that the Hackett family in 1910 contemplated what seemed an expanding future in a settled and organized world, the outbreak of the Great War still four years away and not contemplated.

With such parents and with such a background, the outlook for the young Shan was propitious in the extreme. An only son with three older sisters, endowed with qualities of great potential and surrounded with every incentive to succeed at whatever he took up, there must have been a feeling of predestination about the course of his life. When he was two, one of his father's most cherished projects came to fruition with the founding of the University of West Australia, John Winthrop being appointed as its first Chancellor. Before Shan was four years old, the Great War that was to destroy the *Pax Britannica* broke out, changing the face of Europe for ever and altering the future direction of the whole world. The response of the Australian people was one of intense loyalty towards and enthusiastic support for the Mother Country, as it had been at the time of the Boer War of 1899, when a considerable force of mounted troops took part in military operations in South Africa, using their skills in horsemanship with great dash and daring, earning from among their number no fewer than six Victoria Crosses. During the decade that followed great efforts were made to build up a strong and well-trained defence force. The build-up of a large volunteer militia was begun, supported and reinforced by the introduction in 1908 of compulsory military training for all males between the ages of 12 and 26 and requiring the setting-up of cadet corps in schools that had not already, on their own initiative, formed their own. The result was that by 1914 a national militia with a total strength of 230,000 men of all ranks was in place as the raw material from which volunteers could be drawn to form an overseas expeditionary force that could go to the aid of the imperial power. The scale of the Australian contribution to the Allied cause was staggering; by the time the Armistice came some 330,000 had volunteered, of whom two-thirds had become casualties, 60,000 of them killed.

An event much closer to home was to have substantial effect on the future course of Shan's life. The death of his father before his sixth birthday removed a powerful influence from the developing awareness of a young and impressionable child that, and the circumstance of a boy growing up in the wake of three older sisters taken together, was perhaps the root of what was to be one of Shan's determining characteristics, the belief that he was the principal architect of his own fate, that, in his own later words, it was he who should become accustomed to determining the course of his own life.

Within two years his 'beautiful and beloved widowed mother' was married again, to Frank Moulden, a successful Adelaide barrister, later Sir Frank and Lord Mayor of the city. The whole Hackett family, all five children, moved with their mother to the large Moulden house in North Adelaide, where it was decided that the young man's formal education should begin. A pre-preparatory school was chosen, presided over by a headmaster whose name, with the aid of very little alteration, could be pronounced as Whack'em Good. Shan's view in much later life was that the disciplinary practices at his first school, while occasionally painful, never otherwise did him the slightest harm.

Shan came to love his new stepfather whom he saw as a good man, with whom his mother had found happiness and her family security and great well-being. Frank Moulden's situation meant that they were all at the centre of the social life of South Australia. When, during his Commonwealth tour just after the First World War, the then Prince of Wales arrived in Adelaide, the Mouldens gave up their house to help provide accommodation for the Royal entourage, acting as the host and hostess of Lord Louis Mountbatten and his party. Shan's schoolboy memories of his first meeting with Royalty and its circle were, 'What a very nice lot of people they all turned out to be'. He recalled being shown later what he described as the longest bread-and-butter letter he ever saw in his whole life, written in the most effusive tones to his mother by the Prince of Wales' cousin, the principal guest in their house.

Soon after his tenth birthday it was time for the young Shan to be sent away to boarding school. For someone who was already giving clear signs of his considerable learning abilities, the choice was an easy one. Geelong Grammar School in Melbourne, established over forty-five years earlier, had gained a glowing reputation with its high standards and a long and outstanding record of academic and sporting achievement. Accordingly, Shan was entered into the Junior House for the first term of 1921, making the five-hundred-mile journey alone by sleeper from Adelaide to Melbourne and, not being expected at the school so early, spending the day exploring the unfamiliar city. Almost from the moment he set foot in his new school, Shan sensed that he had arrived in a place that would be of immense importance to him and the eight years he spent at Geelong, formative years, as he himself described them, were happy and productive. Formative they certainly were, in laying the foundations and building the first storey of his life-long passion for language and for the origins, derivations, meanings and usages of both the spoken and the written word.

He was fortunate in his first master in the Junior House. R.V.Jennings was a man of charm and humanity, who was skilful in nurturing the burgeoning interests of his pre-teen charges. It was a time when people all over the world were becoming aware of the miracle of wireless telegraphy and, to the young particularly, the feeling of being in unseen contact with strangers many miles, perhaps even continents, away, was an excitement of altogether other proportions. Upwards of a dozen of the sixty-odd pupils in the Junior House had caught the wireless bug and, as part of his work of encouragement of the young, the Housemaster had set aside a room in which a number of the primitive receivers (which were all that were generally available at the time) were set up. Shan was one of those who found an enormous fascination with the mysterious inter-action of cats' whisker and crystal and, with earphones clamped to his head, he listened enthralled to the rapid messages in morse code which patient manipulation of the wireless receiver could capture. Self-taught, he gained enough knowledge of the dots and dashes to be able to distinguish the call-signs by which transmitters in the different Australian States identified themselves, but, to his lasting regret, reading the messages themselves was always beyond him.

Water-colour painting was another of the young Shan's interests that he was to practice from his first days at Geelong. Academically, his early leanings were on the science side, with a bias towards chemistry and, with the habit of the young in drawing up a whole life's ambition with precocious certainty, he thought that when he grew up he would be a biochemist. This to him, as he made steady progress up the learning curve in his favourite subjects, seemed in his view to bring together the value of sound scientific knowledge with an appreciation of humanity and its problems. He was to be drawn away from this path and, who knows, perhaps for someone of the level of ability he was plainly beginning to show an eventual Nobel Prize, by a growing interest in history. It was mediaeval history and especially the mediaeval history of England that drew his attention and in even the limited contents of his House library there was enough to set him along a new path. By this time he had moved on at the age of fourteen to Cuthbertson House, one of the three senior houses, and he was beginning to give some thought as to what his academic career might be after Geelong. It was supposed that the more scholarly would go on to university, which to the comfortably-off pupils of Geelong meant either Oxford or Cambridge. There was plenty of information, either printed or anecdotal, about what was expected in an Oxbridge undergraduate and Shan saw that his increasing interest in history would have to be buttressed by a sound knowledge of classical and modern languages, building on such Greek and Latin as he had managed to acquire. Having come to a decision on his future direction, it was by an unfortunate coincidence that at about the same time the classics master at Geelong, Mr Barber, should have been enticed away by the offer of an academic post of greater importance in his eyes than the one he then had. This left the school without a classical specialist at a crucial point for Shan but this problem was solved by sending him on regular weekly visits to the girls' grammar school nearby, where a highly qualified lady teacher gave him lessons in Greek.

There were other excitements and distractions for the fourteen-year-old. What is traditionally the stuff of schoolboy dreams did in fact come about when Shan and his eighty fellow-pupils in Cuthbertson were mustered for a roll-call on the house cricket ground to watch the ineffectual efforts of the fire services to prevent the burning-down of their house. Again in the manner of the young, he formed an extremely deep friendship with one particular member of his house, D. M. Sullivan, known as 'Pump' Sullivan. This close relationship continued for the whole of Shan's remaining time at Geelong but faded away as soon as they went their separate ways on leaving school. Another aspect of Geelong life that appealed greatly to Shan was the regular Saturday excursion when groups, usually of two or three boys, were given picnics and allowed to make a bicycle expedition for the whole day into the countryside. On these occasions 'Pump' was an invariable member of Shan's party.

An essential element of the public school ethos was the need to take part enthusiastically in sport and to strain every sinew to excel in it. Shan, as a member of his House cricket side, became a useful spin bowler but his greatest success was in football by Australian rules, where he played on the wing for the School XVIII. In his last year he was also school champion at fives. Academically, he enjoyed considerable success, winning scholarships and regularly being in the lists of school prize winners in history and in classical and modern languages, culminating in being given in 1927 the major prize for the best all-round scholar at matriculation level. He was also active in a wide spectrum of school life; as Curator of the Geelong Grammar School museum, as a member of the committee of the *Corian*, the school magazine and, an augury of things to come, as secretary of the Literary and Debating Society.

All in all, Shan found Geelong, set in one hundred acres of beautiful country on the shores of Coria Bay, an enchanted place where he was extremely happy for the whole of his time there. He seems to have been fortunate in being in the care of civilized and enlightened masters who unlocked his considerable latent intellectual powers and gave him solid educational foundations on which he would go on to build so effectively and so rewardingly.

A few months after leaving Geelong at the age of eighteen Shan was required to give an address at the laying of the foundation stone of Hackett Hall, another of his father's legacies, at the University of Western Australia. Piously, he chose to speak as if he were standing in for an unavoidably absent father and, in describing John Winthrop's attitude toward learning, succeeded in defining his own philosophies. He quoted some of the words used by Socrates in his defence when on trial for his life: 'A life without enquiry is not worth living'. To Shan, enquiry meant intellectual curiosity, which to him was the source of all real progress and a proper way for human civilization to develop. He saw the intentions behind his father's philanthropy and his different legacies as being to give to many others, through future generations, the means to satisfy their own intellectual curiosity and to apply the findings during their lives' work. This Shan felt to be his own duty too.

It was now 1929. His secondary schooling over, it was time for Shan to move on. Confident in his ability to use the formidable tools with which he had been endowed, he set sail from Fremantle for Europe in the company of his stepfather, Sir Frank Moulden.

Chapter Two

ACADEME AND THE ARMY

Before embarking with his stepfather on one of the P&O liners that maintained a regular connection between Australia and the United Kingdom (although 'England' was the term that most Australians would use), Shan paid a visit to the Zoo in Perth. The endowment of the Zoo was one of the many benefactions his father, John Winthrop, had made to the city where he had built his considerable fortune and the Director, conscious of the standing of his young visitor, invited him to choose something from the collection of fauna to take to England for the London Zoo. Shan was much taken with the idea of asking for one of the young lion cubs that the Zoo had recently acquired, but, since they had already been weaned and were on a diet of raw meat, one of them was not thought to be a suitable companion for a long sea voyage. A much more practicable choice was a baby snake, an anaconda that might eventually grow to a length of fifteen feet, but, being at this time only twelve inches long, could travel in a shoe-box beneath Shan's bunk. This indeed it did, fed through an eye-dropper with the milk that came daily to the cabin with his morning tea.

When much younger Shan had for a while sung in the church choir and had gained an easy familiarity with Hymns Ancient and Modern. As the ship approached Ceylon, by one of those curious quirks of memory, some lines came uninvited into his head. The mischievous thought struck him that he might test how far his fellow-passengers could match his pious knowledge and so he asked his steward, with whom by now he was on close terms, whether he could procure a packet of powdered spice. This acquired, Shan spread it liberally one morning on the promenade deck, in the hope that its aroma would be noticed by passengers taking their daily constitutional and that they would be irresistibly reminded of the words: 'What though the spicy breezes blow soft o'er Ceylon's isle, where every prospect pleases and only man is vile'. Alas, the experiment was futile. Not one person appeared to notice anything unusual and no one questioned why there should be a smell of spice in

14

the air; certainly no one, as they passed to and fro by the attentive Shan, could be detected quoting, however *sotto voce*, the lines he was waiting to hear. Not for either the first or last time in his life, his fellow man failed to match Shan's expectations.

It was now that Shan was to have his first direct acquaintance with a part of the world that would become important for his future and, in time, decisively mould the man and lay the foundations of the great reputation as a soldier he was to gain. When the ship arrived at Suez it was announced that arrangements had been made for those passengers who wished to see something of Egypt to disembark, be taken to Cairo and to re-embark at Port Said the following day, after their vessel had completed the transit of the Suez Canal. While at Geelong, Shan had read Graves' *Lawrence and the Arabs* as well as *Revolt in the Desert*, Lawrence's own abridgement of *Seven Pillars of Wisdom*, and had felt the first stirrings of an interest in the Arab world. The impression that Lawrence's book made upon him may be judged from the recollection, which stayed with him into old age, of it being the first book he read straight through twice. It had never been difficult for the educated Englishman to develop positive feelings of Arabism and, despite the Arab awakening in the post-1945 world and the development with it of an increasing Muslim fundamentalism, it is something that for a long time existed in the English character and consciousness and perhaps still does to this day. There are those who would say that anyone who had endured the English public school system might have found himself sympathetically drawn to the way of life of the desert Arab and the parallels with his schooldays that could be drawn from it. Be that as it may, Shan in his turn was no less susceptible to the romance of the Near East than anyone else of his age and background and it was with great excitement during his brief time ashore that he experienced the sights and sounds and unforgettable odours of the Egyptian capital. By the time he climbed up the gangplank to go back on board he knew instinctively that sooner or later, he would be back in the that part of the world with a part to play in it.

Sir Frank Moulden and his stepson were to leave the ship at Marseilles, a port by that time only a day or two away. Whether or not the prescient snake felt the approach of this event or whether the frequent daily movements of the shoebox from under the bunk had split the container's seams, when feeding time came, the reptile had gone. Neither Shan nor the steward could trace it anywhere in the cabin and nor were sightings made elsewhere on board; Shan afterwards had fantasies of his pet, by then grown to full maturity, furtively jumping ship by way of the mooring lines on some sultry evening in a tropic port.

15

On disembarking, the two were met by Shan's sister Joanna, then an undergraduate at Grenoble University, who, after their short reunion, saw them off to Paris at the Marseilles railway station. The men had an agreeable stay in the capital, made memorable for Shan by the evening they spent together at the Café de Paris. Here one of the hostesses tried to create an interest not in her own charms but in those of her companion. 'You cannot say that you have really seen Paris, if you leave without sleeping with my friend.' Shan was able to resist the temptation.

Once arrived in London, they stayed in Shan's mother's flat in Ashley Gardens, a place intended as much as anything else for the use of any of his sisters who found themselves, for whatever reason, having to spend time in London. His eldest sister Verna, studying medicine at the Westminster Hospital, had lived there until she met and married one of the registrars, an up-and-coming young surgeon called Wallis Kendall. The second sister, Patricia, reading for the bar, was installed there when they arrived and they moved in with her. Shan enthusiastically started at once to explore the possibilities of the imperial capital, one of his first outings being to Covent Garden to see the Diaghilev Russian Ballet dance *Petrouchka*.

Some inklings of the shape and pattern of his future life were beginning to form within Shan's mind. His father, over sixty when his only son was born, was by now a fairly distant childhood memory; he had a great affection for his stepfather and admiration for his mother's independence of action in her business career and the spirit and energy with which she engaged in it. All the influences that surrounded him tended to develop in him a strongly individual attitude to life, to reinforce in him his earlier conviction that he himself had prime responsibility for the major decisions that would set the course he would follow in the future. He had at one time toyed with the idea of going to Trinity College Dublin, the old college of many of his forebears, but the independent and strongly Roman Catholic Irish state that was now in place had brought about considerable change to the social and political climate of sixty years before, when his father had been up. The Hackett family background was firmly Protestant and for him to attempt to study in Dublin, even if it were his own true ancestral country, was probably unwise.

A strong connection had grown up between Geelong Grammar School and Winchester College in England and it had become something of a practice for a number of Geelong boys to spend the senior years of their secondary education at the English school. Shan's family had chosen not to do this, but as someone in the top flight at Geelong, when the time came to look for somewhere suitable for his university education, New College, Oxford, with its long association with Winchester, was an

16

obvious choice. They were approached and in February 1929 Shan was offered, subject to matriculation, a place at New College for the Michaelmas term of that same year. The offer was readily accepted and it was with this purpose that Shan and his stepfather had set off together for England.

Arrived and installed by early summer, there was ample time before going up to Oxford for Shan to make a few exploratory wanderings down paths that excited his curiosity. One of these was the thought that one day he might make a career as a painter, but a short period he spent during those months at the Central School of Arts and Crafts in London was enough to convince him that his destiny did not lie in that direction. That time was not, however, wasted. It gave him a lifelong amateur's pleasure in the creative act of painting and to the end of his days he would recall the talents and the influence upon him of his tutor, one Walenski, with admiration and affection.

There were still other things to be done. In London he found someone to give him extra private tuition in Greek and he also felt an urge to improve his French beyond the point of being able to fend off importunate nightclub hostesses. He saw an advertisement in *The Times* offering classes in the French language at the Château Boulain near Fontainebleau and announcing that applications might be made to their head of administration, who would be in London during certain dates. So Shan duly presented himself to this person, who expressed some surprise at having to deal not as was generally the case with the parent or guardian of a potential student but with the student himself, but nevertheless he was given a place on the summer course. He arrived at the Château to find the names of others who had arrived before him already posted on their bedroom doors. The notice at the room next to the one allotted to Shan indicated that his immediate neighbour was the Hon D.E. Hely-Hutchinson, which some instinct told him augured well. So it did. They became firm friends and their relationship was further strengthened when it turned out that Hely-Hutchinson was also to go up to New College at the same time as Shan.

The combination of circumstances that brought about the offer to Shan of a place at New College and the considerations that led him and his family to accept it together determined the pattern and direction of the whole of the rest of his life. It consolidated in him his natural spirit of intellectual curiosity; it entrenched his desire for learning and his fascination with the power of language and gave him a love for Oxford and the academic life that never left him. He made enduring friendships and perhaps above all these things, superimposed upon his strong Australian foundations what he perceived to be the basic virtues of

Englishness. The period he spent in Oxford, from 1929 to 1933, was in itself a remarkably significant one, lying as it did between the twenties when the establishment, at least, continued to be able to enjoy a comfortable standard of life, to retain confidence in the rightness of its duty to manage the affairs of the nation and to hold strong in its belief in the imperial certainties, and the thirties, when foreign ideologies were growing stronger and stronger and their dictatorial leaders were leading the slide towards another world war. New College at that time saw its own purpose with complete clarity; it was produce men of a calibre fit to take their place in the highest levels of service to the State, in all their manifestations. While its undergraduates were no longer entirely drawn from Winchester, as had been the case a century earlier, the large Wykehamist element set the standard against which the intake from other schools was measured. The atmosphere was one of striving towards academic achievement and intellectual growth, without the hedonism and conspicuous extravagances of the undergraduates of certain other colleges yet enjoying within their own world a life of decent comfort, regulated by civilized and long-established customs. Shan was to be transformed, during his four years at Oxford, from a well-educated and highly intelligent Australian of Irish ancestry, into an English gentleman, albeit one always able to judge the actions and thought-processes of others from a distinct and other-than-English point of view.

Buttressed by the sum of £1412.4s.3d paid into his bank account by his mother from the proceeds of her tantalite mining enterprise, Shan took up his place at New College. He began to build a circle of close friends, one of them, a fellow undergraduate who would come up the following year, was Prince Constantine von Lichtenstein, who always referred to Shan as 'our little Australian bushvacker'. Another at nearby Magdalen was later, as Lord Lovat, to achieve great fame in Hitler's war as a commando leader and one of the very first ashore in Normandy on D Day. In their company and that of other friends he began to take part in the sporting pursuits of the establishment; hunting with hounds, riding in point-to-points, fly-fishing, stalking and grouse-shooting, sailing, polo, race meetings and betting at race meetings.

Shan seems to have made the transition from the discipline of the school classroom to the independence of his tutor's rooms with considerable ease. One reason must have been his upbringing by two successful and powerful men, his father and his first stepfather and by a capable, determined and loving mother and the self-reliance that had grown with it. Another was in the quality and nature of those in whose hands lay the responsibilities for maintaining the standards of New College. Its head, Warden Fisher, H.A.L. Fisher, author of the great *History of Europe*, which he was to be engaged upon during most of Shan's time as an undergraduate, had been the Minister for Education in Lloyd George's wartime Cabinet. Supported by a capable and hospitable wife, he acted the dignified father-figure, wise, tolerant and understanding, aware without being interfering and knowing how much direct contact with the affairs of each individual in his charge was excessive and how much exactly right. Shan was also fortunate in his history tutor, the highly regarded and much revered Christopher Cox. As a man he was easily approachable, with a strong sense of fun; as a teacher able and encouraging. Like most of Cox's charges, Shan developed a strong rapport with his tutor and kept up a correspondence with him that lasted until the older man's death.

Someone else on whom Shan greatly depended for guidance and advice was his college scout, Metcalfe, who attended to his domestic needs and each day, when there was no pressing social engagement, would bring him his half-commons lunch of bread, cheese and a pint of beer. These scouts, or college servants, were generally charged with the care of the undergraduates who had rooms that led off one particular staircase and in many cases they took over the position in the lives of their young men that the nanny had occupied in their earlier lives (and perhaps still did from the upstairs room to which she was retired when her regular nursery duties were over and which would be the first port of call of the son of the house on his return for the holidays from his preparatory or public school).

After passing his Mods in his first, the Michaelmas, term of 1929 (with the exception of Latin, which he took during the following term), Shan had free time before starting to read Greats and Modern History. This he used to further his already strong interest in English mediaeval history and with H.W.C. Davies' *Mediaeval England* in his hand, wandered the countryside, identifying sites and exploring historic towns and villages until he became, in his own judgment, more knowledgeable on the subject than any of his English contemporaries. There were also fellow Australians to be sought out and cultivated and he found a sufficient number in the different Oxford colleges with similar sporting interests to provide the eighteen needed to make up a football team under Australian rules and to challenge their counterparts at Cambridge to an inter-varsity match. No blues or half-blues seem to have been awarded for this outlandish activity and there is no record of it in the sporting archives of New College. Shan did win a half-blue at a sport more conventional in Oxford eyes as a member of the University lacrosse team, victorious against Cambridge during the 1932 season.

Something that came early in Shan's time at New College was an invitation from the headquarters of the University Officer Training Corps (the body that encouraged undergraduates to take part in some sort of part-time military training during their time at the university) to call and to discuss over a glass of port, which branch of the armed forces he would volunteer to give his time. An undergraduate who joined the OTC could expect to be given a supplementary reserve commission in the branch in which he had chosen to serve, converted to a regular commission should he on graduating decide to make a career as a regular officer. Surprisingly, in the light of his subsequent history, Shan appears to have made the Royal Air Force his first choice and arrangements were made for Acting Pilot-Officer Hackett to follow a training course during the summer of 1930 at the de Haviland flying school at Stag Lane aerodrome near Edgware. What guided Shan in this decision can only be speculated upon. Although by the late twenties those who had come up after fighting in the Great War had long since graduated and departed, there would have been among the tutors many who had gone through the horrors of trench warfare and it may be that Shan had listened to their reminiscences and thought the sublime detachment and individual responsibility of the pilot a better and more appropriate occupation for him. This was not his mother's view. Despite herself flying about Western Australia, often in dangerous conditions, when surveying for precious metals as part of her work as director of her mining company, as soon as she learned what Shan proposed she fired off an anguished letter imploring him for love of her to abandon the plan. This he dutifully did.

Shan's choice of service in the RAF Volunteer Reserve was unexpected, given that there had previously been at the back of his mind the thought that he might eventually join the Army as a regular officer, 'to enter the military condition', as he himself put it, although it seems that his family may not wholeheartedly have shared his ambition. Certainly, late in 1931 his stepfather, by then a very sick man, had written to Shan urging him to change to reading law and saying that he already ought to be eating his dinners in one of the Inns of Court. After Sir Frank Moulden's death the following year his mother earnestly hoped he would return to Australia after Oxford and make his life in what had been the family newspaper business and in which they still held an interest.

His great-grandfather John had gone into the 8th Light Dragoons as a cornet in 1784 and, ancestral precedent aside, Shan had the conviction, shared widely among his contemporaries, that a second war with Germany was inevitable. His supplementary reserve commission, converted to a regular commission, would bring him the benefit of back-dated seniority reflecting time up at university. His classical studies brought him in touch with the role of the soldier throughout history and he felt at ease with the military ethos and with the free and willing acceptance of a code of conduct shared by all. Perhaps too, for a native Australian there was some attraction in the separateness of the soldier within British society, someone whose assumed task set him on a moral plane above the generality. Another of the effects of his background, even taking into account the ancient Irish element that was part of it, was a ready sympathy with the imperial imperative, the belief shared with generations before him that British rule over other peoples and other lands was broadly beneficial wherever it was applied and infinitely superior to any imaginable alternative.

So in 1931 Shan took his supplementary reserve commission in a 'good' horsed cavalry regiment, The Bays (2nd Dragoon Guards), and began to spend part of the long vacation in Tidworth and in Shorncliffe, where the regiment was variously stationed, carrying out his military training. A receipted bill from the regimental saddler dated 26 August 1931 records that Mr Hackett bought a pigskin Sam Browne belt, a leather-covered cane and a chin strap, for a total cost of £1.12s.6d. It is a small military curiosity that the Bays, traditionally and to this day, use pigskin for all these military accoutrements, a leather not known for its ability to take the high degree of polish associated in other British regiments with the turnout of a properly dressed officer.

The six weeks of training that each supplementary reserve officer was obliged to give every year could be arduous and not only on the military scene. Writing during the long vac of 1932 to his tutor, Christopher Cox, from the officers' mess of the Bays, Shan described a fraught and unsuccessful attempt to sail in very bad weather to France in an ill-found craft he and a friend had chartered, the tiller breaking away from the rudder, the dinghy having to be cast adrift and other damage being done to the boat. The sequel was a solicitor's letter recording the owner's distress at the condition of his craft on its return and demanding the sum of £8 to restore it.

In 1932 Shan was awarded a second-class honours degree in Greats and the following year another second in Modern History. Armed with a note from the Warden, H.A.L. Fisher, telling him not to be disappointed at only gaining a second and that he would find his years at the University of great value to him throughout the whole of his life, he went down from Oxford and, having either overcome or overridden his family's wishes, took up at the age of twenty-three the career as a soldier that was to occupy his next thirty-four years. Family loyalty overtook any fond feeling he might have developed during his two heavy cavalry years with the Bays and he decided to join the successor to his great-grandfather's regiment, which had become the 8th King's Royal Irish Hussars (8H). He was given additional seniority of two and a half years, his commission being back-dated to 29 January 1931. This practice, although both welcome and extremely useful to the university entrant into the Army, was not always popular with fellow-officers who had earned their commissions after two gruelling years at Sandhurst and whose seniority counted from the day they left the Royal Military College. They felt, perhaps with some justification, that their own full-time training was of rather greater value to the Army and to their own regiment than the occasional, short-term periods spent on attachment with some entirely different unit. It is possible that Shan's own commanding officer shared these sentiments in some degree, as, having after a short acquaintance got the measure, as he thought, of his new university entrant, he told Shan 'that he would never be a soldier, never anything but an armed civilian'. The comment was probably less a criticism of Shan's dedication to his calling, which was complete, but more a tribute to his erudition, which he probably took no great pains to conceal.

The system that gave those extra years of seniority and the higher entry in the Army List that came with them were undoubtedly of benefit to Shan as he made his way, within ten years of joining his regular regiment, to the rank of brigadier and command of a parachute brigade in action, at an age that would have been unthinkably young in peacetime.

8H were about to begin the peacetime overseas posting to which all regiments of the British Army were, in their turn, liable. For the cavalry, the practice was to start with four years in the Cairo Cavalry Brigade, followed by seven years in India. At the time, the Cairo Brigade was made up of two horsed regiments, or 'mounted' as the official designation had it, and an armoured car regiment, the latter the 12th Lancers (12L) until they were relieved by the 11th Hussars (11H). For the young officer in Egypt during those pre-war days, life had all the formality and rigorous protocol of Edwardian England; deviation from any of its many particulars brought, according to the degree of the offence, social doubt, derision or, worst of all, a permanent black mark. An essential part of his equipment was an adequate supply of visiting cards, whose layout and wording were strictly laid down. Calls had to be made by the newly-arrived on the High Commissioner in Egypt, (effectively, despite the nominal existence of an Egyptian government, the governor of the country), the head of the Egyptian Army, (a seconded and senior British Army officer) and the General Officer commanding British Troops in Egypt, as well on many of the more important appointments in the cavalry brigade. Two cards had to be left, (or 'dropped'), the second of them being for the notable's wife, and cards also had to be dropped whenever the individual left the country. An unconscious reflex action developed invariably by butlers and occasionally and regrettably by their masters was the running of a fingernail backwards across the card to confirm that it had been properly die-stamped and not merely printed. A discovered lapse of this gravity would gravely affect the standing of the unfortunate delinquent.

The consequence of all this calling was to hope to receive, in the fullness of time, invitations to at homes, dinners and garden parties and so on and thus to enter a firmly established British society, however foreign the place might be in which it found itself. In a letter written to Christopher Cox not long after the arrival of the regiment in Cairo, Shan describes the beauty of the desert but deplores how, although abroad, he and his fellow-soldiers have all the trappings of home and that, but for the heat and the light, they might within the barracks think themselves in England. Perhaps to remind his tutor of the place his four years at New College held in his affections, he says he thinks he is happy in Egypt, with his responsibilities for a troop of thirty mounted soldiers but says that he understands his principal concern is to be the fitness and well-being of the horses. 'The men,' he wrote, 'matter less!'

Life within the regiment followed patterns that reflected genteel behaviour in upper circles of the Home Country. Broadly, the officer was part of a family, one with understood and freely accepted civilized values. Christian names were invariably used between officers of any rank, other than to the commanding officer, who was addressed as Colonel; there was no bar in the Mess, all drinks being brought by a mess servant to wherever the officer was sitting and noted down, to be paid for through a single mess bill at the end of the month. Standing someone else a drink was forbidden in the Mess, but this strict rule was not allowed to prevent the normal politenesses, by the simple and understood device of allowing an officer to offer another a drink, the person offered being allowed to accept, but of the cost of each drink being charged separately to the officer who had consumed it. Shan recalled later the culture-shock of a short attachment to an infantry battalion in Mersa Matruh during the Italian scare of 1935. He was amazed to find officers in the mess calling those senior to themselves 'Sir' at every opportunity, of being invited to sign a chit for every drink and of being politely reprimanded for his temerity in sitting inadvertently in the armchair reserved for the second-in-command of the battalion. [Nothing was to change; the author recalls how on joining his regiment on being commissioned some three years into Hitler's war when the country's fortunes were probably at their

23

lowest, being given as the central piece of advice to a newly joined young officer, the invitation to treat the regiment 'as if you were at a country-house party of which your Colonel was the host'. Practices in the mess were, happily, exactly the same as in the pre-war 8H.]

Within the territory of Egypt, the British Army kept a low profile. It was a time when nationalism was on the increase and the Wafd party, which espoused it, was increasing its political importance. Outside barracks and when off duty, British soldiers wore civilian clothes and were forbidden to be armed (although some officers thought it prudent to have a stout stick somewhere about them). There were occasional disturbances and small riots, although nothing on the scale of the period after 1945, which culminated in 1951 in the battle of Ismailia police station and, in Cairo, the Turf Club massacre. For the officers their social life was tranquil. A regular feature was the Saturday night dances at Shepheard's Hotel, when white tie was *de rigueur*, day dress a sufficient reason to be barred entry and every private dinner party black tie at least.

None of this sense of exclusiveness prevented the young Shan from finding friends outside his own regiment. To the puzzled amusement of his fellow-hussars, he even had acquaintances in the Royal Engineers and the Royal Corps of Signals. All this was part of his firm intent to become a good officer, although he would say to the end of his military service that he had not joined the British Army but the 8th Hussars, which happened to be part of the British Army. His youthful inclinations toward Arabism made him a keen student of Arabic and he also sought to improve his military skills and knowledge in every way possible. The climate of Egypt in those pre-High Dam days was greatly influenced by the annual flooding of the Nile during the summer months, always preceded during the month of May by the *khamsin*, the hot, sand-laden winds from the desert. Serious military training therefore had to be confined to the cooler and less humid months between October when the floods would have begun receding and the following April. The Army worked hard and Shan was proud that, even in their outmoded horsed-cavalry way, his regiment reached a very high standard of efficiency.

Summer was reserved for leave, which was generous. Each officer in Egypt was entitled to three months each year, to anywhere that it might please him to go, although it was usually taken in two parts. Those keen on fishing would go back to England and follow Ascot with a few weeks of their favourite sport, while the shooting fraternity would combine Goodwood with the opening of the grouse season. A married officer with young children out from school in England might take his family off to the cooler beaches and forested mountains of Cyprus or perhaps to the better air and onshore breezes of Alexandria, to where the High

Commissioner and his staff decamped each year. Whatever the inclinations of the officer, taking leave was considered a serious matter that had to be seriously planned. For Shan leave was also an opportunity to continue the academic work that the vigorously enquiring side of his nature was never to allow him to neglect. He was intent on completing his thesis on Saladin and his campaigns of 1189 AD before the Third Crusade and so he divided one leave between England, where long periods were spent in either the Bodleian or the Reading Room of the British Museum, and Syria and Lebanon. Here, mounted on a mule, he made an expedition up the Orontes Valley, the location of Saladin's campaign. Once back in Cairo with the Regiment, he wrote up his paper without, as he later proudly recorded, missing either a single party or a single chukka of polo. Nor, in the agreeable atmosphere of his officers' mess, did this extra-mural activity of an apparently unmilitary nature excite the slightest curiosity or mockery in his fellow-officers, a circumstance in which Shan took very great pleasure. It confirmed yet again the content he felt in the military condition, particularly in what he saw as that blessed part of it that was his own regiment. The thesis, once completed, was duly sent off to Oxford and Shan received his BLitt, being especially gratified by the accompanying encomium from the Regius Professor who had assessed it.

The Abyssinian crisis of 1935, when the Cairo Cavalry Brigade was deployed in the Western Desert towards the Italian defences on the Cyrenaican frontier, had consequences for the whole of Shan's future career. The futility of attempting to confront Italian tanks with British horses soon became obvious to the High Command and in November 1935 a rudimentary programme of mechanization of the cavalry regiment was begun. The soldiers' mounts were now Ford V-8 pickup trucks, with a section of soldiers in each and a machine-gun, on a mounting of the regiment's own devising, positioned behind each driving cab. While this modest concession towards the realities of twentieth-century warfare may have made the British Army's situation in any confrontation with the Italians in the Western Desert the more tenable, when the Indian Government heard of what had happened they announced that they had no interest in receiving a mechanized cavalry regiment for a tour of duty on the sub-continent but would accept only horsed regiments. In anticipation of their long Indian tour, 8H had, before leaving England, pooled regimental funds and the private financial resources of its officers to acquire a considerable string of unschooled polo ponies from Australia, one hundred and twenty of them in all. The plan had been to train the ponies up to a high standard and to take them to Egypt for this most prestigious of mounted sports. There was every expectation that the regiment would do so well at polo that, when the move to India took place, it would have with it a number of well schooled ponies of high reputation, which would find a ready and lucrative market among the maharajahs and the Indian cavalry regiments. That at least was the plan and so, before 8H left Tidworth for Egypt, an advance party under a riding-master was despatched to accept the ponies at Suez on their arrival from Australia, to see them safely to the barracks the regiment was to occupy in Cairo and to begin their schooling. The news that the posting to India would no longer take place was met with consternation and a feeling of potential financial disaster. As had been the plan, the 8H polo team had become accustomed to winning all the local tournaments in which it took part and succeeded in doing so, in large part because its string of ponies had been trained up to the standard of competition it could expect in India. There was no longer the justification for continuing to raise the qualities of their ponies to a point that might make winning the local tournaments a simple matter, for such high-quality mounts were virtually unsaleable in Egypt. Accordingly the regimental polo team was despatched to California, to Austria and Hungary and to Hurlingham back in England, to play in matches that would demonstrate the quality of the ponies and stimulate the sale of as many of them as possible during the sporting tour.

Despite all these efforts, a large number of ponies remained with the regiment and at the outbreak of war in 1939 Shan, although by then far from Cairo and 8H, was still officially the owner of two. During the summer months it had been the practice for the regiment to move its polo ponies to Alexandria, where each year a 'married families change of air' camp was set up and officers not out of Egypt on leave and still on Cairo duty would commute from Cairo to Alexandria each weekend to play polo, travelling either by train or by the newly-instituted DH Dragon service of Misr Airlines. Other single officers might be sent to Alexandria ostensibly to help with administrative duties at the married families' camp, but in reality to devote their energies to the welfare of the polo ponies and their exercise on the polo field.

Despite, or perhaps because of, the regiment's recent arms-length confrontation with the Italians in Cyrenaica, Shan decided early in 1936 that it was an appropriate time to advance his linguistic skills, specifically in the Italian language. He applied for and was given four months' language leave and, with the help of the military attaché at the British Embassy in Rome, it was arranged that he would stay for a month in the home of an Italian professor and then proceed to an attachment to a mounted regiment stationed in Rome, the Italian 4th Dragoons. This turned out to be a most agreeable time for Shan. The programme drawn up by the military attaché made it possible to spend the first few weeks of absence from the regiment skiing in Sestrières. On his eventual arrival at the professor's house, Shan realized that his stay there would be in no way marred by the presence of an eighteen-year old daughter who, as he later wrote, became a most delightful companion to him in his studies.

He was to describe the cavalry regiment where he took his attachment as being made up of little men on big horses; Shan, no hulking six-foot giant himself, must have felt at home. From Rome he went direct to London to sit his interpretership examination in Italian, which he passed and then returned to 8H in Cairo.

One embarrassing consequence of his time with the Italian cavalry was to find himself ordered, as soon as he had got back, to attend riding school for some remedial training. It was the Italian military custom to ride very short and, while in Rome, Shan obviously conformed to his hosts' customs, whereas 8H, in common with all other British cavalry regiments, employed the traditional English hunting seat with its long stirrup leathers. 'Shan, you ride like a monkey on a stick,' said the Adjutant to him, 'and we must get that out of you.'

The Regiment's contented way of life was about to experience another hiccup. The small excursion at the time of the Abyssinian crisis was regarded in retrospect as a training exercise and an amusing diversion from ordinary life. Other events in Europe were, however, beginning to cause ripples which were to spread far out across the Eastern Mediterranean. By 1936 Hitler and the Nazi Party had been in power in Germany for three years and his malign intentions towards the Jews were clear and being actively and brutally applied. The pace of emigration of these unfortunate people accelerated and large numbers of them made their way to Palestine, a country that at the time was governed by the British under a League of Nations mandate. The stated and admirable policy of the British Government was to attempt to develop a multi-racial country where the different cultures of its inhabitants could, under sound and efficient administration, learn to live harmoniously together and work towards eventual independence. But the ideas on a desirable rate of progress towards independence between the governing power on the one hand and the governed peoples on the other were no less diverse in Palestine than they were in any other colonial or quasi-colonial country and, perhaps because of ethnic and historical factors, were probably greater there than elsewhere. Further, the Muslim population looked with growing apprehension on the increasing numbers of Jewish immigrants. They saw and envied the quasi-independence of Egypt and Iraq and the moves towards it in Syria; the mandate, as they understood it, was intended as a staging post on the road to an independent state of

Palestine. A serious rebellion in 1929 had been put down by vigorous action requiring the deployment of troops from Egypt and Malta and use of all three of the armed services. A smaller rising in 1933 had been more easily suppressed, but the growing problem of Jewish immigration seems by 1936 to have persuaded the Palestine Arab Muslims that they had to act or be overwhelmed. The Balfour Declaration, which twenty years earlier had viewed with favour the establishment of a national home for the Jewish people in Palestine, provided it were understood that nothing would be done to prejudice the civil and religious rights of the non-Jewish population, was proving to be less and less the protection of the indigenous peoples that its authors may have persuaded themselves that it would be. The increasing flow of Jews into Palestine was a fact that could not be ignored and money from Europe and the United States was pouring in with them to buy Arab land on which they could settle.

Most people in his circle would probably have shared Shan's views on the problem of Palestine. Those Jews he would have met during the course of his life in Australia and in England were likely to have been thoroughly established in the countries in which they, or their ancestors, had chosen to settle, moving freely and contentedly in their adopted society and being very like their fellow-countrymen in appearance, manner and outlook. Such people were unlikely to be ardent Zionists and many among them felt strongly that the Jewish condition would be best served by avoiding the duties and responsibilities that a secular Jewish state in Palestine would impose on the worldwide Jewish community and by continuing to make a life within the culture and customs of the country in which they found themselves. Until the emergence of Hitler, the situation of the Jews in Germany had seemed to have been one of successful and reasonably harmonious integration, but, with the rise of the Nazi party, hopes of continuing such a situation had become a mockery for them and the condition of those elsewhere in Eastern Europe, with the long histories in those countries of pogrom and ghetto, was also precarious. Only in the West, if only for time being, did there seem to be any sense of security.

In mid-April of 1936 serious Arab rioting broke out in Haifa and two days later, under the spiritual and political influence of Haj Amin, the Grand Mufti of Jerusalem, a general strike was called. The Palestinian demands were for the cessation of Jewish immigration, prohibition of the sale of land to the Jews and a measure of self-government as a step towards full independence. The High Commissioner decided on a policy of conciliation and negotiation, perhaps necessarily as he had little with which to put the rebellion down other than two garrison infantry battalions.

During the next four months reinforcements of some nine further infantry battalions and supporting troops arrived from Egypt and Malta. 8H went up from Cairo at the end of June, followed at the end of July by the armoured cars of 11H. They were there to carry out that duty familiar to any serviceman during the period of Empire and the winding down of Empire, duties in aid of the civil power. The regiment was given a sector closest to the Egyptian border with Palestine – Gaza and Beersheba and the Sinai. Here, in support of the Palestine Police, they carried out patrols in their Ford pickups, searched villages for arms and provided armed escorts for military convoys. Mines and booby traps were a particular hazard for 8H and eight of their trucks were, at various times, blown up. With negotiations between the High Commission and the Arab authorities making no progress and with growing deterioration in civic order, it was decided to deploy more troops and 1st Infantry Division under General Dill (later to give great service to his country as the senior British military representative in Washington after the United States entered the war) was brought in during September 1936. The GOC decided that the best means of imposing his authority would be by a show of strength and as part of it, he would drive boldly around his area of operations. Shan, whose Arabic had by this time reached a considerable fluency and who had been seconded to intelligence duties, was attached to his staff as escorting officer. The General's rapid progress, courageously standing upright in his staff car through the towns and villages lined with (he thought) applauding Palestinians chanting greetings, was, he concluded afterwards, a success. To Shan, travelling in a second car and receiving most of the badly-aimed projectiles from the then inexperienced stone-throwers, it was a different story. He could understand what was being shouted and it was not expressions of loyalty and respect. It took all Shan's diplomatic skills to conceal from his master the true nature of the triumphal progress and to allow him to remain convinced that a successful public relations exercise had been carried out.

A Royal Commission came out and recommended partition, a solution rejected by the Palestine negotiators. The general strike ended late in 1936, but the revolt dragged on with inter-communal strife until 1939. The calling-off of the general strike allowed 8H, and Shan with it, to return to Cairo and resume training as a mechanized cavalry regiment. For Lieutenant Hackett there was the satisfaction of having put his foot on the first rung of the honours and awards ladder, with a mention in despatches for his service in Palestine.

Chapter Three

ARABS AND OTHERS

His foray into Palestine with the Regiment had increased still further Shan's interest in Arabs and the Arab world. His Arabic was by now very competent and there was also perhaps more than a pang of regret in his mind about the recent mechanization of 8H, much as he accepted the necessity for it in the likely conditions of what seemed increasingly an inevitable war. Apart from the occasional formal regimental parade, he saw his riding being limited in the future to polo and other recreational activities and this he took as a matter of great regret. His thoughts began to turn to the possibility of a posting to where there would be both Arabs and horses, the Trans-Jordan Frontier Force.

The nature of the British involvement in the affairs of Palestine was briefly touched upon in the previous chapter. Peace negotiations that followed the Great War of 1914–18 had to deal not only with the problems of the principal enemy nations, now defeated, but also with the future of their previous colonies and dependent territories, removed by defeat from their control. Among them were the administratively separate parts or *vilayet*s of the old Ottoman Empire that formed the eastern end of the Mediterranean between, roughly, Egypt and Turkey, the territories of Syria, Lebanon, Palestine, which included the area known as Trans-Jordan, and Iraq. These *vilayets* became mandated territories of the League of Nations, in effect countries whose right to independence was recognized but were judged not yet ready for independent self-government. They were included in the list of League of Nations mandates, a mandate describing the device of handing over responsibility for the government of countries or territories considered to be fit at best for a limited independent self-government to the care of one or another of the more advanced, or perhaps developed, of the victorious allies. In this way both Syria and the Lebanon became French mandated territories while Palestine, Trans-Jordan and Iraq became the responsibility of Great Britain.

The difficulties and contradictions the mandatory powers would face

30

in carrying out their tasks were simple to predict. The rate of progress towards independence would always be too slow for the nationalist elements, possessing as they did the weapon of appeal to local sentiment. In Palestine proper there was the existence of the Jewish problem. The secret wartime Sykes-Picot agreement between the British and French governments had defined the relative spheres of influence of the two countries in what was still known then as the Near East, while the Balfour declaration, in which the British government looked with favour upon the establishment of a national home for the Jews in Palestine, provided that the political and religious rights of the indigenous Arab population were not infringed, (made, some said, as an expression of gratitude for Dr Weizmann's discovery of new methods of manufacturing nitro-glycerine at the time of the shell shortage on the Western Front) rendered almost certain an increasing hostility between Jew and Arab in Palestine. Everywhere there existed fierce tribal loyalties, often underpinned and inflamed by sectarianism. Under Turkish administration, tribal leaders had grown accustomed to holding sway over what they regarded as their own territories and of fighting their neighbours when their assumed rights looked in danger of being infringed. There was also a lively drug traffic that had to be uncovered and, if not eliminated, at least held under strict control.

The twin British mandate of Palestine and Trans-Jordan came directly under the Colonial Office, which set up police forces in both of the territories. In 1921 the legendary Arabist, Peake Pasha, who had fought with Lawrence in the Hejaz, was charged with the formation of a mobile gendarmerie in Trans-Jordan to act as a reserve to the regular police force. In 1926 this gendarmerie was split into the Arab Legion and the Trans-Jordan Frontier Force (TJFF), the former with largely a policing role in bringing to order the unruly Bedouin tribes of Trans-Jordan and the latter more of a regular army for the territory, ensuring the integrity of its frontiers and providing military aid to the civil power. The Arab Legion remained under the command of Colonel Peake until 1939, when he handed over to his second-in-command, Major (later Lieutenant-General) Glubb. The TJFF was commanded by a seconded regular colonel of a British cavalry regiment whose term of office was usually of three or four years, unlike the open-ended tenure of the other British-officered force which, in the long years between the formation of the Arab Legion and the abrupt dismissal of Glubb Pasha by the young King Hussein of Jordan in 1956, had served under only two commanding officers.

The TJFF was a body that gained from its earliest years the highest of reputations for loyalty, *esprit-de-corps* and justifiable pride in its military

31

efficiency. The nucleus of regulars seconded from the British Army, both officers and warrant officers, was augmented by local junior officers promoted through the ranks. Competition to be accepted into the TJFF, whether from members of the British Army or from the inhabitants of the mandated territory, was intense and no man left the force without the feeling that he had passed, while wearing its uniform, through a significant and thoroughly worthwhile period of his own life.

The uniform they wore was distinctive and made sure they would stand out among their fellows. From the tall black hat made of astrakhan fur, slashed with crimson and gold, to the khaki frock coat and the broad scarlet sash worn around the waist, to the cavalry breeches and riding boots, they were a dashing sight and did not care who knew it. In part horsed cavalry for the whole of the force's existence, they exhibited, whatever their rank, that innate air of superiority which the mounted soldier never bothers to conceal from his colleagues who fight on foot. A high standard of horsemanship was insisted upon and maintained, apart from military exercises, by regularly playing polo or taking part in point-to-points or show-jumping.

Answerable ultimately to the Colonial Office, in their own territory they came under the operational command of the Royal Air Force, responsible directly to the Group Captain commanding RAF Amman and overall to the Air Officer Commanding RAF Palestine and Jordan. The RAF had manned armoured cars as early as the campaigns of 1917 and 1918; when Imperial policing had to be undertaken in remote areas difficult of access, such as Afghanistan or Iraq, aerial bombing became a preferred method of pacification and it became considered a natural order of things for the Royal Air Force to take charge of this important aspect of the white man's burden. It was not until 1941, some eighteen months into the Second World War and because of the onset of the Syrian campaign that the Colonial Office handed over its control of the TJFF to the War Office.

During the first half of the thirties the TJFF continued its work of maintaining military efficiency and its frontier defence operations, the latter mainly directed at drug smuggling. It also took part in relief work during the disastrous flooding at Tiberias in 1934. By 1937 the force, which, apart from its British contingent, was recruited from Arabs, both Muslim and Christian, Circassians, Sudanese and even a few Jews, was organized into an HQ, three cavalry squadrons and two mechanized companies. The force HQ was at Zerka, not far from Amman, the capital of Trans-Jordan, where there was also the depot and the training establishment. Of the five active units, one sabre squadron and one mechanised company were also at Zerka, the others being dispersed to

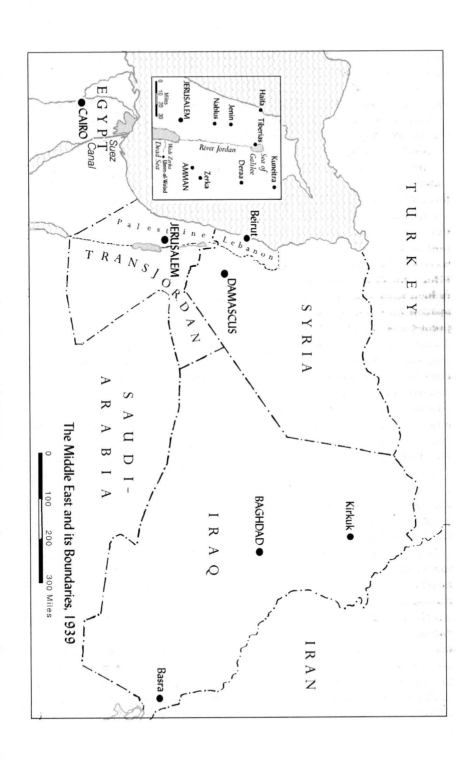

The Middle East and its Boundaries, 1939

various locations in Trans-Jordan. Each was under the command of a British major and divided into half-squadrons and half-companies, commanded by a British subaltern enjoying the temporary rank of captain. The mounted half-squadrons held two sabre troops and a Hotchkiss machine-gun troop, commanded by junior officers, all recruited locally and all promoted through the ranks. The half-companies were made up of a light armed car troop (these were light four-wheeled vehicles with a Vickers gun on each roof and a crew to man it) and a mechanized troop of three sections of eight men in pickup trucks, armed with rifles and a single Bren light machine gun.

Life in the headquarters at Zerka was orderly and comfortable. Outwardly it resembled a typical British Army cantonment, neatly laid out, each path lined with white-painted stones and overall a general air of an efficient and self-sufficient organization. There was a swimming pool, squash and tennis courts, a polo field and football and hockey pitches. Life in the officers' mess was civilized and club-like, while within the married officers' quarters the impression would be gained of finding oneself in the house of a comfortably-off English gentleman somewhere in the shires, in the winter a fire blazing in the grate, two Labradors stretched out on the carpet before it, the pictures on the walls and the furniture in the rooms often having been brought from home.

This was the world in which Shan now wished to find himself. The first step was to obtain his Colonel's permission to apply for a secondment to the TJFF. This done, it was only a matter of time before Shan had to travel to HQ at Zerka for an interview with the force commander, a regular colonel of the 13th/18th Hussars and, in Shan's view, a thoroughly decent man, a regular officer of the highest integrity. Shan had with him another hopeful applicant, a young officer of a Greenjacket Regiment who had been with his battalion in Malta. From his own direct observation, Shan considered that his companion was probably as handsome a young officer as might be found in the entire British Army. Colonel Chrystall indicated at once to them both that as far as he was concerned, for him the TJFF was his entire life and that he could not envisage a finer posting anywhere in the King's service. He told them that they were at the outskirts of Empire and had the duty of exemplifying its finest virtues and that he knew that no one applied to join the TJFF except out of a burning desire to serve King, Country and Empire to the very best of their abilities. Impressed as he was by this expression of noble purpose, Shan knew perfectly well that he himself had been much influenced in his decision to apply by the considerably higher rates of pay that officers in the TJFF enjoyed under the Colonial Office and the help he hoped this would be to him in settling a number of pressing debts at Ladbroke's.

He also knew perfectly well, and thought it unlikely that Colonel Chrystall did, that his good-looking companion had been advised that an extended absence from Malta might do much to restore a degree of emotional calm among the Naval wives whose husbands were so often absent at sea. Nonetheless, they listened gravely to their future commander, impressed by the strength of sincerely held views and recognizing the truths that lay within them.

Both Shan and the rifleman were accepted for their four-year secondment to the TJFF and given command of half-squadrons, Shan in a sabre squadron and the other in the mechanized unit. Shan found that he had been given responsibility to lead, as the only British officer in his detached unit, about sixty men and seventy horses. He was entering what would be a happy and militarily satisfying few years; times were relatively peaceful, the Arab general strike having been called off under pressure from the princes of neighbouring states and the life of the unit revolving around routine patrols and training. His soldiers were keen and secure in their standing in the Arab world, where the carrying of arms brought respect and to do so mounted on a horse heightened respect. In all matters the highest standards were willingly and eagerly striven for, in the care and maintenance of mount and equipment, in horsemanship, in skill-at-arms and in discipline. Their horses were bred from Arab stallions and local mares, to give something sturdier than the Arab but smaller and more nimble than the English horse. The distinctive turnout of the TJFF has already been described and Shan's half-squadron on the move must have been a striking sight, every man carrying a sword in addition to his rifle, on his head either the winter *kalpak*, the tall circassian hat made of black lambskin or in summer, a fringed white scarf-like *khafiya*, held in place by the black rope band of the *hagal*.

As an arm of the Palestine Government, the TJFF was maintained by an annual allocation of funds from this source. Within the sum of money he had been given, the force commander would be expected to draw up a budget that would cover all the expenses of headquarters and five operational units, food and accommodation, training, equipment and the provision of uniforms, everything other than the pay of British officers and warrant officers, which was made direct from the Colonial Office. The budget was administered by a small staff, some British and some local; the paymaster, for example, was an Armenian, the chief clerk a British warrant officer.

This settled existence was about to be severely jolted with the murder on 26 September 1937 of the District Commissioner of Galilee, Mr Andrews, a particularly able and well-respected official. The attack took place against the background of the Peel Commission, which had been sent from London in an attempt to make proposals for the future of Palestine that would satisfy both the Jewish pressure for an increased presence and ever-growing resistance by the Arabs to what they saw as the threat to their hopes of an independent Palestinian state. The death of Mr Andrews was the signal for a resumption of violence by armed Arab bands and for renewed attacks on Jewish settlements. The squadron to which Shan belonged, under the command of Major Richard Hooper, a gunner, was sent off to the Jenin-Nablus-Tulkarm triangle north of Jerusalem, a particularly troublesome and disaffected part of the country. It is interesting to contemplate the almost eighteenth-century way in which the TJFF were sent on active service. The horses, the means of the squadron's mobility, were considered as a first responsibility. They were provided with two day's feed in the form of barley, carried in saddlebags; re-supply was ensured by arranging a series of rendezvous at designated times and named points on a main road, where a truck would dispense replenishments. As far as the men were concerned, nothing was done to provide them with rations and they were expected to live off the land. Fortunately, the rules of Arab hospitality were binding and made the welfare of the soldiery a relatively simple matter. During each afternoon a local officer and an escort would be sent forward to the next village announcing the approach of one hundred and twenty men and one hundred and thirty horses all requiring food and accommodation. For the men a chicken per head would usually be provided and it was also customary to slaughter a sheep for the officers. The food would be served up on beds of rice in great brass dishes and the men would squat in groups around the dishes, eating with their right hands under the gaze of their hosts, some of whom may have been engaged during the day in whatever hostilities were proceeding in the neighbourhood, or would be the following morning. None of this would have seemed the slightest bit strange to either host or guest. Such a thing greatly appealed to Shan, who, perhaps in common with a general feeling among British soldiers, could separate humanity from enmity and appreciate the transcendent value of the recognition of the difference.

Shan was to experience other examples of seeing the man behind the weapon. Rashid, his senior local officer, was first cousin to the leader of an armed band that the half-squadron spent much time in pursuing. Sometimes, when the TJFF were being tiresomely harassed at night by the Arabs, Rashid would, in stentorian tones, call out his cousin's name and remind him forcefully of their co-sanguinity, at which point hostilities would usually be called off. On another occasion Shan asked Rashid to get a message to his cousin expressing his British officer's feelings of indignity at being fired at so ineffectively by ragged-arsed Arabs with bent rifles and poor ammunition and inviting a party from the rebel band to go down to the base camp at Beisan for some musketry training, after which hostilities might resume on a more professional basis. The courteous reply was handsome in its thanks but regretted that his better marksmen were rather busily engaged and could not for the moment be spared. He expressed the wish that the invitation might be extended again at a later date. Unfortunately within a few weeks news came that Rashid's cousin had been killed by his own side, whether as the result of some ancient feud or some present rift was never discovered.

Some while later Shan's half-squadron was attached to a brigade of the 1st Infantry Division to carry out a combined operation with battalions of the Royal Ulster Rifles and the Dorset Regiment against an Arab band of around a hundred armed men. Shan, attending the order group when his part was explained to him, listened with growing dismay to a ponderous plan that he knew would succeed only on striking where the Arabs had been and not at the place to where they would have slipped away. He wished that instead of the task he had been given, of using his two troops to patrol the gap between the British battalions taking part, he could have had twice the number of mounted cavalry and the freedom to pursue the Arabs as they made their escape.

It was perhaps fortunate for Shan that the opposition the TJFF did find themselves facing during that operation did not include riflemen trained up to their own high standards of marksmanship and care of arms. While on patrol in the hills, Shan found himself separated by some distance from his own men. Suddenly, from higher up the hillside came a shot, followed a few seconds later by another. Both missed but he was able from the smoke of the discharge to identify exactly the rock behind which his attacker had concealed himself. Quickly moving out of the direct line of fire, he tethered his horse and set off to stalk his quarry, realizing as he did so that, because the stitching on his pistol holster had come undone, he had been obliged to stow the weapon in his saddle bag and that he was therefore moving off unarmed. Before long he had arrived undetected at the far side of the rock behind which his man had positioned himself and, slithering to the top, found himself above his attacker, still watching intently down the valley. Shan jumped, forcing the man to the ground and, wresting his rifle from him, held him at his own gun's point. Hands half-raised, the Arab then began to fumble in his clothing, Shan thought perhaps for a knife or some other weapon and made gestures with the rifle that he was to stop. The man nevertheless drew out a small cloth bundle, which he unwrapped to reveal two rather battered cigarettes; these were offered to his captor, perhaps as a gesture of submission, perhaps as a token of admiration for Shan's superior skills in fieldcraft, perhaps as a gift between two human beings who had by chance and unhappy circumstance come into each others' company. Whatever, Shan refused the offer and marched his prisoner down to the valley track where the TJFF column was now assembled and handed him over to the Palestine Police officer marching with them.

The weapon he had captured in hand-to-hand fighting turned out to be a British Army short Lee-Enfield rifle left over from the war of 1914–1918, when, from the engraved lettering on a brass disc let into the butt, it had apparently belonged to a member of the West Somerset Yeomanry. The sequel was that the Palestinian, who by bearing arms against the Mandatory Power had committed a capital offence, was tried, found guilty and sentenced to death by hanging. Because of his own close involvement, when the day of execution came round, Shan was asked if he wished to act as the official military observer, but, with the picture vivid in his mind of the hand holding out a cigarette towards him he refused this offer too.

It was during this time that Shan made the acquaintance of Orde Wingate, an officer possessed of strong views and idiosyncratic attitudes. He had already made a reputation by carrying a Bible in one hand, to indicate his fervently held religious beliefs, and an alarm clock in the other, to show the passage of time. Strongly pro-Zionist, he had organized his own Jewish irregular force, which was given the task of patrolling part of the oil pipeline that ran from Kirkuk in the Iraqi oilfields across northern Trans-Jordan and Palestine to the port of Haifa on the Mediterranean coast. Since Shan's Arab soldiers were carrying out similar duties, it was prudent for the two units to keep well clear of each other and this they took care to do. Shan could never make up his mind about his fellow British Army officer; his philosophy and methods seemed bizarre to Shan's more straightforward views on where his own duties and military commitments lay, but he gave Wingate full credit for the intense loyalty he generated in those who served under him, a loyalty which must have underlain the later successes, in the appalling conditions of the Burma jungle, of the Chindits under Wingate's leadership.

In the middle of 1939 Shan went to England with a number of other officers of the TJFF and the Arab Legion to attend an investiture held on 11 July of that year at Buckingham Palace. Here he received the first of the many awards he was to be given during his long career as a soldier, being installed as a member of the military division of the Most Excellent Order of the British Empire (MBE). On the same occasion Peake Pasha, just retired as commander of the Arab Legion, received a CMG and other TJFF officers a CBE and two MCs.

Shan's absence from his unit gave him more time to ponder on the rights and wrongs of the Palestine problem and to attempt to define where his own sympathies lay, a problem never far from his mind while he had been on active service with his half-squadron. The Palestinians were there by right of ancestral occupation but he knew that many of them were merely third or fourth generation Arab settlers who had migrated from the desert to the fertile Mediterranean littoral. They could make good, loyal soldiers and their clannish tribalism was appealing, but they could also exasperate. The Jews' right to Palestine and Trans-Jordan, which territories together they called the land of Israel, was more mythical than documented and the Zionists were divided from the great mass of Jewry, including the orthodox, in their desire for an independent, secular Jewish state. Yet, as Shan understood the Koran, the coastal plain was the rightful home of 'the people of the Book' and these were certainly not the Muslim Palestinians. The persecutions in Europe were bringing and would go on bringing more and more Jews to Palestine; they were efficient and hard-working and often brought valuable technological skills with them. His heart, on balance, was with the Arabs, but in his head he foresaw clearly the inevitability of a widening chasm between the aspirations of the two Semitic races and an increasing ascendancy of the better equipped, better financed and technologically superior Jewish people.

By the time Shan returned from the London investiture war was about to be declared with Germany and with it the Arab revolt drew to a close. On 3 September 1939 Shan was in his twenty-ninth year, over a year short of the age when it was considered acceptable for a regular officer to ask permission of his commanding officer to be married, which, if granted, led to qualification for a house and marriage allowance. Unlike the United States Army, where a newly-commissioned officer might immediately marry in the chapel of the same West Point Military Academy where his years as an officer-cadet had just been concluded, the British Army thought it best for the young officer to gain experience and skill in command and leadership before taking on the domestic responsibilities of wife and children.

There is no suggestion that Shan saw the eventual approach of his thirtieth birthday as a reason to begin planning his own wedding; there was now a full-scale war to be fought and Shan's great pride in his calling made certain that military duties would, as they had in the years of semi-peace and preparation for war that followed his arrival in Egypt with his regiment in 1933, come uppermost in his mind. While serving with his half-squadron in the Jordan Valley, he had from time to time, in the company of fellow-officers of the TJFF, taken to crossing over to visit

Tiberias during off-duty periods, where in parts life was closer to the European model than in the Arab lands where most of his time was spent. Here he had met a young Austrian widow, the mother of two infant daughters, who in 1933 had married her German husband and gone with him to Palestine, where her in-laws were the owners of a hotel in Tiberias. The outbreak of hostilities brought many difficulties to their developing friendship. Margaret Frena became an enemy alien and, together with her daughters and her mother-in-law, was interned in a camp set up in Sarona, in the community of German Templars. It was fortunate, as it turned out, that she and her family were not sent off to Australia, as were all the male Germans. This unhappy turn of events, as far as Shan was concerned, in no way indicated the end of their developing relationship nor even the putting of it on hold until the war should be over. Whenever it was possible Shan would appear in uniform at the internment camp to visit Margaret and to find out how she and the children were bearing up to their enforced confinement. Soon they decided that they would marry without any more delay than the war would inevitably put in their path.

It might be thought highly improbable that a regular British army officer would ever be given permission, during the course of a war that was not going well for the United Kingdom, to marry a citizen of the country's fiercest enemy. Shan did not hold to that opinion. First there was the obstacle of the approval of his commanding officer or, rather, of his two commanding officers, because it would be a matter of common courtesy to refer to the CO of 8H, then serving in the Western Desert and to which unit he would expect to return when his four-year contract with the TJFF came to its end. Normally the granting of approval to marry would be a formality; it was likely that an officer's intended wife, or at least her family, would have been known to the commanding officer, and where not, it would be assumed that the hopeful applicant could be trusted to see that regimental standards would in all respects be upheld. Here was something entirely outside the experience of those being asked to make a decision and, not surprisingly, Shan's request was turned down flat. Appeals were of no avail and so Shan decided there was nothing for it but to go straight to the very top. He had on a number of occasions met General 'Jumbo' Wilson, a Green Jacket and the General Officer Commanding-in-Chief of Ninth Army, under which the TJFF fell, and it was to him that Shan next turned. The General, a shrewd and civilized man, knew the quality and soundness of judgment of the supplicant young officer. He acceded; 'Go ahead, my boy.' Shan and Margaret were married in Jerusalem Cathedral on 21 March 1942.

Events are running ahead of themselves. It is September 1939 and there is a war to be fought. Shan was sent off to the first of the truncated courses at the Staff College at Haifa and returned to a TJFF organizing itself for its larger wartime role. It was no longer sufficient to command and administer the Force with a regimental headquarters stationed in a base depot; something more suited to the needs of a field formation engaged against a conventional enemy would be required. Shan was appointed to the post of general staff officer grade 2 in his existing rank of temporary major and put in charge of operational duties at TJFF HQ. Developments in Europe began to show the pattern of the likely threats and dangers to the Middle East Command. The overwhelming German offensive in the West, which began on 10 May 1940 and led within a few short weeks to the evacuation of the British Expeditionary Force from Dunkirk, the collapse of the French, the armistice and the formation of the collaborationist Vichy government, posed serious potential problems in the countries adjoining Palestine. The actions of Churchill's government to try to prevent the French navy from falling into the hands of the Germans, the declaration by de Gaulle in London of a Free French movement in exile and perhaps some underlying resentment in certain French circles that the British had not capitulated in June along with their erstwhile allies, meant that relations with Vichy were bad from the beginning. Elsewhere in the Middle East, the opportunist declaration of war by Italy, (it must be presumed that Shan's pronouncement after his return some years before from his attachment to the Italian army, that he would confidently take part in any conflict in which the Italians were on the other side, had not got to the ears of Mussolini), brought a large and hostile military force up to the western frontier of Egypt and threatened British control of the Suez Canal.

In 1941 the Levantine pot finally boiled over. In May a revolt fomented and led by the pro-Axis Rashid Ali against the government of Abdullah, the Regent of Iraq, drew swift German support and the *Luftwaffe*, together with the Italians, began to fly in both supply and battle aircraft. This required overflight by the Axis air forces of the Vichy territories of Syria and Lebanon, to the British an intolerable situation exacerbated by evidence that quickly came to light that French airfields in those countries were refuelling and resupplying German planes en route to Iraq. It was also strongly suspected that the Rashid Ali revolt had been strengthened by the transfer to Iraq of Vichy French arms and equipment that had passed under the control of the Axis armistice commission in Syria. That the British would react soon became clear and Vichy responded early in June, despite having had warnings from Washington of the dangers of collaborating with the Germans in Syria/Lebanon, by issuing a defiant statement that the borders of Syria,

41

Lebanon and Tunisia would be vigorously defended against any British aggression. General Weygand was in overall command of the defence of the Vichy French Levant and reinforcements were despatched from metropolitan France.

Thanks to determined resistance by British forces stationed in Iraq under the terms of the 1930 Anglo-Iraqi treaty and the timely arrival at Basra of a strong force from India, the Rashid Ali revolt collapsed, but, nevertheless, conscious of the danger of any further attempts by Germany to control the oil-producing lands of the Persian Gulf, the British proceeded with plans to invade and occupy the two French mandates. Although the start of Operation Barbarossa, the German invasion of the Soviet Union, was still two weeks away, the signs of its imminence were clear to Whitehall and the possibility of German inter-ference in the Gulf States through the Caucasus, however improbable it might have seemed at the time because of the immense distances to be covered, was within its collective consciousness. That apart, the Middle East situation was dire. Greece and Crete had been lost and the great winter victories of Wavell in the Western Desert against the Italians had been cruelly reversed by the arrival of Rommel and his Afrika Korps and his swift and effective counter-offensive against British forces in the Western Desert.

Accordingly a mixed force of British, Indian and Australian units was assembled in Palestine, to which the TJFF was joined. Planning proceeded on the assumption that the French would offer only a token resistance to save face and then surrender. There had been some defec-tions into Palestine from French Circassian regiments, but otherwise few of the French troops in Syria and Lebanon had crossed over to the Free French, either at the time of the 1940 armistice or subsequently. It was also believed that General Weygand himself had expressed doubts on the wisdom of out and out resistance to the British. The report in *The Times* on 5 June 1941 that during the latest air raids on London, the famous Punch table had escaped damage, may well have played its part in main-taining morale on the British side.

Shan, though, was not without some misgivings. He had come to know from his work with the TJFF along the Syrian frontier of the quality of the French-led troops and there were also reports of a strong Foreign Legion presence. He also felt some concern about the proposed use in the campaign of the Free French troops stationed in the Canal Zone. The operation to eliminate the danger of a German occupation of Syria and the Lebanon went ahead and on 8 June 1941 the Allied force crossed the northern frontiers of Palestine and Trans-Jordan. Good early pro-gress was made, Tyre and Deraa being quickly captured. The advance was then directed on Beirut and Damascus, with the Australian Division advancing up the coast road and the TJFF and the Free French aiming towards Damascus. Vichy French resistance stiffened considerably, progress became disappointingly slow and it became clear, with strong counter-attacks that succeeded in penetrating deep into Allied positions and threatened the recapture of Kuneitra on the Damascus road, that earlier hopes of a token Vichy response, followed by capitulation, could be put aside. The ability of the Vichy air forces to strafe and bomb Allied troops was also a matter of concern, along with the damage and casualties that they seemed capable of inflicting.

Two actions in which Shan was involved deserve mention. On 22 June a cavalry charge by the TJFF succeeded in capturing the railway station at Umm-al-Walad, which allowed Shan to claim that he might be the last British officer ever to have gone into action with drawn sword on a horse. Later he found himself in command of a mixed force charged with the assault and capture of a Beau Geste-type fort, (as he described it) outside Damascus. A hard-fought action eventually secured the surrender of the garrison of troops of the *Légion Libanaise*, but not before both sides had borne heavy casualties. Shan was wounded and all the other Allied officers engaged in the action were either killed or wounded. While he was in the Jerusalem military hospital to which he had been evacuated, the Syrian campaign drew to its eventually successful end. On 10 July the Vichy French asked for an armistice and all fighting ceased at midnight on 12 July. The occupation of the whole of Syria and Lebanon up to the Turkish border began and, against the express wishes of the British Government, de Gaulle appointed General Catroux as High Commissioner for the occupied territories, to govern in his name and in the name of the Council for the Defence of the Free French Empire. An Allied control commission to supervise the armistice was set up, which Shan was ordered to join after his short period of convalescence.

Two things stuck in his mind about that period of his life. The first was walking down a street in Beirut with his right arm in a sling to see, approaching him, a French officer with his left arm in a sling. Intrigued at the coincidence, they fell into conversation, only to find out that they had both been wounded in the same action but on the opposite sides. This was too good an opportunity to be lightly passed up so they found a café and sat down to fight the action all over again, Shan quietly confident of receiving professional congratulations on his conduct of what had been a successful action. His French counterpart had no such intention. In considerable detail, he listed the tactical errors he thought Shan and his force had committed and invited his late enemy to justify what, to his view, was an incompetently fought action. 'I thought at the time,' the Frenchman said, 'that Marshal Foch must be spinning in his grave!' For once out-argued, all Shan could think to do was to point out that at least he had been on the winning side. 'And that,' was the retort, 'was the most distressing part of the whole business!'

The second concerned the flag flown from the front mudguard of the Control Commission's vehicles to indicate the identity and the importance of the occupants. It was black, bearing the two white initials 'CC'. It soon came to Shan's ears that to the French it signified *'Congrès des Cons'*!

The campaign had cost the Allies some 4,600 casualties in killed and wounded and on both sides together the total came to over 11,000. One avenue down which the Axis powers might have attempted to occupy and exploit the oilfields of the Persian Gulf had been closed to them. The truth that no wars are as cruel as civil wars was once more asserted in the bitter enmity felt by the Vichy forces in Syria towards their compatriots who had chosen the side of de Gaulle, and Shan mulled once more over the wisdom of pitting Frenchman against Frenchman. But in the immediate aftermath of Greece and Crete and with Rommel asserting himself so successfully in the Western Desert, Allied resources were stretched to their limits and every man was needed. That the campaign had not advanced the Allied cause in the minds of Vichy became clear after it was over. The offer of repatriation of the surrendered French to metropolitan France was largely taken up, but not until the return of Allied prisoners of war taken in the campaign and who had been removed to France had been secured by the effective device of locking up General Dentz, the erstwhile Vichy governor-general, and his senior officers until the safety of the Allied soldiers had been assured.

For his part in the campaign Shan was awarded the MC and a second mention in despatches. His four-year contract with the TJFF was by now past its full term and as soon as he had fully recovered from his wounds he was posted to the headquarters staff of Ninth Army in Basra as GSO2 (Ops). This seemed to him to be drifting into a backwater. He agitated for a return to his own regiment, 8H, heavily engaged at that time in the Western Desert as part of 4 Armoured Brigade of 7th Armoured Division, or the Desert Rats as they became popularly known from the device employed as the divisional insignia, the long-tailed little mouse, or jerboa, of the region. His first stop was in Palestine to be married, at St George's Cathedral in Jerusalem, an event that went off happily despite his best man, Pat Hore-Ruthven, managing to break his arm a day or two before and having to be hastily substituted for by a fellow TJFF officer. There was just time to enjoy a brief honeymoon and then

Shan went up to the Desert and 8H, where he was given command of C Squadron. The newlywed was sent on his way from Palestine with the following verse:

A Ruthless Rhyme (With apologies)

Hackett, of course, was always bent
On going to his regiment,
But I shall never understand
Why he should thirst for blood and sand,
When he could drink and love and laugh
Till ripe old age upon the Staff.

Besides, my batman says the Huns
Have just brought up some whopping guns,
And no one, face it, really thanks
Misguided men who die in tanks,
A human 'Crêpe Suzette in Honey'*
With Shan as pancake, isn't funny.

'One crowded hour of glorious life
Is worth an age without a name'.
The poet's right. Let's hope Shan's wife
In widowhood, may feel the same!
A pity if they bump off Shan;
I always liked the little man.

* The name of an American light tank, then just coming into service with the Eighth Army.

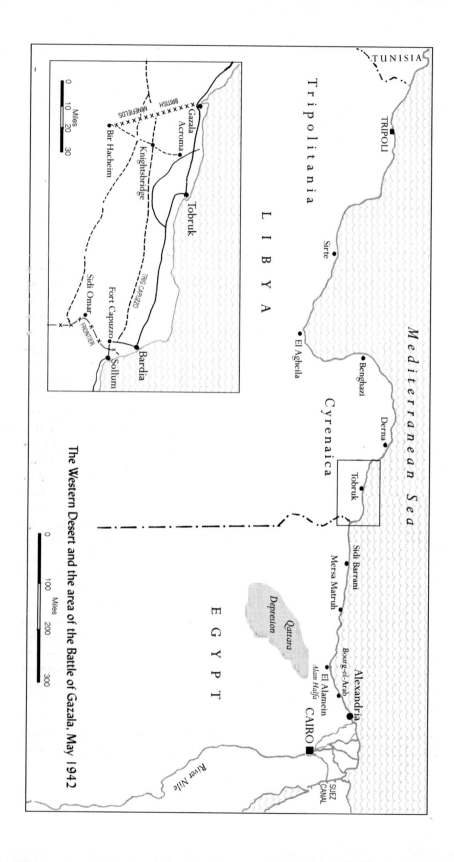

The Western Desert and the area of the Battle of Gazala, May 1942

Chapter Four

PAST ALAMEIN TO AIRBORNE

In February 1942 Shan's regiment, 8H, which he had yet to rejoin, was equipped with armoured cars for the reconnaissance role, but during that month it was decided that it should reorganize as an armoured regiment. New American tanks were arriving in the Middle East and at the end of the month the regiment drew its first batch of the new equipment; four Grant medium tanks and four Stuarts (Honeys), light tanks, and immediately began the re-organization of the regiment into two squadrons, (A and B) of Grant tanks and one light squadron (C) of Stuart tanks. The Grant was the immediate forerunner of the Sherman, eventually to become the main battle tank of the Allied armies in Europe and carried its main armament, a short 75mm cannon, in a side pod that gave it a limited degree of traverse. This gun, although packing a heavier punch than any other tank armament on the British side, was no match for the German long 75mm with which later versions of their heaviest tank then in the desert, the Pkw IV was being equipped, nor for that matter was anything like a match for the main German anti-tank gun, the long-range and extremely powerful 88mm. This weapon, which was to be of immense value to the German armed forces during the whole of the Second World War, had been designed originally as an anti-aircraft gun but although in 1942 not self-propelled but towed by a lorry, its manoeuvrability and ease of handling, the high muzzle velocity and flat trajectory of its thirty-pound shell and its long range, made it of great value against ground targets, in particular tanks and fixed fortifications. The 88 was treated with the utmost respect in every theatre in which it was deployed and in the Western Desert, where there was little cover and visibility was usually very good, it was particularly effective. Later it was to appear on a self-propelled armoured chassis and to be mounted in the Tiger and King Tiger tanks, but these did not fight in the Western Desert.

It was not only in heavy weaponry that the Germans held a demonstrable advantage on the battlefield. The ebb and flow of the desert war gave each side ample opportunity to capture and study items of equipment of all sorts and the qualitative advantage at many levels that the Germans enjoyed could be seen by all on the Eighth Army side. One stark example was something in daily use, the humble petrol can. On the British side this object, without which military operations could not continue, was a flimsy tin container, easily prone to damage in the rough and hasty handling and re-handling it had to endure on the long supply line between base and the front line. It was intended to make a single journey only and those cans that arrived with contents intact were frequently opened in the often frantic conditions in the field by piercing with sharp blows of a bayonet or some other tool to hand. The crude spout that was the result often led to further waste as the precious fuel was poured into fuel tanks. The Germans had developed a practical container that later became known as the jerrican and which would be adopted by Allied forces in every theatre of war. A sturdy and re-usable steel container, with a lever-action cap to its pouring spout, a sensible handle and a shape that permitted easy stacking and handling, it was robust enough to withstand multiple journeys to and fro and, suitably marked and delineated, could be used to transport any of the fluids needed by the troops. Easily recovered and refilled, it became a ubiquitous piece of equipment that could find a common use by the opposing sides and there must have been many jerricans that alternated regularly between the British and Commonwealth and the Axis forces.

Shan was to arrive in the Desert from a period in his military experience when the horse had been his only means of providing mobility on the battlefield to find himself in a theatre of war of great distances, largely featureless landscape, harsh climate, scant population, long lines of communication and an almost total absence of any natural or man-made resources of use to a fighting army. He had little knowledge and no direct experience of armoured warfare, but now found himself on a battlefield where the tank and the anti-tank gun were the dominant land weapons.

The desert campaign was, by the time Shan was to join it, almost two years old. It had been a time of fluctuating fortunes for both sides. The first move in 1940 had been by the Italians who employed their greater numerical strength in a cautious foray across the frontier wire into Egypt, penetrating as far as Sidi Barrani, a distance of forty miles or so and, content with this achievement, took root there. Wavell's offensive during the winter of 1940 routed the Italian forces and by early February 1941 had driven them back over five hundred miles to El Agheila on the border dividing Cyrenaica from Tripolitania. The response of the Axis powers was to introduce Rommel and his Afrika Corps into the equation. He landed at Tripoli with a force that in tanks and anti-tank guns was undoubtedly qualitatively superior to those of the British and

Commonwealth units opposing it, supported by a strong *Luftwaffe* component including Stuka dive bombers. Furthermore, Wavell had been ordered to send a number of his best divisions to reinforce Greece, then under imminent threat from the German Balkan offensive. By the end of March Rommel was ready to make his move. What was at first taken to be a reconnaissance in strength swept aside the weakened British armour defending El Agheila and, brilliantly exploiting his opportunities, Rommel led the Axis forces to the recapture of the whole of Cyrenaica up to the line of the Egyptian frontier, leaving only Tobruk as a besieged fortress in British hands.

In November 1941 the British again took the offensive and, after heavy battles, relieved Tobruk and once more drove the Axis forces back to El Agheila. The familiar situation repeated itself of the advancing forces moving further and further from their bases and resupply becoming more and more difficult, while, for the retreating troops, their lines of communication became shorter with each day's march until the strengths of the two sides reached a rough balance and the side retreating became able to stand and hold the weakening attackers.

The situation at the turn of the year, in the period before Shan returned to his regiment, was that, the Axis forces having been forced out of Cyrenaica, a confident General Auchinleck, the latest Eighth Army commander, was busily engaged in refitting and building up supplies in preparation for resuming the offensive with, this time, the intention of capturing Tripoli and clearing the Axis forces out of North Africa. However, Rommel, the wily desert fox, struck first in January 1942 and with his customary boldness and dash, forced the Eighth Army, in no little disarray, back a distance of three hundred miles to a line running from Gazala on the Mediterranean coast to Bir Hackeim almost fifty miles to the south in the desert. All the territory hard-won in 1941 was lost and the 1st Armoured Division, not long out from England, effectively destroyed. Here Eighth Army stood, to lick its wounds and to rebuild its strength, holding a defensive line that placed the British and Commonwealth troops in a series of fortified positions heavily protected by minefields, the armoured forces and the whole of XXX Corps in reserve in rear. This was the Eighth Army's situation when the re-equipped 8H, with Shan in command of C Squadron, moved up from Egypt to join the order of battle. On 12 April the Regiment de-trained at Fort Capuzzo on the Egyptian-Cyrenaican border and immediately moved off some eight miles to the west to form a leaguer. These leaguers, which had become an essential element in the tactics of desert warfare, were self-contained bases, quite often with artillery and other support under command, which were formed at whatever defensible location in the desert the units concerned found themselves. They had to be capable of offering a strong defence and from them also, offensive action could be taken. The Regiment straightway continued its training as an armoured regiment and carried out a number of exercises with a Green Jacket motorized rifle battalion and elements of the Royal Horse Artillery (of course, despite its traditional title, fully mechanized), in which Shan and his light tank squadron enjoyed themselves in their wide-ranging role as flank guard. On 20 April there was a move west to the general area of Bir Hackeim, where the Free French brigade under General Koenig had occupied a strong defensive position, and then, a few days later, together with the rest of 4 Armoured Brigade, a further thirty miles to the south-east. Here the regiment stayed until well into May, enduring periods of unpleasant weather and extreme heat; the *khamsin*, the hot wind from the south that brought sandstorms with it, was blowing. Despite the conditions, combined training with other arms continued and also live firing practice against the wrecks of tanks and motor transport that littered the desert all around them. Swimming parties went down to the coast and, for the fortunate few, short leaves in Cairo or Alexandria were granted.

This state of limbo went on until on 21 May, when the commanding officer received a warning order of a possible enemy attack within the following fourteen days, covering the period of the full moon. The Regiment, like all the units in the desert, began to maintain a higher degree of alertness by standing-to each day at dawn and dusk. The war diary for 26 May notes that it was a normal day.

That night, Rommel struck once more with a wide outflanking movement to the south, aimed at a direct engagement with the British armour positioned behind the main defensive line. The first the 8H knew of it was a message received at 0330 on 27 May placing the regiment on fifteen minutes notice and reporting that the Germans, taking full advantage of the bright moonlight, were on the move in strength and at speed. 12L, the reconnaissance regiment, had deployed its armoured cars in front of the British line some miles to the west of Bir Hackeim and, as it got dark on 26 May, had reported the noise of considerable enemy movement somewhere ahead of it, but for some reason, possibly another occurrence of poor wireless communications, the information never reached 8H.

The British defensive positions were based, as has already been indicated, on a deep defensive minefield running south from the Cyrenaican coast at Gazala and protected by infantry formations, down to, on the extreme left flank, the strong garrison of 1 Free French Brigade holding the key position of Bir Hackeim. Some twelve miles to the south and east, 8H, together with the rest of 4 Armoured Brigade, was in position to challenge any movement of the Afrika Corps around it to the south, although it was the opinion of Eighth Army that the main panzer thrust would be in the north and that any armoured movement in the south would be either diversionary or a probing action. Here they were to be proved wrong. At first light the following morning Shan, whose light squadron was in the regiment's forward position, received a wireless message from his commanding officer, Lieutenant-Colonel Kilkelly. The news was serious. The CO said that the Germans were moving much faster than had been anticipated, that they had already bypassed Bir Hackeim and were approaching the Brigade's position. At almost the same time 12L reported that they had what seemed to be the whole of the Afrika Corps in front of them and moving very fast. It was, in fact, to turn out to be the main German thrust.

Shan was ordered to move his squadron up to a ridge ahead from which he might observe the approaching German armour. What he saw fully confirmed the information that 12L had sent back a short time before. The Germans were indeed moving very fast, having taken advantage of the moon to make the forty-mile approach march from their jumping-off position during the night. The first Eighth Army formation to suffer the blows of this devastating armoured attack was 3 Indian Motor Brigade deployed in the desert to the south-east of Bir Hakeim, its role to delay the enemy and to force it to move into a position where it could be attacked by British armour. The destruction of this formation barely delayed the German tanks, which turned north-west to manoeuvre behind the British fortified line and assault the British armour. 8H were next to bear the weight of the attack. Wireless communications in the field were, in the British Army at least, never really dependable at any time during the war but in the desert they were a particularly unreliable way of passing orders and information during an engagement with the enemy. The fragility of the thermionic valves that in those days activated all wireless sets (not only military ones), the heat and violent movement of a moving tank in the desert, the sand and dust that permeated everything, all combined to make it more likely than not that the chances of receiving an intelligible message through the tank commander's headset were evens at best. To allow for this, a flag system had been devised by which simple commands could be transmitted and acknowledged visually between units within sight of each other. Shan duly hoisted a black flag, the signal to attack, and his squadron moved towards the dust cloud that was the approaching Afrika Corps. In the heat of the battle and about to have his first violent contact with the German Army, Shan committed the understandable error of not immediately taking it down. The Germans had long since learnt that any British tank flying a pennant was likely to carry a commander and so it was Shan who drew the greater part of German fire and whose tank was the first to be knocked out during the engagement. Despite suffering burns, he immediately moved himself to another of C Squadron's tanks and resumed command.

The battle went disastrously for 8H. The effectiveness of the main armament of its two squadrons of Grant tanks, the side-mounted 75mm, came as a surprise to the Germans and the regiment was confident that it would be able to inflict considerable casualties on the German armour. A Squadron drew first blood by scoring a direct hit on an 88mm gun, but its success was short-lived. In quick time all but two of its Grants were knocked out by an enemy strength estimated at one hundred MarkIII and Mark IV tanks, closely supported by a powerful force of anti-tank guns. B Squadron, on the right flank and thus not the first to suffer the German's attentions, were soon under attack and lost every tank, but, by great good fortune, casualties among the troops were very low, unlike the unfortunate A Squadron. All the tanks of regimental headquarters were destroyed, the adjutant, Captain Baldwin, killed and Major Phillips and Lieutenant Gimblett, respectively second-in-command and signals officer of the regiment, captured. It was by now 0900 on the morning of 27 May and 8H had to all intents and purposes ceased to exist as an effective fighting unit. For those left on the ground as the spearhead of the German attack went on through it was a time for quick thinking and swift action if they were to escape being killed or captured. The efforts of the enemy were focused on reaching its forward objectives and on the encirclement and destruction of the British armoured formations on the way; clearing up the battlefield and collecting the prisoners was, for the time, of secondary importance. Captain Huth, an officer of C Squadron whose tank had been shot from under him, found himself cut off with a party from the Regiment, a number of whom were wounded. Having attended as best they could to the wounded, he then set about disabling some of A Squadron's Grants that appeared to him might be within the enemy's power to salvage and repair. The next task was to collect what food and water could be found on the battlefield and distribute it; he then ordered the party to disperse and hide up in the vicinity until it got dark. By great good fortune they escaped any close attention by enemy units during the day and at dusk he rallied the fit among the party to him and they set off to walk in the hope of finding British forces. During the night they covered sixteen miles, passing on the way two German leaguers without being detected. In the morning they were picked up by a troop of South African armoured cars.

Later that day the same officer volunteered to go back to collect the wounded and borrowing two trucks from an Indian medical unit, set off. He arrived safely at his previous night's hiding place to find the wounded still there and under the guard of a single German sentry, who was promptly taken prisoner. The evacuation began and a first party of five was sent away, but the rescue was interrupted by the appearance over a ridge, some distance off, of a German armoured car, which at once opened fire. Not wishing to endanger the wounded further, the officer deemed it best to take himself off and, together with the first party, managed to get back safely to the Regiment. Over the next few days a considerable number of the Regiment straggled in, including the second-in-command.

The remnants of the Regiment withdrew to the east, its B echelon (the supply column) taking advantage of the state of extreme confusion on the battlefield and getting a surprising number of its transport vehicles back. By the following day the survivors were once again at Fort Capuzzo; the unwounded and those still fit for battle were reformed into crews, replacement tanks and vehicles drawn from the ordnance depot and 8H set about doing what it could to restore itself into some semblance of a battleworthy fighting unit.

By the end of the first day back in Capuzzo C Squadron had been made up to the point where it could once more be considered operational, the general situation on the battlefield being such that every man capable of taking his place in a front-line unit was needed and needed urgently. The rest of the Regiment was still some way short of being fit for battle and so C Squadron was placed under the command of 3 Royal Tank Regiment of Colonel 'Pip' Roberts, a tank soldier who had already won himself a high reputation in action and who was to go on to become the successful and greatly admired commander of 11th Armoured Division in Normandy. The Squadron went straight back into action under their new commanding officer but without Shan. The wounds he had suffered when his tank burst into flames during the contact battle were becoming troublesome; he had borne them with fortitude for the first two days of carnage and confusion, but on 29 May it was decided that he should be evacuated for treatment. This was done successfully, although his journey to the Royal Naval Hospital in Alexandria was hazardous and extremely uncomfortable.

Although Shan's time in action in the Gazala battle was short, it was sufficient for him to draw some firm conclusions about the Afrika Corps and its commander. The soldiers he thought tough, well trained and highly motivated, while, as for Rommel, he admired his dash, his ability to see a tactical advantage and his quickness in seizing it. He was later to deplore the situation on the British side during Gazala, when General Lumsden, with his reassembled elements of 1st Armoured Division, had accurately judged the point and time where he might have thrust decisively against Rommel and caused him to retreat. But he was frustrated by the insistence of General Messervy (an old-fashioned Indian cavalry officer, in Shan's opinion) to a delay in committing his own armoured division alongside Lumsden, when the opportunity was lost. Shan was later to find himself in complete agreement with the German view that the main faults of Eighth Army in the desert were a cumbrous organization and sluggish reactions to events.

In Shan's absence, his C Squadron under 3 RTR went on fighting a withdrawal battle, taking heavy casualties. On 30 May a C Squadron officer, badly wounded in the head, was rescued by having his tank towed out of action, under fire, by another officer who was himself to be reported wounded and missing two days later. By 6 June C Squadron was down to five tanks. The old A and B Squadrons of 8H had meanwhile been reformed into a composite squadron as a sort of divisional reserve that was moved from regiment to regiment around the battle, wherever the need was greatest.

The hours of darkness brought little rest for the battered Regiment. Apart from the need for repairs and maintenance so as to be able to field the maximum possible from the dwindling number of tanks still partly battleworthy, the *Luftwaffe* was very active and their night bombing highly disruptive. Two days from 8 June out of contact with the enemy gave some relief but it was short-lived; by 13 June the composite A/B Squadron was down to three tanks and in the German attack the following day the last of the tanks of 8H was destroyed. The remnants of the Regiment were withdrawn to Bardia to reform.

Shan returned to the desert from the Royal Naval Hospital at Alexandria on 21 June to find 8H, even after replacement, at a strength of fifteen tanks and a few of the soft-skinned trucks of B echelon. He reformed C squadron the following day and received twenty light tanks three days later, but that very night German bombers found their leaguer and two men of his new squadron were killed and a dozen wounded. The withdrawal that would eventually end at El Alamein had begun and Shan's squadron did good work in the extremely fluid situation that existed all over the battlefield. One day, operating independently of the rest of the Regiment, which now had a strength of eleven officers and one hundred and fifty other ranks, he located and attacked a large concentration of German transport, inflicting very heavy casualties. During much of Eighth Army's retreat, Shan's C Squadron operated in a reconnaissance role before being withdrawn on 1 July to rest and refit, getting up to their war strength of sixteen tanks. By 14 July they were back in the line.

Rommel's successful offensive put him once again in possession of Tobruk and carried him deep into Egypt towards Alamein, where the almost impassable sand sea of the Qattara Depression approached closest to the Mediterranean coast. Here Auchinleck rightly judged was his best chance of defending Egypt and the Canal Zone from the seemingly unstoppable Axis armies. Rommel's achievement had been staggering. The extent of his booty, in arms and ammunition, in stores and supplies of every sort and especially in petrol was enormous and was to do much to compensate for his ever-lengthening lines of communication that, despite his being in possession of every port in the theatre of war except Alexandria, stretched back all the way to Tripoli.

The two armies now faced each other on a front of forty miles and the rest of the month of July passed in a series of attacks by one side or the other to maintain or improve tactical positions of advantage and by counter-attacks to regain what might just have been lost. During this phase of the desert battle the rump of Shan's regiment was combined with the rump of the 4th Hussars to form, temporarily, the 4/8H, their area of operations being at the southern end of the British position. By the month's end some sort of stalemate had been reached and both sides settled down to re-equip, reform and ready themselves for the next phase, which Rommel had decided would be his final battle of the desert war, a German offensive that would bring him into the Delta, the capture of Alexandria and Cairo and the occupation of the Canal Zone. Beyond that his imagination carried him, with the British forces totally destroyed and all their enormous supply depots captured, deep into Syria and Iraq and to a junction in the Gulf oilfields with German armies advancing south through the Caucasus. He believed he would be ready to launch his attack on 30 August. On the fifteenth of the same month General Montgomery replaced General Auchinleck as commander of Eighth Army.

What followed became known as the first battle of Alamein. Montgomery had disposed four of his infantry divisions behind a minefield, with another infantry division and his armour deployed on and around the Alam Halfa ridge, some fifteen miles further back. The Eighth Army's commander accurately read his enemy's intentions as being broadly similar to the battle of Gazala some three months before, a penetration in the south of the British line (although this time the Qattara Depression would restrict an outflanking movement), followed by a sweeping right hook to the sea to cut off and destroy the British armour, leaving Egypt open to him. To encourage Rommel in this course of action, Montgomery deliberately left a weakness on his left flank. The enemy's plan turned out exactly as foreseen. Again the chosen night, (30 August) was moonlit, so that his engineers could with less difficulty lift thousands of British mines to create the gaps in the defences through which his armour would expect to pour into the rear of the main British positions. In the event progress was slower than planned and a new factor had entered the equation; the Royal Air Force was much stronger than it had been during the summer battles and was able frequently to establish areas of local air superiority. German forces on the ground, in the front line as well as their supply depots and replenishment columns, were being attacked with unprecedented ferocity and increasing success. This time Rommel's intentions would not succeed in giving the desired results, as they had at Gazala.

The job given to 4/8H was to cover the withdrawal of the armoured car reconnaissance regiments through the gaps the British had left in the minefields, laying mines to close them to the enemy and then to pull back to take station with the remainder of the British armour at the Alam Halfa ridge. Here, hull down in sound defensive positions, they waited for the arrival of the German tanks, confident that the *Luftwaffe* was less likely to be able to interfere. The German armour duly appeared, expecting the British tanks to sally out and engage in the mobile desert warfare in which they had so often been defeated by superior German tactics, better tanks and heavier firepower. They did not and this time it was the Germans who were defeated, calling off the battle and retreating back through the minefields to go once more on to the defensive.

Shan would later recount two episodes of the battle that had stuck in his memory. The first was a visit at Alam Halfa of a keen and efficient sapper officer, to enquire whether it had been Shan's squadron that had laid the mines to close the British gaps after the armoured cars had passed through. On being told that it was, he asked whether the detailed map showing the location of the mines laid and which Shan had no doubt drawn at the time could please be handed over to him. The bemused Shan, who had not been trained in minelaying and had, to his knowledge, never been asked to make a map, was only able to give a graphic description of the dangerous circumstances in which he and his men had, under fire, so courageously carried out this unfamiliar activity. The second was a visit after the battle of a general who appeared in a staff car at regimental headquarters, where his driver and ADC proceeded to set up a large blackboard that they had brought with them, on which it was explained to the assembled officers how he, the commander of XXX Corps, had achieved victory over Rommel in the late battle of Alam Halfa. It turned out to be the colourful General Horrocks (or Jorrocks, as he was familiarly known to the British Army), whose life was to be intertwined with Shan's in the Arnhem battle two years later. On this occasion Shan was not convinced by the general's tale, it being quite clear in his own mind that the honours of the day lay with 4 Armoured Brigade and particularly within that formation, 4/8H. How much this doubtful observation on General Horrocks, recalled by Shan in later life, was coloured by the failure of XXX Corps in 1944, still under the same commander, to carry out successfully the tasks given to it in Operation Market Garden and join up with 1st Airborne Division in Arnhem can only be speculated upon, but Shan always considered his initial reservations about Horrocks at their first meeting in the desert to have been justified.

The few months in 1942 Shan had spent back with his Regiment between the Battle of Gazala in May and the Battle of Alam Halfa in the last days of August had been busy but were soon to come to an end and as it transpired, he was not again to serve with 8H as a regimental officer. He had conducted himself well in battle, as was officially recognized by the award of a DSO to go with his MC and the pre-war MBE. Events away from the main desert battle were to take him into new and unfamiliar duties and responsibilities, this time as a staff officer.

Arising out of their long and glorious maritime tradition, the British in wartime had always sought to create an open flank by exploiting the mobility that, whenever and however temporarily it could be won, was given them by control of the seas within the theatre of war in which the Royal Navy was operating. The general situation in the Mediterranean during the desert war was, by and large, favourable to this strategy. The Italian Navy, despite some spectacular successes with midget submarines, had not been able to control the broad seas, nor, a matter of great concern to the Germans, had it been able to protect the tankers and supply ships on the Tripoli run, vital to the support to the Axis desert armies. This was despite the power and effectiveness of the German *Luftwaffe*, which certainly up until the Battle of Alam Halfa was the more likely to have control of the air over sea and land. The sheer extent of the battlefield, the long and vulnerable lines of communication that were the inevitable outcome of rapid advances over great distances, gave great strength to fast-moving, self-contained fighting groups that could appear without warning in places they had never been expected and disappear into the desert with little fear of effective pursuit. This was the terrestial dimension of the military philosophy of the open flank and led to the considerable employment in the campaign of what were generically referred to as raiding forces and popularly as 'private armies'. They were highly mobile and relatively lightly armed units, organized both outside and independent of the formations of battalions and regiments making up brigades, brigades making up divisions and divisions forming army corps, which was the structural pattern of armies worldwide. These semi-irregular units, viewed with great suspicion by the staff because of their lack of tight control over their activities and disliked by commanding officers who would find their best men poached from them in the bars and canteens of Alexandria and Cairo by the lure of that semi-amateur type of military life that seemed to appeal greatly to the British temperament. They came from all varieties of background; the Greeks provided a tough band of marauders known as the Sacred Squadron and the Special Boat Service under George Jellicoe, specializing in nocturnal raids from the sea, numbered sponge fishermen with intimate knowledge of Aegean coastal waters in its ranks. Another unit renowned for its toughness was recruited, other than for its British officers, entirely from German-Jewish refugees. A Turkish-speaking band of desperadoes was known as the Kalpaks, while the Long Range Desert Group, among the first of the private armies, gained a high and fully justified reputation for its efficiency. Almost invariably under the command of some colourful and idiosyncratic personality, these unconventional units were employed during the campaigns of North Africa, sometimes with great effectiveness, in deep penetration by land, sea and from the air behind Axis lines, on tasks of reconnaissance and intelligence gathering or the destruction of enemy men and equipment, including attacks on headquarters with the aim of killing or capturing senior commanders and disrupting the work of their staff. It was said that certainly during the first two years of the desert war, David Stirling's SAS had destroyed more enemy aircraft on the ground than the Royal Air Force had managed to shoot out of the air.

During Rommel's advance up to El Alamein and the gates of Egypt a group built around a reinforced Highland battalion made a seaborne raid in strength to deny to the enemy the use of the port of Tobruk and of the mountain of supplies left during its capitulation in June, a week or so into the Gazala battle. The plan was for a landing from the sea, supported by LRDG and SAS and Jock Haselden's German Jews. The operation was a complete disaster. The Highland battalion and Haselden's unit were almost totally destroyed and the other private armies severely mauled, while the Royal Navy lost two Tribal class destroyers, *Sikh* and *Zulu*. The inevitable post-mortem revealed that the three-service operation had been planned by a committee representing the three services engaged; the planning inevitably incorporated all the compromises demanded by services not answerable to a single commander with a clear and single-minded sense of purpose, prepared to impose his will upon the supporting arms. In the operation itself each arm felt itself to be subordinate to its own senior commander, each of whom looked with partisan eyes at the role its own units were to play in the overall scheme of things. The conclusions drawn by GHQ Middle East were, first, that a properly coordinated command and control structure would need to be put in place for all combined operations and, secondly, if the raiding forces were to realize in full the contribution they could make to the desert war, their distinct strengths and weaknesses had to be assessed and understood and placed under an overall command structure. Accordingly, an HQ Raiding Forces was set up and the search begun for an able senior staff officer to give it strength and purpose. Major-General Freddy de Guingand, lately arrived in the Middle East as Montgomery's chief of staff, proposed Shan for the appointment, a thought that did not in the slightest appeal to the candidate. At the time he was, as has been said, in the southern part of the Alamein defences in the area of the Himeimat Ridge, close to the great sand sea of the Qattara Depression, vastly enjoying himself in what was generally conceded by many who took part as the last of the gentlemen's wars. The soldiers on either side, sharing as they did the harsh and demanding conditions of a barren desert and a vast battleground and realizing the close balance of a campaign that favoured first one side and then the other, did not hate each other and in fact held each other in grudging respect. Meticulous attention was paid to old-fashioned niceties of conduct; the provisions of the Geneva Convention tended to be scrupulously observed and a captured officer was, as like as not, to find himself invited to dine with his captors and to share reminiscences and opinions over a bottle of wine before being sent to the prisoner of war camp. A small, if possibly, oblique observation on general attitudes to the proper conduct of a war fought between professionals, with an almost total absence of civilians, was an incident during the negotiations for the surrender of Tobruk to the Germans in July 1942. The number of Allied prisoners was enormous and the South Africans made a request that their captors should see that the black troops among them were strictly segregated from the whites. This Rommel rejected outright, saying that there was no need to make a distinction in captivity between those who had fought side by side in battle.

As Shan later described it, his life in the Alamein line was agreeable. He would saunter out in the early mornings with the purpose of dominating the local battlefield, searching out light German armour of about his own weight and then would follow a stalking game in and out of the hollows of the undulating desert, in which occasionally either side might have a shot at the other and sometimes there would be casualties. This, to Shan, was a thoroughly satisfactory way of occupying himself and his chaps until the next offensive should come along and the thought of giving it up for a staff appointment and a desk at GHQ in Cairo was not something he felt he could readily accept, even if it did mean his promotion to the rank of lieutenant-colonel. He fired off a vigorous protest to the chief of staff at GHQ, General Dick McCreery, a 12th Lancer he had known well in the Cairo Cavalry Brigade when his own regiment had first come out to Egypt in 1933 and when that was seen to be of no avail sent a personal appeal to de Guingand, his proposer for the appointment. He was aware, as was every other soldier in Eighth Army that a great offensive at Alamein was in preparation and he had every intention of playing his part in it. It was made very clear to him that further argument was futile, so back he went to the Delta where he straightway set himself to his tasks as he understood them, first of looking into the lessons that might be learnt from the failure of the Tobruk raid and then of defining the special qualities and capabilities of the different units that fell under the umbrella of raiding forces, so that they might be deployed with the greatest possible effectiveness. He was also responsible for seeing that each of his units was properly armed and equipped for its particular role, but perhaps what was most to occupy him was the job of explaining to senior commanders what benefits raiding forces could bring and of persuading them to agree to their use.

One of the earliest of his new acquaintances as GSO1 Raiding Forces was a White Russian major called 'Popski' Poliakoff, wounded during the Tobruk raid and with much to tell about it, who had recruited a group of his own that had been given, by whoever was responsible at GHQ for such things, the title of 'No 1 Long Range Demolition Group'. It might have been an accurate enough description of the unit's purpose but neither he nor Shan was happy with the name and they agreed to come up with something better. Shan had a sudden inspiration; 'What about,' he said, 'Popski's Private Army?' And so it became for the rest of its existence, playing a part through the great advance of the Eighth Army to Tunis and the defeat of the Axis forces in North Africa, through the whole long length of the Italian campaign, right up to its disbandment when the fighting war was over. But Shan and Popski had not yet finished with each other.

One of the first conclusions the newly appointed general staff officer came to was the need to delineate clearly the areas in which the different constituents of his empire were to operate. So a north/south boundary was set up to divide the territories of the SAS and LRDG and to keep them out of each others' way and avoid the possibility of a carefully concealed observation post set up deep in enemy territory by one unit being compromised by the stirring-up of the Germans by the arrival of another unit intent on some work of destruction in the same area. The raiding parties were theatre troops, reporting direct to GHQ Middle East and consequently not answerable to Eighth Army, but nonetheless there was the need to have the sympathetic cooperation of Montgomery and his staff, something that could not be taken for granted. Shan recalled an occasion when he wished to make a call within the desert units for volunteers to make up the strengths of various of the raiding forces within his responsibility. A message came from Eighth Army that a request for battle-experienced NCOs to be transferred to the SAS as troopers had been passed up to the GOC in C and that, if Shan wished to carry the matter to a satisfactory conclusion, he would have to come to their HQ, bringing one of his commanders with him and discuss it with the great man himself. So Shan and David Stirling took themselves up into the desert, to Eighth Army's tactical headquarters at Bourg-el-Arab where Montgomery, with characteristic directness, said, 'And tell me, Stirling, why do you suppose that my men will fight better under you than under me? In any case, they will not be trained in time for the battle.' Incautiously, the visitors accepted that they might not but they would certainly be ready for the following battle and all Eighth Army's future battles. This was too much for Monty. He banged the table with his fist and barked out a brusque, 'There will be only one more battle in Africa!', stabbed the map with his finger on the Alamein line and added, 'And this is where I shall destroy Rommel and his whole army!' This was too much for David Stirling, an officer not renowned for deference towards those senior to himself. 'All very well, General, but the last GOC in C told us that and the one before him, too.' That abruptly ended the interview and the two recruiting agents came away on that occasion empty-handed from Eighth Army. Monty's small explosion soon died away and he harboured no rancour against his plain-speaking visitors, nor did he allow his anger to affect his estimation of the value and abilities of the two officers, as, in Shan's case, events were soon to prove.

As everyone knows, the Battle of Alamein duly took place and its results are now history. As the Axis forces began to withdraw, disappointment began to be felt in Cairo that Eighth Army was having little success in getting around and behind them and cutting them off and that far too many of the enemy, particularly among the German formations, were able to escape. The feeling grew at GHQ Middle East that had a trained and ready parachute formation been available in the theatre and had it been dropped at somewhere like Capuzzo, the Axis retreat could have been effectively blocked and that the bag of prisoners and booty would have been much greater and the destruction of Rommel's armies achieved much sooner. These feelings resolved themselves into a firm decision to proceed without delay with raising such a formation in brigade strength and one day Shan was called into the office of the Chief of Staff to be told of it and offered the chance to build, command and train the new formation. He was given two days to think about it, but, replying that two seconds were more than enough, he accepted on the spot. So Shan set out on the road that was to lead ineluctably to Arnhem.

Chapter Five

AIRBORNE TO ARNHEM

In November 1942 Shan took up his new command equipped with little more than a title, 4 Parachute Brigade, the new rank of Brigadier and a blank sheet of paper. Everything had to be done from the bottom up. Perhaps, however, the paper was not entirely blank. No 4 Parachute Training School was already operational at Kabrit, in the Canal Zone, its duties being to train members of the SAS and agents intended to be dropped in enemy territories. The logical plan seemed to be to form 4 Parachute Brigade around the existing parachute training facilities and so that is where Shan set up his headquarters. To put flesh on his paper skeleton, the already trained 151 Parachute Battalion, which had been formed in India at the end of 1941 of volunteers, many of them regulars, from British units serving in India and which was then part of 50 Indian Parachute Brigade, was moved to Egypt in November as the first of the fighting units of the new formation. When it joined 4 Parachute Brigade, for security reasons it was re-designated 156 Battalion The Parachute Regiment (156/Para) and so it remained.

The following month, with the formation of Brigade headquarters under way, it was time for its commander to become a parachutist and this Shan duly carried out in the company of his senior staff officer, 'Crackers' May, the brigade major. He was thus able to demonstrate to the units in his new command that he was qualified to lead them not only by virtue of his battle experience and fighting reputation, to which the ribbons on his chest attested, but also by the wings on his right shoulder.

While the facilities at Kabrit might have been sufficient for a small parachute training school, they were soon revealed to be inadequate for the raising and training of a brigade. The airfield was small, the surrounding area unsuitable for tactical training and the weather conditions of frequent and sudden wind and dust storms made parachuting more hazardous and injury-prone than was acceptable. A much more suitable area in all respects was northern Palestine and so such as now existed of the Brigade moved and set up camp around Ramat David.

Shan found it agreeable to be back in territory that held so many memories of the TJFF and of his early days with Margaret and the two children.

At about the same time a regular infantry battalion, 2nd Battalion, The Royal Sussex Regiment (2/R Sussex), was selected to be converted en bloc, or at least those within it who chose to volunteer, to become the second of the brigade's parachute battalions, renumbered as 10th Battalion, The Parachute Regiment (10 Para). However, it had then been decided that a regular infantry battalion could not after all be forcibly removed from its regiment and incorporated into the Army Air Corps and that 2/R Sussex would retain its original identity and have the gaps left by the airborne volunteers filled by suitable infantry reinforcements. This was done and 10 Para, under the command of Lieutenant-Colonel Ken Smyth, proceeded with its build-up from the core foundation of some one hundred all ranks of 2/R Sussex who had opted to join the Parachute Regiment. At the same time the support arms began to be formed from scratch, the first two units being 4 Parachute Squadron of the Royal Engineers and 133 Parachute Field Ambulance.

Very soon after the move to Palestine twelve Dakotas of 7 Squadron, US Troop Carrier Command, arrived on permanent attachment and the serious work of raising the Brigade to its full level of operational efficiency could now begin in earnest. Exercises were carried out in Cyprus and around Lake Tiberias, where much more realistic and suitable conditions could be found both in respect of the airborne and parachuting training, and also on the ground.

4 Parachute Brigade, with only two parachute battalions, still lacked a third battalion to bring it up its proper establishment. The low response for volunteers from 2/R Sussex, which had managed to provide only a nucleus of a fighting battalion for 10/Para, had set in train a vigorous recruiting campaign throughout the whole of Middle East Command. Despite the understandable and unconcealed reluctance of commanding officers to part with men and damage the integrity of their own units, this went sufficiently well not only to build 10 Para up to strength but also to allow the formation of 11 Para to begin. This latter unit, which was formed in the Canal Zone, took a cadre from 156 Para, including the second-in command, Major Micky Thomas, who was appointed its first commanding officer. The build-up of the brigade to its full strength and operational efficiency went well and by late May, after the successful conclusion of the North African campaign and when operations on the mainland of Europe were being actively planned, it was, with the exception of 11 Para, the newest battalion, considered to be ready to join its parent division, 1st Airborne, itself just recently arrived in Tunisia. Before it could be considered battleworthy, 11 Para still had much to do

in both its tactical and its parachute training and, when 4 Parachute Brigade left, it moved up from Egypt to Ramat David to take over the better facilities that could be provided there. In the event, it was not to rejoin its parent brigade until it and the rest of 1st Airborne Division were back in England preparing for the invasion of North-West Europe, but it managed to employ its time usefully in the Eastern Mediterranean by carrying out a number of small raiding operations against various of the German-occupied Greek islands in the Dodecanese.

The decision had been taken as early as March 1943, before the North African campaign had finally been concluded in the Allies' favour, that the next objective would be Sicily and planning began with the intention of using the two airborne divisions in the theatre, 82nd US Airborne and 1st British Airborne, in the initial assault. This operation would be the first major Allied airborne operation against the Axis forces and the biggest so far attempted by either side since 1939; much bigger than the daring *coup de main* strikes by the German forces during the 1940 invasion of the Low Countries or the last major and improbably successful parachute invasion of Crete in 1941. The heavy casualties sustained by the Germans in that operation persuaded them that even against a fragmented opposition the losses were finely balanced against the gains and they were never again to use airborne troops to undertake a large-scale drop, their parachute units thenceforth being used as ground troops, albeit of a surpassing military quality.

Shan's 4 Parachute Brigade, being under-strength by 11 Para, still absent in the eastern Mediterranean, and in any case constituting an additional brigade within an airborne division that had arrived complete with its three brigades from the United Kingdom, was held in reserve for the invasion of Sicily, a decision that may not have pleased Shan at the time, but for the fledglings that were his direct responsibility was an extremely fortunate one. The airborne operation, which was to take place overnight on 9/10 July 1943 and precede the seaborne invasion the following morning, was not successfully executed; the achievement of such of the troops who were landed in enemy territory owed everything to their valour and resource after their arrival and little to the effectiveness of their delivery. At that stage in the war many of the pilots of the Dakotas who were to transport the parachute units and to tow the gliders carrying the battalions of 1 Airlanding Brigade and the essential support arms of light transport and anti-tank artillery were embodied civilian airline pilots, accustomed to flying mostly in daylight and in peacetime conditions for pre-determined distances along navigational radio beams and homing in on airport beacons for their approach and landing. They were untrained in aerial navigation by map reading, sextant or sun compass, and, furthermore, the troop-carrying aircraft did not have the benefits of armoured seats for the flight crews nor of self-sealing petrol tanks. In addition, there was already a prevalent philosophy, particularly strong in the minds of those of senior officers who had gone through the carnage of trench warfare during the First World War, that, apart from the need to preserve resources for future operations, action to minimize Allied casualties should be taken where it was possible. Accordingly, elaborate plans that seemed sound on paper were made to allow gliders to be cast off at such a distance off the invasion coasts as would keep the tug aircraft short of the range of enemy anti-aircraft fire but still sufficiently close for the gliders to reach their landing zones safely.

An unwelcome complication on the night was a strong headwind blowing offshore from the invasion beaches. To cope with this additional hazard, it was ordered that the release point for gliders would be reduced to 3000 yards from the coast, a condition that in practice proved too much for many of the aircrew. The bumpy journey, the difficulties of estimating the exact release point during a night lighted up by the exploding anti-aircraft fire apparently immediately ahead of them, persuaded many of the tug pilots to cast off their gliders further out to sea. Almost eighty of the gliders carrying the three British air landing battalions ditched; of the almost five hundred casualties sustained by them in the whole of the invasion, over half were drowned, while the Glider Pilot Regiment crews flying the towed aircraft alone suffered losses of more than one hundred all ranks.

Shan and 4 Parachute Brigade, with its role as reserve formation in the invasion plan, followed the progress of the landings with concern. He was later to recall how glider pilot survivors evacuated back to base in Tunis would go about looking for an American throat to cut in revenge for what they felt, justly or not, was a failure of duty on the part of some of the tug pilots. The situation reached the point at which it was necessary to confine members of the Glider Pilot Regiment to barracks until tempers had cooled and events had moved on.

Once on the ground (or, rather, on the ground and in the sea), scattered and depleted as it was, such of 1 Airlanding Brigade as remained determinedly set about achieving its objectives of securing the vital bridge at Ponte Grande and proceeding on to the capture of the important town of Syracuse, on the south-east coast of Sicily. A party of the South Staffordshire Regiment, carried in a glider that landed several hundred yards offshore, swam, carrying their weapons, to the defended beach under enemy fire, crawled through the barbed wire and, as soon as it was light, moved off to join the rest of their battalion, *en route* capturing two pill boxes, twenty-one Italian soldiers and an anti-tank gun. The fact of the dispersal of the Allied forces over a wide area added to the confusion of the enemy, who believed the invasion to be of far greater magnitude than in fact it was.

The British 17 Infantry Brigade, part of the seaborne landing, relieved 1 Airlanding Brigade, which was withdrawn from the battle and returned by sea to the airborne base in Tunisia. In the meantime 1 Parachute Brigade had been dropped with the objective of capturing the important bridge of Ponte di Primosole, south of Catania. Again the operation was hampered by a dispersal of the airborne troops during the flight; not only were they dropped outside their designated dropping zones but the timing and sequence of arrival of the transporting aircraft also went badly awry. After a confused and messy but eventually successful battle, in which ground troops from XIII Corps also took part and during which the parachute brigade commander was wounded, 1 Parachute Brigade was in its turn withdrawn. By 19 July it was back at its Tunisian base, where, with the other formations of 1st Airborne Division, it licked its wounds, re-equipped, replaced the killed, wounded and missing and waited to discover what part it would play in what they thought inevitably would be the next stage of the war, the invasion by the Allies of the mainland of Italy.

By 17 August 1943 all German and Italian resistance on the island of Sicily was at an end and the Allies were in complete control. In planning the next steps, from the highest levels of the Allied governments downwards, there was disagreement about the course that should be adopted. To simplify the arguments, the Americans had their eyes firmly fixed on the invasion in 1944 of the mainland of North-West Europe from the United Kingdom and they were reluctant to divert resources from it to what they considered sideshows making only subsidiary contributions to the prime and over-riding objective of the defeat of Nazi Germany in its heartland. Churchill's thinking, on the other hand, was much influenced by what he felt might be Stalin's intentions for the future of the central and eastern countries of the Mediterranean, distant as the Soviet ground forces might have been at that stage of the war. In Yugoslavia the struggle for supremacy between the two partisan groups, Tito's Communists and Mihailovic's supporters of the pre-war regime, the efforts of both groups directed not only against the Axis occupiers but also against each other, was tending to move in favour of Tito. He was also aware of the major part being played in the French resistance by the Communist party and he had already warned Roosevelt of the dangers of what he called the 'Bolshevisation' of an Italy in which the Fascist government had fallen, leaving no credible alternative government to fill the vacuum. Churchill's instinct, therefore, was to exploit the momentum built up by the successful completion of the North African and Sicilian campaigns and move on in strength into mainland Italy.

New events within Italy itself were to help determine matters. On 24/25 July, while the Allied invasion of Sicily was barely two weeks old, the Italian Grand Council met and passed a resolution that effectively replaced Mussolini and his Fascist party with a new national government under Marshal Bagdolio. On the orders of King Emmanuel, the now former dictator was arrested as he left the Grand Council meeting and was taken away to what was intended to be a secure place of imprisonment. With the complete and final defeat of all Axis forces in Sicily several weeks later, the invasion of Italy became much more certain.

We should now turn to an examination of the effect of all these events and happenings on the Allied airborne forces in the Mediterranean theatre of operations. The 82nd US Airborne Division, unlike its British counterpart, was not withdrawn but kept in the line, with all its supporting arms and base support transferred to Sicily as suitable facilities were captured and could be made ready. During the campaign the process of reinforcement, replacement of casualties and of destroyed and damaged arms and equipment went on, so when the invasion of Italy became a serious prospect the American division was complete in Sicily, close to the presumed next area of operations and close to the air component that would carry it into battle. By contrast, 1st Airborne Division was hundreds of miles further away in Tunisia, separated from and only in spasmodic contact with their controlling formation in Sicily, the British Eighth Army. The result was that after protracted negotiations between the Bagdolio government and the Allies over the precise terms of the Italian capitulation, going on while fighting continued in Sicily, the invasion began on 3 September 1943 with the crossing by the Eighth Army of the Straits of Messina that separated Sicily from Italy proper. The unblooded 4 Parachute Brigade was chosen to support British land forces and briefed for a landing on two dropping zones in the region of Reggio, only a few miles ahead of the leading troops.

Shan approved of none of this. With the Italian government giving every indication that there could be an early collapse of resistance, with the likelihood of an extremely fluid situation all over the country and of the Germans almost certainly reacting by rushing in reinforcements from the North, his firm view was that it was an ideal opportunity for the strategic use of the airborne forces at the Allies' disposal. He sent for maps of northern Italy and in the map room at his headquarters, planned a landing for his brigade well north of Rome, with the aim of blocking the defiles on the lines of communication through which German forces moving south would have to pass. His grand idea, if even it ever registered in the minds of those senior to him, was never adopted. Instead, the overall Allied plan that emerged was for a new seaborne landing at Salerno, linking up with Eighth Army advancing along the toe of Italy and then having the combined forces push forward in the direction of Rome.

The landings at Salerno were to take place on 9 September 1943 and, in an early version of the plans, the contribution of Shan's 4 Parachute Brigade would be to capture Monte Corvino airfield in the immediate vicinity of the beachhead and hold it for use as a forward base for RAF fighter and ground support squadrons. There was a vivid memory throughout 1st Airborne Division of the problems of the landings in Sicily and the wide dispersal on the ground of the airborne troops, the consequence of the inexperience of the pilots of the US transport aircraft. Shan was determined that, whatever else might happen, he and his headquarters would be put down in the correct place and accordingly arranged to be dropped from RAF Albemarles, an unsuccessful medium bomber aircraft normally used as a glider tug and by no means properly adapted to drop parachutists. The brigade staff found the preparatory training jumps they did from the RAF aeroplanes 'uncomfortable'. In the end an equivalent formation of the US 82nd Airborne Division was given the task, the objectives were changed and, as Shan had feared, the airborne landings were indeed, in the event, seriously dispersed.

On 8 September, as the Salerno invasion fleet was on its way, the Italian armistice was signed and some of the assault units began to have visions of unopposed landings and a simple occupation of their planned objectives. The Germans destroyed such hopes by their customary swift and decisive reaction to events and resistance to the landings was fierce. The Allies, too, could also make contingency plans and on this occasion did so effectively. A major port and naval base on the heel of the Italian peninsula was Taranto, from where, under the terms of the armistice agreement, a considerable proportion of the Italian Mediterranean fleet was to sail to Malta to surrender. Accordingly, all the specialized assault transport being fully occupied with the landings in the Bay of Naples, a plan was devised for 1st Airborne Division to be taken by warships of the Royal Navy and US Navy to attack and occupy Taranto at the same time as the invasion at Salerno was taking place.

No opposition was met at Taranto and the Allied flotillas entering port were able to observe the gratifying spectacle of the Italian battle fleet steaming in the opposite direction to their appointed place of surrender at Malta. The dogged resistance of the island during all the years of the desert battles had not only collectively won it the George Cross but, in providing a base for the devastating attacks on Rommel's sea supply lines that were costing the Afrika Korps the loss of over two-thirds of what was being shipped to them, had been a major contributor to the eventual British victory.

The first troops of Shan's 4 Parachute Brigade to get ashore on 8 September were one half of 156/Para, which had embarked at Bizerta on USS *Boise*. They disembarked during the early evening from alongside the quay without difficulty or casualties, closely followed the by rest of the battalion in HMS *Aurora*. Next to arrive in HMS *Penelope* and go ashore were Shan and his Brigade headquarters, together with 10/Para. Both units moved to the first objective, the railway station at Taranto, brushing aside on the way some Germans who were defending the custom sheds.

Apart from USS *Boise*, five HM cruisers in all were used as troop transports, together with a minesweeper, HMS *Abdiel*. Unfortunately this vessel, while entering harbour during the night through what was supposed to be the swept channel, struck an acoustic mine and blew up and sank with the loss by drowning, from the total ship's passenger list of seven hundred members of 1st Airborne Division, of 129 all ranks from 6 Para, 2 Anti-tank Battery and the Parachute Field Ambulance. She also took down with her a number of the Division's anti-tank guns.

Shan established his headquarters on the quayside and, not long after the Brigade's arrival, the loud hailer on the USS *Boise* was heard calling for General (as US brigadiers were called) Hackett to report on board. Shan, dressed in his slightly travel-weary khaki-drill uniform, presented himself in the captain's cabin where he found the admiral commanding Italian forces in Taranto, in full dress and wearing his ceremonial sword, requesting to be allowed to surrender formally to the senior Allied military commander present. As the youthful but somewhat dishevelled Shan was introduced to the admiral, splendidly and formally dressed for the important and historic ceremony, the Italian could not maintain the solemnity the occasion demanded. Looking at the slight figure of Shan, he burst out laughing and said, "But he's only a boy!" To his astonishment, he received a dignified and appropriate response from Shan in fluent Italian.

The consequence of the Division having been hurriedly lifted to Taranto in fighting ships rather than troop transports meant that the troops arrived with little other than their personal weapons and what they had been able to carry on their backs. It was soon realized that whatever could be found locally would have to be pressed into service and the Divisional administration made use in its supply columns, among other things, of a local train and a steam traction engine and trailer, while any motor transport, military or civilian, that could be found in the vicinity of the port was taken on strength and at once pressed into service. An enterprising staff officer of the Brigade laid hands on a smart Maserati, thinking it would be a suitable mode of transport for Brigadier Shan, but, it being spotted by a more senior officer of the Royal Air Force, he pulled rank and ordered it to be handed over, depriving the brigade commander of a most desirable spoil of war. 4 Parachute Brigade did not, however, come empty-handed out of this exercise of living off the land. An officer of 10/Para, carrying out a routine patrol around the railway station, reported finding a number of goods wagons loaded with cases of Martell brandy, requisitioned from the French by their occupiers to provide warmth and comfort to the German officer corps in Southern Italy. This Shan was determined would not follow his Maserati into less deserving hands and so he ordered it all to be unloaded without delay and added to brigade supplies. A surprisingly large proportion of this booty found its way back to England with the brigade, allegedly packed into the panniers of the Field Ambulance as essential medical supplies and surviving officers remember happily to this day how frequently it seemed possible to serve properly constituted cocktails in the messes during the following Spring and Summer.

1st Airborne Division was directed on Foggia to the north, where there was known to be a considerable complex of airfields capable, when captured, of operating a large Allied bomber force. 4 Parachute Brigade was chosen to lead the advance and 156/Para moved off with the divisional reconnaissance squadron in the early hours of the following morning, 10 September, with 10/Para on a parallel route. To Shan's delight, his old friend from raiding forces days, Popski, together with his small but effective private army, had landed with 4 Parachute Brigade and he was sent off in the general direction of the enemy to find out what he could and to cause such trouble as he was able.

It was soon established that the enemy troops facing 4 Parachute Brigade were part of the German 1st Parachute Division, tough and battle-experienced soldiers who had opposed 1st Airborne Division in Sicily. Although withdrawing, they were determined not to yield ground lightly. One company commander has recalled his admiration for the professionalism of their weapon handling, in particular the astute siting of their machine guns and mortars, which were used very effectively to delay the advance of the British paratroopers. Some sharp encounters took place, during one of which the airborne divisional commander, General 'Hoppy' Hopkinson, had come forward to 10/Para's position, where Shan was typically already installed, to see things for himself. Wearing his red beret and carrying a large pair of liberated German binoculars, the General put his head over a stone wall to observe the battle going on in front of him. Hardly had an apprehensive Shan shouted a warning of the presence of snipers in the vicinity when General Hopkinson was hit by a single bullet through the cheekbone. He fell into Shan's arms, covering them both in blood and was swiftly evacuated to the military hospital in Taranto, where he died later the same day. He was another senior officer in the Hackett mould, one who believed his place to be as much up with the troops in contact with the enemy as in his headquarters further in the rear and who, as his successor at Arnhem did to a lesser extent, paid the price for wishing to see for himself.

4 Parachute Brigade's campaign ended with the capture on 16 September of the airfield at Gioia. This was an objective of which the Allies had stood in desperate need and, within forty-eight hours of the elimination of the last German opposition, was operating a force of six RAF fighter squadrons in support of the Salerno landings. Both 10/Para and 156/Para had had some spirited actions during the week that operations against the German paratroops had lasted. On the second day of the campaign 156/Para were preparing to attack Mottola, a hilltop village some twelve miles north of Taranto, where the Germans, supported by armoured cars, were dug in. Shan, as usual well forward in his jeep with his Brigade Major, turned to John Waddy, his Brigade intelligence officer and said, "We could do with some artillery". This enterprising officer recalled having passed, a mile or so back, an Italian battery position of medium howitzers. Although since the armistice the Italians had become the Allies' co-belligerents, this particular unit had appeared to Waddy, whether from lack of any proper orders or otherwise, to be taking an insufficient interest in the battle going on around them. He drove back to the gun position and in his best pigeon Italian, swiftly secured the 'loan' of a troop of three of the guns, together with their gun crews, the ten-ton tractors and their drivers, and a decent supply of ammunition. The whole lot was handed over to 156/Para, which put them to good use and Mottola was soon captured, as a contemporary report put it, 'in fine style'. Later an Italian major, showing more spirit than his medium howitzer colleague, came into Brigade headquarters and offered Shan the services of his battery of field guns. This reinforcement was readily accepted and when Shan went over to inspect his new supporting arm he was delighted to discover that the battery was horse-drawn. "That," he said, "will add a little tone to our battle!"

The Brigade was relieved by the Division's glider-borne troops, 1 Airlanding Brigade, who continued the divisional advance to Foggia. Shan's 4 Parachute Brigade moved back to the general area of Taranto and took up defensive positions covering the port from the east. It had given a good account of itself against stiff German resistance at a cost across the brigade of one hundred and ten casualties of all ranks in killed, wounded and missing, and, in doing so, had in its first operations against the German Army, gained valuable operational experience. As Otway says in his official history of airborne forces, two main lessons learnt in that short campaign were the value of seizing and maintaining the initiative and of the necessity for effective improvization when supply is difficult or interrupted; the Brigade could little realize that in less than twelve months its noses were to be deeply and fatally rubbed in both of them.

After its formation in the Canal Zone and Palestine, 4 Parachute Brigade had moved to Tunis to join 1st Airborne Division that had arrived in North Africa from England up to its war establishment, with its two parachute brigades, 1 and 2 and its one airlanding brigade of glider-borne infantry. 4 Parachute Brigade therefore constituted an addition to the normal divisional strength. Before leaving North Africa for Taranto, the Division had already been warned that it was likely to be ordered to return to the United Kingdom in order to prepare and train to take part in Overlord, the invasion of Europe planned to take place during 1944. When the definite order came through, it was decided that one parachute brigade would remain in the Mediterranean as theatre reserve, suitably strengthened and reinforced to allow it to operate independently of divisional backing in any airborne operations that might be required during the Allies' campaign in Italy. Contrary to expectations, it was not Shan's brigade, the last to join the 1st Airborne Division, which was chosen to stay behind but 2 Parachute Brigade, one of the Division's original formations.

In November 1943 1st Airborne Division, with 4 Parachute Brigade now a permanent part of its establishment, embarked at Taranto and sailed back to England, so Shan found himself once more in the land that he had left with his regiment as a young and newly-joined officer over ten years before, with Margaret and the children far away in Palestine.

As soon as it could be arranged after the wedding, during the latter part of the time Shan was in the Western desert with his regiment, Margaret went down to Cairo and found herself a flat and a job at GHQ Middle East. She and Shan had a little while together during his short convalescence after being wounded and a longer period of married life during the time he was GSO1 of Raiding Forces at GHQ. When the formation of 4 Parachute Brigade was taking place and Shan had moved to his new headquarters at Kabrit, in the Canal Zone, Margaret left Egypt and returned to Palestine, going first to Haifa and then up to Jerusalem where, with her mother-in-law and the two children, she found a place to live in the German colony in Jerusalem. There she stayed all through the time that 4 Parachute Brigade was in Tunisia and Southern Italy and for its first few months back in England where, in the fine hunting country of Leicestershire and Rutland, it proceeded with the rest of 1st Airborne Division to prepare itself for the invasion of North-West Europe.

It would not be until the late spring of 1944 that the orders would arrive for her passage with the children to England, which began with an uncomfortable and seemingly interminable railway journey from Jerusalem down into Egypt, where at Port Said the three of them embarked and set out to rejoin Shan in a new and strange country.

Chapter Six

TO THE MARKET GARDEN

1st Airborne Division had returned to England to take part in what was to be the supreme Anglo-American effort of the Second World War, the invasion of Fortress Europe, or, to use its German title, *Festung Europa*. While not on the scale of the epic battles taking place on the Eastern Front, where up to two hundred divisions had been engaged on either side, it was nonetheless intended to be the decisive blow that would bring about the collapse of Germany and an end to the war against Hitler. The Atlantic Allies were relying for their success on the extent to which the commitment of the German Armies in the titanic battles against the Soviets would constrain their ability to defend in the West and to building up an advantage in numbers with the new American divisions and the weapons and equipment flowing across the Atlantic from the enormous armaments industry into which the United States had transformed itself. Its onetime stranglehold on the Atlantic sea-lanes now greatly diminished, the German U-boat fleet was less and less able to impede the massive build-up of the invasion forces.

The scale of the enterprise was immense. Elaborate and effective deception plans were put in place to persuade the enemy that the main effort would take place across the short sea route leading directly to the Pas de Calais, while at the same time unconventional weapons were being developed to pass invading troops over defended beaches and through fortified shorelines. Artificial harbours were designed and built in great secrecy, to be put in place on these same beaches and allow the landing of the huge tonnages of supplies needed to sustain the Allied forces once they were established ashore. By removing the need in the first wave to capture a major seaport, where strong German defences could be expected, the planners increased their own freedom of action in deciding where the main effort would be made.

A vital element in the final plan, codenamed Overlord, was the landing of the Allied airborne forces closely behind the invasion beaches to secure vital communications and to disrupt the movement of enemy reserve forces in the immediate area of operations. By their nature and with the technical and material resources of the period, airborne troops could take into battle with them only the arms and equipment that they could carry and what could be got to them by canisters dropped from aircraft and such heavier weapons as could be delivered by Horsa glider or by direct parachute-cluster drop from four-engine bomber aircraft such as the Halifax. These loads, in the middle of 1944, usually amounted to wheeled transport in the form of jeeps and whatever could be mounted on them – light 75mm pack howitzers of limited range of action and weight of shell and the six-pounder anti-tank gun, a useful weapon at shorter ranges and against the less heavily protected areas of German tanks. The larger and much more effective seventeen-pounder anti-tank gun could only be landed from the bigger Hamilcar glider, which could also carry the (very) light Tetrarch tanks which were part of the equipment of the airborne divisions' armoured reconnaissance regiments. This meant that, even in a perfect drop in which all troops arrived on the allotted dropping and landing zones and no equipment was lost or damaged, airborne troops would still be at a considerable disadvantage from the more powerful tanks and artillery it could be expected that the enemy would deploy against them. Consequently an underlying principle in the planning of all airborne operations was to achieve an early link-up with ground forces so that the airborne units could be reinforced and supplied over land routes.

By the time 1st Airborne Division was moving into its training camps in the English Midlands four airborne divisions were potentially available to take part in the invasion of Europe. Two were British, the 1st and the 6th, and two were American, 82nd Airborne, which, like 1st British Airborne, had taken part in the fighting in North Africa and the Mediterranean, and 101st Airborne, lately arrived directly from the United States. From the time of its arrival back in England and during the first months of 1944 1st Airborne Division undertook intensive training in all aspects of their likely future tasks, from weapon and signals training at unit level up to full-scale exercises involving the dropping of the whole Division, followed by a ground exercise in which it operated as the enemy against 6th Airborne Division.

As with everyone else, for Shan and his Brigade it was a time of intense and exhausting activity, which demanded that all the resources of the formation in manpower and equipment were to be brought to a state of readiness with which every unit would acquit itself well in the battles to come. No one underestimated the scale of the task ahead of them; the German Army was still strong and equipped with weapons that had been refined and developed in the demanding circumstances of the Eastern

Front. In terms of armour, infantry and anti-tank weapons of all sorts, the Wehrmacht almost certainly had the edge in terms of battlefield effectiveness while those of the Allies who had been in action against German units had no doubt of the battle-hardened qualities of the troops, of their ability to react swiftly to changing circumstances, to organize strong defensive points and to be quick and decisive in organizing counter-attacks whenever they had been driven off their positions. Shan saw with total clarity the task he had to accomplish to make his Brigade fully battle-worthy and he set about it energetically and in full awareness of all the different things that he had to achieve; honing the leadership skills of his unit commanders at all levels, making sure that communication could be maintained under battlefield conditions, testing administrative and supply services, making cooperation between different arms a matter of instinctive reaction and, above all, developing high morale and deep feelings of comradeship and a sense of common purpose in all the units under his command.

The condition of 4 Parachute Brigade when it finally took its place on the battlefield at Arnhem shows how well he accomplished his tasks. In the later months of the Brigade's time in England he was sustained by the arrival during April 1944 of Margaret and her two young daughters. She has described how after a voyage in convoy through the Mediterranean and into the North Atlantic, enduring endless boat drills on the way, (the U-boat menace was by no means entirely over) they disembarked on a grey, wet day in Liverpool, to arrive in England for the first time into the drab sadness of that bombed city. From there the family went to London where they stayed with friends and where Margaret was able to get on with such practical arrangements as schooling for the two girls (they were packed off to High Trees School near Woolacombe, an early and sharp introduction to the English way of bringing up children). From London, Margaret went up to join Shan in the house he had taken for both of them in the small town of Oakham, in Rutlandshire. They found when they moved into School House that a grandfather clock came with it and for the two of them it became an object of affection and in some way a talisman within what was their first true family home. Here they were able, however temporarily, to resume a married life that had scarcely begun, although they had been fortunate in suffering less separation than many wartime marriages. Their wedding had taken place in the theatre of war in which Shan was serving and had gone on serving; Margaret had not been sent to the safety of South Africa, as many military wives stationed in Egypt had been and they had, fortunately, had time together in Cairo. In England, they now faced the prospect of a further separation with 1st Airborne Division firmly written into the order of battle for the forthcoming invasion of German-occupied Europe.

The various units that made up 4 Parachute Brigade found themselves dispersed into billets in various locations around Leicestershire and Rutlandshire. To many, it was a return home after years abroad in India and the Middle East and the pleasure in that outweighed such of the privations of life in wartime England as impinged upon them. Their main occupation was in training for their tasks in the coming invasion of German-occupied France, which they carried out locally or, for the larger-scale exercises, on the Yorkshire Moors. Social life was not neglected and the participation of the US aircrews attached to the brigade, with whom they did their parachute training and who would fly them to whatever operations the brigade was eventually committed, added a welcome extra dimension to the parties that were a regular feature of off-duty life.

A serendipitous addition to the social scene was the presence within the brigade area of the Army Remount Depot at Melton Mowbray. Not only was this a means of recreation for those who wanted to ride but its wartime establishment included sixty young female riders and grooms. This proximate source of female company was not neglected by the bronzed veterans of the Middle East and the Taranto landings and more than one of them found his future wife from it and, with wartime urgency, made certain to be married before they left for battle. Once the landings in Normandy had begun, life throughout 4 Parachute Brigade and the rest of 1st Airborne Division became increasingly tense, as the Division was placed on frequent standby for operations that were successively overtaken by events on the ground before they could be mounted. The confinements to billets, the packing and unpacking of stores and equipment, preparations that sometimes found units sitting in their aircraft waiting to take off, only to be stood down and deplane, were all demanding on morale and personal commitment and it was not surprising that there should have been an increase in absences without leave. The effect this succession of disappointments had on general morale was readily apparent to all the unit commanders, who managed to handle it successfully and sympathetically. This may well have led the planners to a state of mind where any operation actually mounted was better than yet another cancellation.

The broad outlines of a plan for Overlord, the invasion of North-West Europe, had been agreed at the Quebec Conference of 1943. It envisaged a three-division assault from the sea on to the beaches of Normandy and, when the plan was presented in detail to Generals Eisenhower and Montgomery as Supreme Allied Commander and Commander of the allied invasion forces respectively, they both felt it too limited an effort to allow them to succeed in their strategic goals of the early capture of Cherbourg as a main port and of Caen as the pivotal strongpoint at the eastern end of the chosen operational area. Accordingly, the seaborne assault forces were enlarged to five divisions, supported by two US airborne divisions, these to be dropped in the elbow where the Carentan Peninsula, at the northern head of which lay the prize of Cherbourg, joined the east-west beaches of Normandy, where the main invasion was to take place. To gain the maximum effect from this American operation, it was of necessity that the airborne force be landed in as concentrated a form as resources allowed, which is to say in a single lift. The demands this condition imposed on the available Allied air transport squadrons, substantial a force as this was, meant that the British 6th Airborne Division, already assigned a vital role at Overlord's eastern end in the capture or destruction of vital bridges and coastal defences to prevent German interference with the landing troops and to maintain the integrity of the left flank of the beachhead, was restricted in the number of transport aircraft that could be made available to it. This meant the British division would have to carry out its tasks in two lifts, separated by the amount of time needed for the first wave aircraft to return to their bases in England, refuel and re-arm, load up the second lift of 6th Airborne and fly back to its designated dropping and landing zones. The effect of all this was that since there were no aircraft left that could be made available to 1st Airborne Division, there was no way in which that formation could be given any sort of task in the very first phases of Operation Overlord. The division was placed in Army Group reserve and kept in a state of high alert, ready to react to whatever contingency might arise with the invasion forces in what was expected would be a fluid and rapidly developing situation as Allied troops built up and enlarged their beachhead. As will be described later, Shan's 4 Parachute Brigade was placed in particular state of readiness.

In the event 6th Airborne Division's operation was judged to have been a great success, in particular the *coup-de-main* operation on the Orne bridges by a reinforced company under Major John Howard of the Oxfordshire and Buckinghamshire Light Infantry, one of the three glider-borne infantry battalions of the airlanding brigade.

The drop of the main body of parachutists, which also took place during the hours of darkness, was far more dispersed than had been intended by the air plan and although superhuman efforts were made by those dropped in the wrong places to regain their correct rendezvous, the effect this dispersal had in reducing the size of the forces that could be directed on each ground objective undoubtedly made the degree of success achieved that much more praiseworthy. It is a tribute to the determination, skill and élan of the airborne soldiers that they did accomplish so much of what had been demanded of them.

The lessons of the British airborne contribution to the success of Overlord were carefully studied and the results disseminated by HQ Airborne Forces. Clearly success in the tactical objectives of each unit taking part in an airborne operation depended upon it being delivered as close as possible to the exact place demanded by the plan. By the very nature of the way airborne forces were then organized and deployed, only those arriving by glider did so as formed bodies; the parachuting troops, even if the order to jump was given in the exact place above the dropping zone that had been intended, are leaving in succession an aircraft moving over the ground at a speed of some forty-five metres per second, which imposes a degree of dispersal even in ideal circumstances. The first task of the arriving troops, having collected the weapons dropped with them and having armed themselves for combat, was to assemble into formed and disciplined units susceptible to proper command and control, able to proceed to the attack upon their allotted objectives. This had to be done despite gaps in unit strengths that might have been suffered *en route* from accident or enemy action and from hostile receptions on the dropping and landing zones. In dealing with the twin problems of inaccurate delivery and undue dispersal, much faith had been placed in the use of pathfinder units of the SAS squadron that was a vital part of each airborne division. Dropped in advance of the main bodies in order to guide the troop-carrying aircraft accurately to their correct dropping and landing zones through the use of electronic or visual signals, success was dependent on the pathfinder teams being dropped in the correct locations and on all their guidance equipment arriving safely with them. On D-Day there were certainly incidences of the absence of equipment leading to ineffectual messages being directed towards incoming aircraft and one of a pathfinder team being dropped away from its correct location but persuading itself that it was in the right one, with the consequence that they performed their task exactly as ordered but brought the units they were guiding into entirely the wrong dropping zone.

In those days before global positioning satellites and other highly-developed navigational aids, when the aircraft of airborne divisions had to navigate in close formation through cloud and often through enemy anti-aircraft fire as well, it is understandable that, despite the dedication of the British and American aircrews, the accuracy of delivery of their human and material cargoes was not always as high as might have been hoped. There is a fundamental weakness in airborne operations from the potential fallibilities of the transport methods and the consequential wastefulness, something that was to be unfortunately proved during the crossing of the Rhine by 6th Airborne Division in March 1945, when the number of troops and the amount of vital equipment lost to enemy action while still airborne or in the immediate aftermath of landing, reached serious proportions. The effective strength of the glider-borne units that reached the ground in that operation in a condition to fight was about fifty percent of those who had set out that day from England and would have been lower still had a navigational error, this time a fortunate one, not dropped a regiment of the US 17th Airborne Division, whose objectives were on the right flank of 6th Airborne Division, on top of a battery of German 88mm guns covering the glider-landing zone of the British division.

Another lesson, learnt on D-Day and observed at the Rhine crossing, was that where enemy resistance is known to be present in any strength airborne forces should be dropped within range of supporting artillery fire and at a proximity to the battlefield that will allow an early link-up with friendly ground forces.

In the period leading up to D-Day, senior Allied commanders, and no doubt many of all ranks in the units waiting in their concentration areas to embark or to emplane, were thoroughly aware that the success of the first assault and the advance inland to the objectives laid down by the planning staffs could by no means be taken for granted. The German general's dictum that no military plan survives the first contact with the enemy would have found few dissenters among those in the British Army who had already been in action in this war. Consequently a whole series of contingency plans were drawn up, some in advance of the Allied landings in Normandy, to attempt to deal with the situation should things not go according to plan. The first of these was Operation Tuxedo, which placed 4 Parachute Brigade at four hours notice from D-Day onwards, to drop anywhere within the invasion area where a major threat was seen to be developing and that might threaten the success of, or seriously jeopardize Allied operations. It was followed by a plan which would have employed the whole of 1st Airborne Division in a similar role: others followed thick and fast, usually triggered during the first weeks of the invasion by particular incidences of German resistance that were causing delays to the timetable of successive Allied position lines that the planners had set down before D-Day. During the first two months after the landings on 6 June 1944, by the end of which time the breakout from the bridgehead was under way, some seven separate operations were proposed, but the later ones, including a planned operation three airborne divisions strong and codenamed 'Transfigure', to land south-west of Paris and cut off the German retreat, were all overtaken by events on the ground. The dash and speed with which General Patton's Third US Army advanced around the southern edge of the theatre of operations and made their way to the capture of Paris, while the bulk of the German army in Normandy was closely engaged with the British and Canadians to the north, was such that even as airborne planners were unrolling their maps and deciding on another series of dropping zones, American troops were dashing through the intended objective.

It will be recognized that each of these proposed operations had required, right up to its moment of cancellation, detailed planning of every aspect, from the air plan which covered all movement of transport aircraft and supporting fighters and fighter-bombers, maps of the anti-aircraft defences menacing chosen air routes, the precise complement and load of every parachuting aircraft and glider, as much intelligence as could be provided on the strength and disposition of enemy forces that would be met with on the ground, the tactical plan to be followed once the troops had been landed, the support to be given to them from both the ground and the air, the medical and administrative elements of the plan, the liaison and control groups to ensure that the artillery and air support made available was directed to provide effective help to the airborne units once arrived on the ground. It must have seemed to all those staff officers and others toiling on the treadmill of necessary but, in the event, unproductive effort, as every postponement and cancellation was received from higher headquarters, that the war would have ended before 1st Airborne Division had been able to carry on the work it had begun in North Africa and had briefly resumed in Italy almost a year before.

In the series of interviews on his war that Shan gave to the Imperial War Museum late in life, he speaks of a total of twelve aborted or unrealized airborne operations planned between D-Day and Market Garden, of which Transfigure had been the seventh since D-Day. This was in addition to other proposals for the possible use of airborne troops in support of the Allied advance on the ground, which remained as suggestions and did not get to the stage of detailed planning. The five that followed Transfigure were all identified by codename, having successively as their objectives the capture of Boulogne and the areas from which V1s (or flying bombs) were being launched against England; support to the ground troops in crossing the River Seine; to land ahead of the Allies advancing beyond the Seine; to capture Tournai and the bridges over the River Escaut and finally a landing on the Walcheren Islands to assist in opening up the port of Antwerp. The fact that none of these plans came to fruition did not perhaps unduly worry General Eisenhower, the Supreme Allied Commander in Europe. He was by no means a whole-hearted supporter of airborne operations, seeing them as very well trained troops of high fighting qualities, but troops who were expensively equipped and who demanded the use of a considerable amount of air transport, which he would perhaps have preferred to see deployed in supplying and maintaining the momentum of Third US Army, by now well out of the bridgehead and advancing briskly across great swathes of France.

Then, in twelfth place, came Operation Comet, the first of the two plans to capture the bridges over the main rivers of the Maas, Waal and Lower Rhine and, incidentally, over all the smaller rivers and canals that ran through that part of the Netherlands.

The second was Market Garden. For Operation Comet it was deemed sufficient to commit only the British 1st Airborne Division and the independent Polish parachute brigade, Shan's 4 Parachute Brigade's task being to capture the bridges over the first of the major river obstacles, the Maas. It is difficult in retrospect to see how such a relatively small force as a single airborne division, given objectives well ahead of the then forward positions of Montgomery's Twenty-First Army Group, could have had the slightest chance of success against anything other than a negligible German presence on the ground. Shan, who had a healthy respect for the German ability to bounce back, was among those who had begun to suspect that higher up the military chain there were officers who chose to believe intelligence reports about the enemy that were favourable to the immediate military intention and to disregard or downplay those that were not. Another sceptic was General Sosabowski, commander of the Polish Independent Parachute Brigade Group and a veteran of the Austro-Russian front of the First World War, who, when at the point in the divisional commander's briefing for Operation Comet, questions were called for, could only say, "But the Germans, General, the Germans!" Misgivings about the scale of the tasks given to the different units were felt lower down the chain of command and there were few in 1st Airborne Division who were deeply disappointed when in the early hours of 10th September, just four hours before the first aircraft carrying the troops were due to take off, the operation was cancelled. During the afternoon of the same day, General Urquhart and his divisional staff had began to plan for their part in Operation Market Garden that had exactly the same objectives as Comet but was strengthened by the two US airborne divisions, 82nd and 101st, which had taken part in the D-Day invasion along with the British 6th Airborne. Ominously Market Garden was the thirteenth plan to be proposed to the airborne forces of the Allies and the first of the sequence that was destined actually to take place.

The events that began in Holland on Sunday 17 September 1944 are now colloquially known as the Battle of Arnhem, although the operations of 1st Airborne Division and the Polish Independent Parachute Brigade in and around that town were only part of the much larger action, Market Garden, where two other airborne divisions and the larger part of British Second Army took part with a degree of success denied to 1st Airborne Division at the furthest limits of the operation. To take the only failed part of the largest airborne operation of the entire war and use it as a description of the whole is perhaps illustrative of a British tendency to take a reverse pleasure in defeat, a tendency that might have its origins in the first few years of the War, when what went well for us was greatly outweighed by what went badly wrong. Nevertheless, it is necessary to be thoroughly aware of the factors, the decisions and the course of events leading up to Market Garden in order to understand how they all led inevitably to the destruction of Shan's 4 Parachute Brigade.

It might be helpful at this point to attempt to set the wider scene in which such momentous events were being planned and would shortly take place. After the hard slog of the Normandy beachhead, especially on the British and Canadian left flank, where the deliberate intention to draw to that part of the bridgehead the great bulk of German armoured formations had been only too successfully achieved, the breakout had taken place and the Allied armies streamed over the River Seine and across North-West France in pursuit of the retreating and, to superficial judgement, disorganized and demoralized German Army. The scenes during the liberation of each successive town or village seemed, to the Allied troops taking part, to offer the fullest justification for taking part in the war against Hitler's Germany and for the casualties, destruction, pain and loss that had been endured over the long years of what, by general agreement, had been a just war. The relief and delight of the liberated men and women as the Allied advance through France and Belgium proceeded at what seemed an unstoppable pace, the long-hidden bottles of champagne unearthed and poured unstintingly into soldiers' tin mugs, the desire to press any gift, however small or however incongruous, as a bottled-up expression of deep gratitude for the ending of the four-year-long dark night of occupation, induced in the liberators a sense of euphoria that led inexorably on to the thought that surely, at last, the war was over. The thought grew into a conviction that shut off from itself the realities of the Allied troops' own experience on the battle-field and the conclusions that should have been drawn from it. Even those whose first experience of being in action against the German army

84

had been in the Normandy bocage or in the open plains south of Caen could not have failed to have been impressed by the tenacity of the enemy in defence, by the speed and skill of his counter-attacks, the quality of the weapons with which he was equipped and his ability to react to adversity with speed and resolution. At the start of his magisterial record of the Second World War and the part he played in it, Winston Churchill sets out four tenets as being the moral of the crowning work of his life. They are: in War, Resolution; in Defeat, Defiance; in Victory, Magnanimity and in Peace, Goodwill. How the Germans might have behaved had they achieved final victory they never had the opportunity to demonstrate, but there is no doubt from their actions that they not only believed in but also practised the first two of Churchill's precepts. What might have appeared, particularly to the Press, to be an unstoppable Allied advance from the River Seine right up to the borders of Holland was not without its small but ominous indications.

In the German Army of that time the extent to which a commander at whatever level would show initiative and accept responsibility for his part in the battle in which he was engaged tended towards the exemplary, possibly because a German called upon to carry out the duties of someone more senior than himself would not expect, during the time he was performing them, automatic promotion to the higher rank. In the British Army the situation was otherwise, perhaps in an effort to circumvent the Treasury's stranglehold on military pay, as promotion invariably brought with it, however temporarily, the greater monetary reward of the higher rank. To illustrate the point, it is necessary to imagine the German Army in retreat somewhere east of the Seine, being pursued by an Allied armoured division. At some important crossroads a German officer (or warrant officer, or non-commissioned officer), finding no organized defences in place, positions himself in the middle of the road and proceeds to stop other members of the German Army moving back along the same axis. You are now members, he announces, of *Kampfgruppe Schmidt* (or whatever his name might be) and before long he has built his little battle group into a sizeable force that he believes will be strong enough to delay the advancing Allies for a sufficient length of time to have made his efforts worthwhile. If he has been fortunate, he might have acquired a tank, a self-propelled gun or an anti-tank piece and the ad-hoc group he has assembled by force of personality, the judicious waving of his pistol or lurid threats of the degree of eventual punishment for doubt and hesitation, will proceed to hold up the approaching armoured division for as long as seems possible and will then slip away to repeat the performance, if he is lucky, further along the line of retreat.

The reaction of a British soldier stopped in a similar manner may be imagined. He would be likely to glance at the cap badge of CSM Smith and, if different from his own, say that he was nothing to do with your lot, mate, and continue on his way.

It could also be contemplated that the German retreat was due not only to the pressure of the Allied advance but also to the enemy's reasoning that North-West France was in any case indefensible and that the nearer the German Army got to its own frontiers the stronger its resistance could become and the stiffer it would be conducted.

On the Home Front the desire of the British to see the war at an end was palpable. Directly after the great sigh of relief that D-Day and the invasion of Europe had finally happened, a great area of South-Eastern England had to endure assault by the first of Hitler's weapons of revenge, the V-1 or flying bomb. These terrifying devices, a worrying proportion of which seemed to be able to penetrate British air defences, with their unmistakeable putt-putt engine note and the heart-stopping realization of those on the ground beneath its flight path that when the engine cut out it was about to begin its plunge to earth and the detonation of its one-ton warhead, were a burden that a tired public felt was one too many. Unlike the London blitz of the winter of 1940/41, when the greater part of the destruction had been wrought on the dockland areas and the working-class districts of the East End, the flying bomb dispersed its dreadful destruction across Greater London and the Home Counties at random. One particularly shocking episode among many, right at the beginning of the German V-1 attacks, took place at the Guards' Chapel in Birdcage Walk where a service of thanksgiving for the success of the Normandy landings was hardly begun in the presence of a large and distinguished congregation when a flying bomb exploded on the roof of the nave, causing very heavy loss of life. By a bizarre coincidence the event was witnessed by Mrs Winston Churchill who had that morning decided to visit her daughter Mary, who was serving as a member of the ATS with an anti-aircraft battery in Hyde Park. Together they watched the black object plunge from the clouds and explode, as it seemed to them, in the direction of Downing Street. To the soldiers engaged across the Channel and receiving the national papers with their rations on the day after publication, it was disturbing news and would go on being so during the next three months, until the advancing Allies had overrun the launching sites in North-West France. Then, of course, came soon after in September, the new menace of the V-2, the rocket against which, once launched, there was no possible defence, its one-ton warhead exploding on the ground before the sound of its approach had been heard and whose launching sites in occupied Holland had yet to be captured. In addition to nearly two thousand five hundred flying bombs, London was to endure five hundred of the unstoppable rockets, a number which could have been far greater but for the delays in its development as a result of the highly successful RAF raid on the V-2 research and development establishment at Peenemünde a year before.

The Allied advance had the unwanted consequence of bringing our own troops and the newly-liberated population of Belgium into the target area of these weapons. Although those in the front line were, because of their proximity to the enemy, safe from attack (although they could see for themselves the vapour trails of the launched rockets as they climbed into the stratosphere and hear, after some delay, the rumble of its liquid-fuelled engines), it was those further back who were to feel for themselves the ordeal of South-East England. Antwerp, Brussels and Liège were all put under attack and, in a ghastly reprise of the Guards' Chapel disaster, a cinema in Antwerp, filled with Allied servicemen, suffered a direct hit from a V-2.

It was on the background of this canvas that planning for Market Garden began on 10 September. The British people had just entered the sixth year of their war against Hitler, the Americans were still in their third. Only the Germans had been fighting longer and that by only two days. The hard years when the British were fighting alone had taken their toll and they, understandably, were approaching exhaustion. More worryingly, manpower resources were getting very thin and units and whole divisions began to be broken up to fill gaps in remaining formations, while Army reinforcements began to be found from the most unlikely quarters, men no longer needed by the Royal Navy and the Royal Air Force. The relative strengths of the two Allied armies ashore in France had gone from a greater 21st Army Group presence during the first weeks to a US preponderance that would only go on getting larger as new and fresh American divisions arrived from the United States. There was an intense desire to be over with the whole thing that coincided with a belief that, perhaps at long last, a situation had arrived that was going to make it possible. Such feelings, together with an optimism induced by the rapid advance of the Allied armies on a broad front and the belief after the 20 July attempted assassination of Hitler that cracks were beginning to appear in the edifice of the Nazi state, must have been present to a greater or lesser degree in the minds of the airborne planning staffs and it is to their work one must now turn before examining its results on the ground, particularly as they affected Shan's 4 Parachute Brigade.

The inter-Allied command structure for the airborne forces, to which the planning staffs belonged and to which they reported, was multi-layered and subject to inevitable constraints in terms of objectives, resources, time and force of circumstances that produced, inevitably, plans of compromise. After their successful operations from D-Day onwards, the two American and one British airborne divisions taking part were kept in the line and fought as specialized infantry formations under the command of the senior American and British ground force commanders. There was a considerable airborne capacity as yet un-committed to the battle, consisting of 17th US Airborne Division, newly arrived in the United Kingdom, the British 1st Airborne Division and the 52nd Lowland Division, (an air-transportable infantry, not an airborne division), and the Polish Independent Parachute Group. To use these Allied formations to the best advantage and to ensure proper co-ordination of their operations and the establishment of common operating and administrative procedures, Supreme Headquarters Allied Expeditionary Forces (SHAEF) issued the order on 2 August 1944 to bring them all under the umbrella of the newly-formed First Allied Airborne Army, which was to be divided in turn into two airborne corps, one containing the American Divisions and the other the British and Polish formations. It also included IX US Troop Carrier Command and, when specific operations took place, 38 and 46 Groups (troop-carrying) RAF. The Army Commander was an American, Lieutenant-General Lewis Brereton, a US Army Air Corps officer who had already seen action in the Far East and Middle East, and who, during the Normandy invasion and subsequently, had been commanding Ninth US Air Force, the tactical American air arm in North-West Europe. (At that time the American air force was not an independent service like the Royal Air Force but two quite separate services, one forming part of the US Navy and the other of the US Army.) His deputy and the commander of 1 British Airborne Corps was Lieutenant-General 'Boy' Browning, one of the pioneers of British airborne warfare but perhaps better known at the time as the husband of the author Daphne du Maurier. Within the Airborne Army headquarters each commander or senior staff officer, customarily an American, had a British deputy.

In practice, 1 Airborne Corps was to be allocated to one or other of the Army Groups where the airborne arm could be used most effectively and placed under its command for the duration of the operation. Proposals for the actual operations to be undertaken could come from SHAEF, from one of the Army Groups, from the Allied Expeditionary Air Force or from Corps itself. A feasibility study would first be done at Corps level in an attempt to limit the number of proposals passed down to the divisions and in that way it was hoped to control the work load on the staff responsible for detailed planning and on the soldiers charged with carrying out the actual operations. In practice this admirable intention did little to lighten the demands on divisional, brigade and unit staffs as, in addition to the twelve unfulfilled and one achieved plan over a period of under two months, various other suggestions for making use of airborne forces were made, some of which may have filtered down to divisional level and required at least an outline perusal of the practical demands they imposed. There was also evidence of a desire by First Airborne Army to get its forces into action, leading to tentative suggestions made by SHAEF and Army Group being passed down to corps and divisional level in an effort to save planning time, before formal approval to go ahead with the operation had been given. This only had the result of seeing planning efforts wasted and mental and physical energies being expended, with no useful result.

When Market Garden finally received the green light it was 10 September, the day on which its lightweight predecessor, 'Comet', had, in the early hours of that same morning, been cancelled. The title encompassed two separate operations, the ground assault into Holland by Twenty-First Army Group being codenamed 'Garden' while the three-division airborne landings were 'Market'. (It is proposed to follow what has become the customary usage and to speak of the whole operation, as well as its two constituent parts, as Market Garden.) There were therefore merely seven days for the detailed planning of a complex airborne assault, made more hazardous than either the D-Day airborne landings or the airborne element of the Rhine crossing the following year, by reason, among other things, of the depth of the intended penetration in Market Garden behind the forward positions held by the enemy. It was also a pitifully short period compared with the two months or more given to the D-Day planners and the full month enjoyed by those dealing with the Rhine crossing. Another consequence of this truncation of time was that, as decisions were progressively made, orders were at once given for the practical implementation of that element of the overall plan to proceed, which made proposals for later changes, however desirable they might potentially have been in the achievement of the objectives, unacceptable on the grounds that steps already taken could not be retraced and nor could alternative tasks be substituted before the deadline of Sunday 17 September.

The overall intention of Market Garden was, in Montgomery's words, to lay an airborne carpet from south to north across the three great rivers traversing Holland, capturing the road bridges intact in the process. Over this carpet was to be thrust three corps of Twenty-First Army Group, XXX Corps under General Horrocks in the lead with the Guards

Armoured Division as its spearhead, followed by VIII and XII Corps, each also containing an armoured division, the 7th and 11th respectively, as well as infantry divisions. The aim was to breach the great water barriers that lay between the Allies and the Ruhr and the North German Plain; the capture of the first would remove the greatest industrial zone in the Third Reich from its control while over the second lay the path to the great cities of Central Germany and the ultimate prize of the capital, Berlin itself. The achievement of Market Garden would require great dash and determination by the ground troops committed, but it was hoped success would bring, to the point of near certainty, the ending of Hitler's war before Christmas.

Such were the glittering prizes held out by Montgomery when he went to present his plan for a single bold thrust to the sceptical Eisenhower, the Supreme Commander and his superior officer. He had proposed an advance on the Ruhr by the northern flank as a strategic idea earlier in the campaign and as the rapid advance of his 21st Army Group yielded both Brussels and Antwerp to him, he felt success for such a move to be achievable and he pressed the plan with increased vigour and with all the considerable confidence in the rightness of his thinking of which he was capable. General Eisenhower's headquarters were at that time in the Cherbourg Peninsula, some four hundred miles behind the point of the Allied advanced troops and communications between them were not good. Finally Eisenhower agreed to fly to Brussels on 10 September for a face-to-face discussion on the single thrust, which, if agreed to, would require the diversion of supplies and resources from the three American armies operating in the centre and on the right flank, with all the possibilities there were of a strong adverse reaction among the American public across the Atlantic. In any case, Eisenhower's instincts lay more in the concept of advance on a broad front, where a possible breakthrough at any part of it could be exploited and quickly reinforced from flanking formations and where supply lines could progressively be firmed up. On the ground Twenty-First Army Group's advance through Belgium was slowing down as it began to run up against the water obstacles that ran transversely across its front, while at the same time the effects of supply lines running all the way back to the Normandy beach-head began to impose severe limitations on how much could be delivered to the forward units. It had been hoped to press the extensive rail network of Northern France and Belgium into service in supporting the Allied supply chain, but interdiction by our air forces, both before and since D-Day, had done so much damage to track, rolling stock and infra-structure that a great effort would be required before any help could be given by this means. More worrying still, the impetus of the British advance, strong as it had been, had failed to prevent substantial bodies of German troops escaping from North Belgium across to the north side of the Scheldt estuary and, more disappointing still, the narrow isthmus that connected Beveland and Walcheren on the north bank had not been cut and so these garrisons still had a firm land connection with the main German forces occupying the remainder of the Netherlands. Until both banks of the Scheldt estuary could be cleared as far as the open sea, there was no question of being able to use Antwerp as a port of supply. Had it been possible to do this quickly, after the arrival of British forces in the vicinity of the city and port of Antwerp, the supply situation of the Allied forces would have been transformed, but it would in the event take months of bitter fighting in atrocious conditions before the Scheldt could be opened up to Allied shipping, something that had lain potentially within the grasp of the forward British elements during the early days of September, but which had eluded them.

As soon as the two commanders met Montgomery began to expose his grand plan to bring the war, under his own direction, to a speedy and certain end with a vigour and confidence that his superior found unappealing. However, the Anglo-Irishman had other considerations in his mind than personal ambition and a messianic belief in the righteousness of his proposals. Only two days before, the first of the V-2 rockets had been directed on London from its launching base in Holland and the British Government was still attempting to assess the possible impact of this new weapon. Monty was quick to point out the dangers of this advanced new German weapon and how a successful advance into central Holland would permit an early clearance of the rocket bases, something that would at the same time eliminate a potential danger to Allied armies in the field and the supply bases that supported them. In the end Eisenhower was persuaded and agreed to place a corps of Brereton's First Airborne Army at the disposal of Twenty-First Army Group in support of its single, war-winning thrust. This corps, under the command of General Browning, would be made up of the two US airborne divisions, veterans of the Normandy landings and the British 1st Airborne Division and the Polish Independent Brigade. 52nd Lowland Division would be standing by, to be flown in once the objectives had been taken and suitable airfields captured and made operational.

At first, acutely aware of a far from resolved supply situation, Montgomery proposed to set the later date of 23 September for the launch of Market Garden. He realized, as did the staff at SHAEF, that every day that passed before his thrust could be made was one day more for German resistance to be stiffened. He was quickly promised that the resources he calculated were required adequately to support his great offensive would be made available to him, if necessary by halting American units and by diverting their supplies. Montgomery now had the assurances he felt he needed to bring the date forward and set Market Garden for Sunday 17 September.

Back in England, the detailed planning for the operation, now only a few days away, continued with frantic haste. Shan began to have feelings of an almost desperate inevitability, as if commanders, staff and the divine power itself were determined that, come what may, Market Garden would take place. He described the plan, once it had been revealed to him, as the depiction of an ideal situation to which the Germans had been added as a sort of afterthought. His concerns were shared, in a more detailed and informed way, by an intelligence officer at Airborne Corps headquarters.

Putting together an accurate intelligence picture of the enemy's strength and dispositions from such pieces of knowledge as may be found from the curious, disparate and invariably limited sources that are available can never be a straightforward task and this was particularly the case with the planning of Market Garden. Of the sources themselves, Ultra, or the breaking of the German Armed Forces Enigma coding machine, was one of the most difficult. Potentially and in practice a provider of the most accurate and timely knowledge of the enemy, including his forward intentions and his actual operation orders, the fear that the Germans would deduce that Enigma had been broken put great restraint on the distribution and use of the material. The effect was to limit very severely and to the highest level the number of those to whom the intelligence information they were given could be revealed as having come from Ultra. Passed on down the chains of command, it tended to become disguised or fragmented and thus perhaps had its value for tactical purposes rather diminished. Aerial reconnaissance could, where the quality of the product was high and the photographs accurately and speedily interpreted, be very useful, as could that provided by the observation of front-line troops in contact with the enemy and by the seeking of information from local civilians. Intelligence from Resistance groups or from SAS and other irregular forces operating behind the lines was often to be had in considerable volume but its use uncorroborated was always dangerous because of the very real fear that an agent or group might have been turned or that wireless sets and code books had fallen into German hands and were being skilfully used against the Allied side. The suspicion in 1st Airborne Division that parts of the Dutch resistance might have been turned by the Germans led, during the fighting around Arnhem, either to a refusal to use information volunteered by the civilian population or at best to a reluctance to seek it and make use of it.

As the picture began to be built up of enemy forces that there might be on the ground where and when the airborne component of Market Garden arrived, there was at the beginning a tendency, in which the euphoric atmosphere brought about by the great German retreat had its place, to downplay the enemy strength and to believe it incapable of any serious resistance to the landings. Although there was known to be armour in the vicinity of Arnhem itself, it was classified overall as belonging to training units (which certainly did exist in the area), or to the battered remnants of one or more badly-mauled *panzer* divisions and, as such, probably unlikely to pose a serious threat to airborne formations. There were those who had justifiable concern that the German armour was almost certainly a great deal more formidable and they made their worries known. One in particular was Major Brian Urquhart, an intelligence officer at the headquarters of General Browning's I Airborne Corps. What he had been able to build up from the material available to him, a lot of it from Dutch underground reports, seemed to paint such a disturbing picture that he arranged for a Spitfire fighter-sweep that was to take place over the general area of Arnhem to include a photo-reconnaissance sortie of the planned landing zones. The low-level photographs he received confirmed his worst fears. German armoured vehicles were clearly visible in the fringes of the woods bordering the areas into which it was intended, in two or three days time, that 1 Parachute Brigade would be dropped. Bearing in his hand what he thought would be conclusive confirmation that the operation as planned was now fatally flawed and would require an immediate and drastic reworking, he went immediately to his superiors in the belief that his pessimism had been vindicated. The reaction was stupefying. What was not wished to be seen could not be seen, became invisible, virtually disappeared from the photographs he had laid upon the planning tables before his senior officers. Instead, he was drawn aside with attempts at persuasion that he was over-wrought, that he had been working too hard and his judgement had been affected and that for his own good, he should immediately take a rest, have a few days leave and quietly recuperate from the long period of overwork which he had been forced to go through. The suggestion became an order and the unwelcome doubter was removed, to have no further influence on the nature of the information upon which the subordinate brigades and battalions would construct their battle plans.

The first of the factors that were to prove fatal to the northern sector of Market Garden and lead to the utter destruction of a superbly trained and totally dedicated airborne division was a failure to pass the available intelligence down to all the operational levels that had need of it. This, wilfully or misguidedly, led directly to a tendency at those levels to underestimate the opposition that the British troops would meet. The rationale was possibly a genuine belief that the sheer weight and power of the airborne army and the overwhelming bomber and fighter air support available to it would be more than sufficient to prevail over a weakened and fragmented enemy, still in the process of organizing itself and its defensive positions. If that was the thinking, it was another example of an inability to give proper weight to the German capacity for swift and effective reaction to each new turn of events. More likely, the planning process had developed its own unstoppable momentum, driven on by the thought that, if Market Garden did not take place, there would be little likelihood of any early employment for the Allied airborne army.

The next factor was the air plan, to which we must now turn. Massive as the air transport resources available to the Allies were, they were not sufficient for the most desirable condition for the success of an airborne operation, that the force should be landed in one powerful blow, compressed into the shortest possible time frame. To be unable to meet the first condition would mean that the commander on the ground would not have his entire force at his disposal during the early period of the operation, while the enemy was off balance, still reacting and least able to defend the objectives of the attacking troops. The more the period over which the landing of the airborne troops on the ground was extended meant the more time the enemy was given to read the intentions of his opponents and deploy his own troops to resist them.

The most fundamental of the considerations that bore upon the development of the air plan for Market Garden was the difference between the British and Americans in the strategies they believed should be adopted to fight the air war in Europe. To the US, offensive operations ought to be conducted in daylight, when in theory and allowing for absence of cloud cover, precision bombing of precisely identified targets could take place by close formations of heavily armed aircraft grouped together in self-defence. To the RAF, night bombing operations were preferred, a philosophy much influenced by the heavy losses suffered in the early part of the war in daylight raids. The belief was that single or small groups of aircraft were much less easily detected and consequently less vulnerable to anti-aircraft fire and night-fighter aircraft. These defensive forces would in any case be made less effective by the cover provided to the attackers by darkness. A high standard of navigational training, increasingly supported by electronic aids to ground identification that were progressively being developed, would ensure that planned targets could be found and attacked with accuracy

94

and economy of effort. To a considerable degree, each distinct philosophy was a product of necessity. The Americans, becoming belligerents during the third year of Hitler's war and building their war effort on the foundation of relatively small peacetime armed forces that would be rapidly expanded with the aid of an enormous and invulnerable industrial capacity, there was a strong desire to get on with it, to get into the position where every enemy could be overcome by the sheer weight of arms that could be brought against them. The British were, on the other hand, very conscious of the limits of their resources and the vulnerability which dependence of the importing over the sea lanes of a large proportion of the nation's essential war requirements imposed upon them, and realized that the most had to be got out of every individual and every item of equipment in case there were no replacement for either. In practice this resulted in the United States air forces being equipped with bombers devoting a considerable part of their payload to heavy defensive armament and the larger crew required to operate it, leading to a relatively small bomb load per aircraft. The tactics demanded close formation flying so that in defence against enemy fighters, each aircraft could provide protection to the others. In turn, each formation was headed by a lead navigator, whose responsibility it was to see that his formation was brought to the chosen target and to give the order to it all to drop its bomb loads together when he had the objective in his sights. The RAF aircraft, on the other hand, was designed to operate singly, to have the ability to defend itself (although to nothing like the capacity of the American aircraft to do so), and to carry the greatest possible bomb load so as to maximize the damage each single aircrew could inflict. To reduce the comparison to its simplest, the RAF aircrew had navigational and night-flying skills that were not shared by their US counterparts.

When it became clear that the number of troops of 1st Airborne Army to be lifted considerably exceeded the number of troop-carrying aircraft and glider tugs available, HQ 38 Group at once proposed that a first drop could be made at or before first light on D-Day, the flight having taken place during the hours of darkness. Their experiences in dropping the British 6th Airborne Division in Normandy on 6 June gave them confidence that they would be able to deliver the paratroops and gliders with the necessary accuracy. The transport aircraft would then return to their bases in the United Kingdom where they would top up with fuel, have a quick serviceability check, embark a second load and complete a further landing within daylight on the first day. This was vetoed by General Brereton, general officer commanding First Airborne Army and, as has been noted, himself an air force officer. The reasons he gave were that there might be losses or damage by enemy action to the first lift which would require restitution; that consequently any second lift might fall short of the numbers required and that in any case, aircrew would be too tired to make two lifts in one day. It would not be surprising if he had not taken into account shortcomings in night-flying ability in some sections of his aircrew, which had caused serious dispersal of the 82nd and 101st US airborne divisions during the Normandy landings. Another factor might have been that, although Allied tactical air forces enjoyed general air superiority over the battlefield, by which it was thought that the *Luftwaffe* would not be able to operate effectively by day, the German Air Force was still capable of night operations, as the frequent bombing of Allied troop positions in Normandy and after testified, and it was possible that some of its formidable night fighter force could have been deployed against the streams of troop-carrying aircraft.

The consequence of this edict was that the lift of the three airborne divisions and their supporting arms was bound to be spread over more than one day, even without taking into account delays due to bad weather conditions. In fact, three days were allotted to the lift of 1st Airborne Division, with Shan's 4 Parachute Brigade due to arrive on the second day and the parachute battalions of General Sosabowski's Polish Independent Parachute Brigade Group on the third day. Another consideration imposed by the decision to carry out all the landings during the hours of daylight was the danger to low-flying and slow streams of gliders and transport aircraft from German anti-aircraft defences. It was here that the precautions the Air Forces saw as necessary to the protection of the air fleets began dangerously to influence the ground plan. The airmen believed, a belief that did not appear to be supported by up-to-date photo-reconnaissance sorties, that the Germans had heavy concentrations of flak around the Rhine bridges at Arnhem and at Deelen, the airfield to the immediate north of the town itself. In fact, heavy bombing of Deelen early in September had put the airfield out of commission and its flak defences had been dismantled and removed, something of which the planners seemed to be unaware. In any case, the greater threat to aircraft in the run up to and over the dropping and landing zones is light flak, which is mobile and more easily concealed from observation from the air and best dealt with by flak-suppressing fighter-bombers. Nonetheless, the planners became convinced that a flight plan from south to north over the town of Arnhem and therefore the dropping of airborne troops close to the main river crossing objectives was completely out of the question. A proposal for a *coup-de-main* assault by gliders on the road bridge, the tactic that had been so successfully carried out by 6th Airborne Division on D-Day, was ruled out for the further reason that the flat polderland to the south of the bridge, criss-crossed with drainage ditches, was judged unsuitable for the landing of gliders. It was reckoned that a parachute landing near the road bridge by the Polish brigade would be possible, but not until the third day of the operation, by which time the town was supposed to be in Allied hands and the junction of 1st Airborne Division and the leading units of the British XXX Corps to have been effected.

It is difficult in retrospect to see how it was that the air tail was allowed to wag the land dog with what turned out to be such devastating effect. Since the capture of the crossings of the last major water obstacles was the *sine qua non* of the whole of Market Garden, it would surely have been supposed that any risk would have been justified in order to make the landings as close to the objectives as was geographically possible. In any case, had German flak really have been in position and operationally effective to the extent that the worst fears imagined, the massive air superiority enjoyed by the Allies would have permitted effective strikes, both pre-planned and of opportunity on all anti-aircraft gun sites potentially capable of being brought to bear on the air transport fleets. In fact, such an anti-flak effort in support of Market Garden was made and was highly successful, the losses to transports and gliders on at least the first day being far below what had been feared; they were such that General Browning, in his report on the landings made by the three airborne divisions on the first day, felt justified in describing them as 'negligible'. It is sobering to contemplate that it might still have been possible to use the same description had landings been made on and around the Arnhem bridges.

The dropping and landing zones finally decided upon for 1st Airborne Division were in the open heathland well to the west of Arnhem and, at their furthest, some eight miles from the main objective, the road bridge. The present-day traveller on the motorway from Utrecht to Arnhem will, when he has the landing sites on either side, see from the road signs that he is still more than ten kilometres from the town. That such distances had to be covered by lightly-armed airborne troops before they could arrive in front of their objectives could have been justifiable in the minds of all taking part only in the belief that no serious opposition was to be expected from the German Army. The Polish general and the young British commander of 4 Parachute Brigade would not have been the only ones who saw the dangers implicit in such assumptions.

It was the morning of Sunday 17 September 1944. In Belgium XXX Corps under General Horrocks was poised to break out of the small bridgehead they held on the far side of the Meuse-Escaut canal and strike north-east to link up in succession with the US 101st and 82nd Airborne Divisions at the river crossings at Eindhoven, Grave and Nijmegen, and, within forty-eight hours, with 1st Airborne Division at Arnhem. In England, at airfields all over the southern and eastern counties, troops were moving to board their aircraft, prepared to take part in the largest operation of its kind of the entire war. The stage was set for a battle that was to end in the destruction of what at the time was, without the slightest doubt, one of the finest and best trained divisions in the whole of the British Army. In the battle would end too, gloriously but bloodily, the short two-year life of Shan's 4 Parachute Brigade.

Chapter Seven

THE END OF
4 PARACHUTE BRIGADE

The tasks given to 4 Parachute Brigade within Operation Market Garden were to drop during the second day on the most westerly and therefore the most distant of the landing zones and to move in to Arnhem and establish a defensive perimeter on the high ground to the north of the town, so as to block the movement of any German forces from that direction. The two other brigades of 1st Airborne Division were to land on the first day, with 1 Parachute Brigade of three battalions having as its objectives the capture of the Arnhem road and railway bridges as a first task and subsidiary to that, the seizing of the pontoon bridge close by. The job of the three battalions of 1 Airlanding Brigade, which would arrive by glider, was to secure the landing and dropping zones for subsequent lifts and to form the western sector of the Arnhem defensive perimeter.

The constraints imposed by the air plan and the serious shortcomings in the intelligence information available to him had given the divisional commander little freedom of action in drawing up his tactical plan for the achievement of the primary objective, capture of the Arnhem road bridge. Shan saw the flaws in the divisional plan clearly: the delays that would inevitably result from the distances between dropping zones and the Arnhem bridge and the opportunity that would give for the customary swift German reaction which he well understood and had good reason to fear, and the lack of availability of troops for attacks on the main objectives through the need to tie up at least fifty per cent of the soldiers landed on the first day in the defence of the landing and dropping zones; all this, he realized, would add to the complications of his own brigade's job.

After giving out his orders, he was moved to give expression to his doubts. At the end he bade unit commanders and senior staff to remain behind and told them, with remarkable prescience and with the trusting openness that they had come to expect from him and that had earned

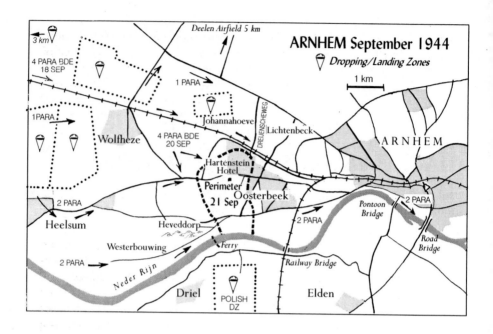

ARNHEM September 1944

◈ *Dropping/Landing Zones*

Deelen Airfield 5 km

4 PARA BDE
18 SEP

1 PARA

3 km

1 km

Johannahoeve

Lichtenbeck

ARNHEM

1 PARA

4 PARA BDE
20 SEP

Wolfheze

Hartenstein
Hotel

Perimeter
21 Sep

Oosterbeek

DREIJENSCHEWEG

2 PARA

Pontoon
Bridge

2 PARA

Heelsum

Heveddorp

2 PARA

Road
Bridge

Westerbouwing

Ferry

Railway Bridge

2 PARA

Neder Rijn

Driel

POLISH
DZ

Elden

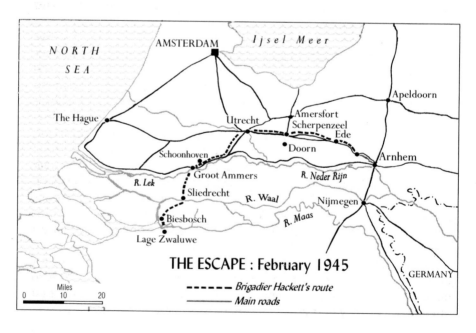

NORTH SEA

AMSTERDAM

Ijsel Meer

Apeldoorn

The Hague

Utrecht

Amersfort

Scherpenzeel

Ede

Doorn

Arnhem

Schoonhoven

R. Lek

Groot Ammers

R. Neder Rijn

Sliedrecht

R. Waal

Nijmegen

Biesbosch

R. Maas

Lage Zwaluwe

THE ESCAPE : February 1945

GERMANY

– – – – *Brigadier Hackett's route*
——— *Main roads*

Miles
0   10   20

for him from all ranks under his command their complete loyalty and deep respect, that their hardest fighting would not be in the defence of the northern perimeter but in getting there.

In the area of 4 Parachute Brigade's airfields the morning of Monday 18 September was foggy and, because of the dangers to the transport aircraft and particularly to the gliders and their tugs in attempting to get into formation in conditions of poor visibility, take-off was postponed from the planned time of 0700 hours. The first aircraft eventually got off at 1100 hours and the brigade's air fleet set out on a route that would leave the English coast at Aldeburgh, cross the southern North Sea and then pass over occupied Holland south of the three main rivers before turning north for their approach to the dropping zones on the west of Arnhem. The day before, the Germans had recovered from the dead body of an officer in an American glider shot down within their lines the flight plan for the whole of the airborne operation. This and their observations of the first day's movement of Allied aircraft allowed them to carry out a rapid redeployment of their flak under the Allied flight paths and the mounting of fighter attacks against the streams of transport aircraft. What, fortunately, they did not know about were the morning postponements and by happy chance the German fighters were sent to attack the landing operations at 4 Parachute Brigade's original planned arrival time of 1100 hours and had all returned to their bases before the Allies arrived. Anti-aircraft fire, however, was much more severe and casualties in the air heavier than on the first day.

Many of those due to jump first, almost invariably the senior officer on board, spent much of the journey standing in the open door of their Dakotas, reassured as they crossed the sea by noticing the regularly-spaced air-sea rescue craft of the RAF. As they got closer, they began to compare the landscape passing beneath them with the aerial photographs and scale models of the terrain that they had studied so intently during the briefings. Shan was being flown by his favourite Texan pilot, someone with whom he had often travelled and who had been promised a bottle of champagne if he managed to put the brigade commander down in the correct place. He also had among those aboard his Dakota, a future Chancellor of the Exchequer, then Lieutenant-Colonel Derick Heathcoat-Amory, serving as an Army staff officer with C-in-C Allied Expeditionary Air Forces and who had come along for the ride, a young French liaison officer attached to the brigade for one of the many aborted operations that might have taken place between D-Day and Market Garden and who had never been returned to his unit (and, as he was to be killed, never would) and a war correspondent. Passengers and onlookers were a long-established tradition of British battles.

No news had been received by 4 Parachute Brigade staff before take-off that morning of the situation of 1st Airborne Division on the ground at Arnhem, which was perhaps excusable with so much already going wrong, wireless communications faulty to the point of uselessness and the divisional commander, Major-General Roy Urquhart, absent from his headquarters. Portents of what was to come were, however, evident during the lively run-in to the dropping zone on Ginkel Heath, when Shan's aircraft was hit several times by small-arms fire from the ground and once by something heavier. Troops started jumping soon after three in the afternoon and German fire was beginning to cause casualties to parachutists while they were still in the air. Shan had the unhappy experience of coming down with, close to him, the eviscerated dead body of one of his own soldiers; he could also see that the air-landing battalion, 7th King's Own Scottish Borderers (7KOSB), which had gone in on the previous day with the task of making 4 Parachute Brigade's dropping zone secure, was closely engaged with the Germans at a number of points around it.

Having picked up his stick, which he had dropped just before hitting the ground and having accepted the surrender of five German soldiers, one in tears because what was happening all around him was taking place on his birthday, he made his way to the rendezvous point, collecting as he went various officers of his brigade staff. They set up the headquarters and swiftly established a wireless link with the three battalions. He was heartened to be told that their losses in getting to the ground had not been heavy and that they were in good order and well organized in their respective parts of the dropping zone. He was also soon joined by his recently appointed brigade major, Bruce Dawson, who had arrived the day before with the brigade advance party. The news he brought was not encouraging. The southern end of the dropping zone had only been cleared by 7/KOSB as the aircraft bringing in 4 Parachute Brigade were beginning their run-in. Elsewhere in Arnhem, although one battalion of 1 Parachute Brigade had succeeded in capturing the northern end of the road bridge, the remaining two battalions had failed to reinforce the position and were held up by a strong blocking line the Germans had been quick to set up on the western edge of the town. The divisional commander and Brigadier Lathbury, commanding 1 Parachute Brigade, were both believed to be somewhere in Arnhem and were out of all contact with divisional headquarters. This unhappy state of affairs was confirmed with the arrival of the GSO1, the division's senior staff officer, Lieutenant-Colonel Mackenzie, who also told Shan that the commander of the airlanding brigade, Brigadier Hicks, had taken over command of the Division, that one of the airlanding battalions, the South Staffordshires, had been ordered to join the attempt to reach the bridge and reinforce 2/Para in precarious occupation of its northern end and that the parachute battalion of 4 Parachute Brigade whose dropping zone was the nearest to Arnhem, 11/Para, was to be removed from his command to strengthen the push to relieve the troops at the bridge.

General Urquhart must have made the decision before he attempted his unfortunate personal reconnaissance into Arnhem that, in the event of his own incapacity, Brigadier Pip Hicks, an infantryman, would assume command of the division in preference to Shan, the younger man though senior to Hicks as a brigadier. It is also clear from his reaction when he did hear of it that Shan could not have been informed of the plan in advance. Urquhart's thinking may have been influenced by misgivings he felt through Shan's lack of background as an infantry commander and it is also clear that the General's desert experiences had not left him with an unalloyed admiration for the abilities of cavalrymen as battlefield commanders. This way of resolving the problem of the absence of the divisional commander did not suit Shan, nor did he relish having the choice of the battalion he was to lose made for him. He felt the situation was becoming untidy and he further pointed out that, although much younger than Brigadier Hicks, he was senior in rank, but told Colonel Mackenzie he would accept the position until General Urquhart returned, when it could be sorted out. What concerned him most from his rapid appreciation of the progress of the divisional battle so far was that the advantage seemed to be moving in the Germans' favour and the British risked being forced on to the defensive well short of having any sort of firm hold on their objectives.

The three parachute battalions of 4 Parachute Brigade quickly organized themselves around their different rendezvous, 156/Para in the north-west corner of the dropping zone, 10/Para in the north-east and 11/Para in the south-east. Shan held a brisk order group, telling 10/Para to hold firm in their present position, which also protected 133 Parachute Field Ambulance in the same vicinity. The medics had already set up their dressing station and were busy dealing with casualties, German as well as British, that had been sustained during the drop and the subsequent sporadic fighting, in which 10/Para were still engaged and sustaining more casualties.

156/Para were to move to the position being vacated by 11/Para as they moved off to their divisional task, and from there were to lead the move east along the line of the Arnhem-Utrecht railway of the now reduced 4 Parachute Brigade. 10/Para and other brigade troops were to follow as soon as the dressing station set up by 133 Parachute Field

Ambulance had dealt with its present casualties and was in a position to move off.

156/Para set off about 1700 hours. The countryside through which they were moving was not the dead flat polderland which most people associate with Holland but more like parts of Surrey, sandy heath and farm land on gentle ridges and hollows, separated by geometrically precise woods. By dusk they had reached a wood north of Oosterbeek, a distance of some six miles from their dropping zone, where the leading company met an officer of 7/KOSB returning to his headquarters. He confirmed the existence of a German blocking line somewhere ahead of them, guarding the western approaches to the town of Arnhem. Night had fallen when the leading company of the battalion under Major Geoffrey Powell ran into heavy enemy machine-gun and mortar fire from positions along the Dreijenscheweg, the track that bisected the wood from south to north. Attempts to outflank the Germans only made plain that the enemy was there in strength and that nothing except further casualties would be gained by attempting to probe through the woods in darkness against what seemed to be a well dug-in enemy. Accordingly, the company was withdrawn to the first defensible position with the intention that 156/Para would advance again in daylight.

By now the various elements of the brigade had collected the transport and stores that had arrived with the gliderborne part of the lift and had reconstituted themselves once more into a cohesive fighting formation. 10/Para were in position between the railway and the eastern side of the dropping zone, while 7/KOSB had moved from their positions around 4 Parachute Brigade's dropping zone to the landing zone that lay just north of the railway and in the centre of the area occupied by the brigade, which the following day was to receive the glider lift of the Polish Brigade and which it was another of their tasks to protect.

At about 2300 hours that night a gunner officer arrived, bringing further instructions from Brigadier Hicks, still acting commander of the Division. Unhappy with the content of the message, Shan went immediately to divisional HQ at the Hartenstein hotel in Oosterbeek where, in the words of one staff officer, a 'blazing row' erupted. Still smarting at being given undiscussed orders by an officer junior to himself, albeit one in a position of superior command by the express wishes of the missing General Urquhart, given before the arrival of Shan and his brigade, Shan found the tasks he had been allotted both imprecise and insufficient. To him, his Brigade, in his own words, 'was being ordered about as if it were a collection of individual companies'. After what must have been a vigorous discussion, a plan to attempt to move on into Arnhem at first light was agreed and Shan undertook to accept the command arrangements, but expressed a clear intention of raising the matter again if the General did not return. He went back to his HQ and spent a night disturbed by enemy bombing which fortunately failed to hit any targets in his brigade area.

The task of 4 Parachute Brigade for the next morning was to seize and hold the Koepel feature, a wooded ridge that rose beyond the Dreijenscheweg and had its highest point about a thousand metres beyond the track where 156/Para had been repulsed the night before. 156/Para, under its commanding officer Sir Richard des Voeux, was to advance with the railway on its right and to the left Lieutenant-Colonel Ken Smyth's 10/Para would keep station, its left-hand boundary the Arnhem-Amsterdam road. The arrival of daylight served only to strengthen the German defences along the blocking line, as it became possible for the enemy to use their armour more effectively against British movement they now had under direct observation. From captured prisoners it became known that the German units that had prevented the advance of 4 Parachute Brigade the previous evening belonged to 9th SS Panzer Division, which, although much depleted, had at its disposal tanks, self-propelled guns and multiple light anti-aircraft guns on tracked chassis, the latter a devastating weapon used against infantry. Again, 156/Para's attempts were rebuffed with heavy losses, especially among officers, two company commanders, John Pott of A Company and John Waddy of B Company, both being seriously wounded and out of action. All their brave attempts to find an open German flank had ended in failure. It was a similar picture with 10/Para on the left, who found that the enemy had reinforced its position overnight and was extending its line to the west along the course of the Amsterdam road, with the apparent intention of boxing in the brigade from the north and, incidentally, to put themselves in a position to attack the Poles' landing zone from direct observation, having been made aware from the captured documents of the intended arrival of the Polish gliders during the morning.

An unwelcome element in the day's fighting was strafing from German fighter aircraft, a reversed situation from the Allied air superiority that Twenty-First Army Group had enjoyed in the Normandy beachhead and during the whole of its advance through France and the Low Countries. The absence of close air support for 1st Airborne Division was inexplicable to the troops on the ground and undoubtedly a heavily adverse factor in what was developing into a battle of sheer survival.

4 Parachute Brigade's successive attacks against the enemy positions astride the Dreijenscheweg were proving very costly and casualties were mounting seriously in both battalions. Food and ammunition

were running short and the RAF's re-supply drops on the pre-planned dropping points, that were still in the hands of the Germans, were lost to the British units for whom they were intended. It became clear to Shan that he had not the strength to continue any attempt to move in to Arnhem along his present axis and he was becoming concerned at the potential threat of German encirclement. Apart from 9th SS Panzer on two sides of him, German units were also pressing him from the west, where he was defended by his squadron of Royal Engineers, necessarily and most efficiently in service as infantry. His only flank not actively threatened was the main railway line to the south. He was relieved, therefore, to get the news that General Urquhart had returned to his HQ during the latter part of the morning and would visit Shan to discuss the overall situation early in the afternoon. Shan saw no alternative but to recommend withdrawal of what remained of his brigade across the railway and, once there, to move east to join the rest of the division in Oosterbeek.

The General arrived not long after 1400 hours, without apparently having any news of the situation of 11/Para, the detached battalion of 4 Parachute Brigade engaged somewhere in the western outskirts of Arnhem, but he did give Shan a graphic account of his own adventures during his enforced absence. Shan's proposals were agreed; there was the complication of the early arrival of the Polish glider lift, which had unfortunately also been delayed by bad weather in England, at a landing zone within the general area where 4 Parachute Brigade was engaged with the enemy. 7/KOSB, as has been noted, was defending that landing zone and, together with the Poles, assuming they arrived, would also have to withdraw south of the railway in line with the revised plan for 4 Parachute Brigade.

Shan's intention was to move 10/Para back first, to secure the level crossing at Wolfheze, through which it was hoped the withdrawing units could be passed, against the very real threat that Germans pressing from the west would get there first. This possibility was uppermost in Shan's mind and would force him into an earlier move than might have been desirable.

10/Para had been given one of the more difficult and least enviable tasks that infantry can be asked to undertake, disengagement and withdrawal while in close contact with the enemy. Their line of retreat was directly across the designated landing zone of the Polish gliders; it will be remembered that the Germans had captured a copy of the air plan and so were thoroughly aware of where and on what day the Poles would arrive. The German units that had pushed west along the line of the Amsterdam road had formed a cap on the north flank of 4th Brigade's area of operations and were by this time in a position to cover the landing zone with fire and to hamper 10/Para's efforts to reach Wolfheze. As the British withdrawal began, the battalion's leading elements found their first rendezvous in German hands and had to fight to clear it. As 10/Para attempted to conduct its fighting withdrawal across the open fields, the noise of approaching transport aircraft began to be heard and gliders started landing into what was already a considerable fire fight. The sight of these tempting new targets caused the Germans to raise their volume of fire substantially and the unfortunate and bewildered Poles had to attempt to deplane and unload the gliders in the middle of heavy cross-fire. Not unnaturally, they could not distinguish friend from foe and those who could use their weapons fired back indiscriminately. This, in the euphemistic parlance of the present day, 'friendly' fire, caused casualties on both sides. The situation for 4 Parachute Brigade, for 7/KOSB and for the survivors of the newly arrived Poles was both chaotic and extremely dangerous and there were many examples of selfless bravery as individuals moved in to try to bring order to at least small parts of the general confusion. Under very heavy fire, some dashed in to help the Poles unload their jeeps and anti-tank guns from the gliders, and others with the use of vehicles moved in and out of the wreckage collecting wounded men. From losses sustained in flight and during the fighting on the ground only two of the ten six-pounder anti-tank guns that had left England with the Polish troops were recovered and able to be used in the subsequent battles.

Taking with them such Polish soldiers as they had managed to pick up, 10/Para eventually reached the line of the railway and moved west along it towards the Wolfheze crossing with the main part of the surviving brigade transport. What remained of its A Company, under the command of Captain Lionel Queripel, was dropped off in a small wood some five hundred metres north-east of the crossing to hold off German attacks coming across the landing zone. The main body found the village and the level crossing clear of enemy and began to set up all-round defensive positions for the night. 7/KOSB, still at that time under command of 4 Parachute Brigade, was also ordered to withdraw south from its defensive positions around the landing zone, in step with 10/Para and it reached and began to cross over the embankment, leaving its B Company to occupy a defensive position in another small wood north of the railway, about a half-mile east of A Coy 10/Para, which had the same protective task. For some inexplicable reason A Coy of 7/KOSB, which had been on the north side of the landing zone, instead of following the rest of its battalion in a southerly direction, moved off to the east and before long found themselves to be surrounded on three sides by German troops and were forced to surrender, only about thirty men managing to escape through the woods to rejoin their battalion. The main body of 7/KOSB got across the railway, to find the rendezvous designated by 4 Parachute Brigade empty and, assuming that the parachutists had been and gone, decided to rejoin the air-landing brigade and moved off to Oosterbeek in conformity with the orders given to them in England that had required them to occupy the western end of what was planned to have been a divisional perimeter enclosing the whole of the town of Arnhem and its bridges. 7/KOSB got to its destination without further incident, reverted to the command of Brigadier Hicks, back in charge of the air-landing brigade since the return of General Urquhart, and took up its allotted part of a distinctly smaller perimeter than had been intended in the orders given out in England before the operation.

156/Para, meanwhile, had also got down to the railway line, intending to pass over it and join the brigade rendezvous. In the confusion of the chaotic withdrawal part of one company and remnants of another became separated and proceeded on to Wolfheze, where they joined up with 10/Para, which after the day's fighting was only one hundred all ranks strong out of the five hundred men that had landed the previous afternoon. The unexpected arrivals from 156/Para were a welcome addition to the defence of the village, as were the few glider pilots and a handful of stragglers who also turned up at the level crossing.

The Royal Engineer squadron commander had in the meantime discovered, a half mile short of Wolfheze, a culvert running beneath the railway line and it proved possible, despite the soft sand at its entrance and exit, to pass through some of the jeeps. It was also invaluable as a means of relieving some of the congestion building up in the columns of Brigade troops making their way towards the Wolfheze crossing and into which Shan and some of his Brigade staff were vigorously and volubly attempting to bring some sense of order. Eventually all the transport that survived and two of the remaining seventeen-pounder anti-tank guns were passed south of the railway by the available crossings and, in some cases, over the embankment itself where a maintenance track, in a less steep place, ran up it.

The attentions of the enemy were not absent while 4 Parachute Brigade was busy trying to reorganize itself and to take up defensible positions. Fortunately, much of the harassing fire was long range and too high to cause much damage, but the actions of enemy groups in about platoon strength and well equipped with automatic weapons, determined to push up to the line of the railway, were more serious and casualties began to be suffered. Just before dark the Brigade Major led a spirited counter-attack by headquarters troops, which seemed to restore the situation. At this point Shan pondered whether to attempt to move what remained of his brigade into Oosterbeek that night, but his discussions over the wireless with divisional headquarters appeared to discourage it and it was agreed that the move in would be made at first light the following day. The hours of darkness passed under sporadic shell and machine-gun fire from the enemy, by now in some strength on both sides of the railway and the noise of heavy tracked vehicles moving about somewhere in the vicinity was quite distinct. Despite information from a prisoner of war that an attack could be expected during the night, nothing other than severe harassment took place, the Germans evidently judging it more prudent to wait for daylight and more complete knowledge of the British positions before mounting their assault with armour and infantry.

Tuesday had been a bad day for 1st Airborne Division. The attempts by 1 Parachute Brigade, by Shan's detached 11/Para and by the South Staffs to break into Arnhem had been completely frustrated by the strength of the German blocking line, and the level of casualties sustained in the town and to the west around the landing zone had effectively destroyed the offensive capability of the whole division. 2/Para were still in their positions on the northern approaches to the road bridge under intense attack, but still denying its use to the enemy, as they would go on doing until early on Thursday morning. XXX Corps were still well away from any possibility of a link-up with the British airborne force; what Shan had feared twenty-four hours before, that the battle was becoming a defensive one, was now a reality. The defensive part of the battle that had been foreseen in the original planning was to have been a short one, taking place around the seized objectives to keep them secure until the link-up with 21 Army Group, racing up from the south, was made. The limit of the Division's capability and of its ambition had been reduced to holding a perimeter around Oosterbeek that included a sufficient stretch of the north bank of the Rhine that might allow the eagerly awaited XXX Corps to force a crossing in strength and to build bridges to allow armour to follow.

For most of what remained of 4 Parachute Brigade it was a sleepless night spent on the alert against German attacks, with such rest as might be possible disturbed by the enemy shelling and mortaring. Where the hastily dug slit trenches could not be provided with head-cover, the mortar-bombs bursting in the trees sent showers of deadly splinters into the least protected dimension of the British positions. It was a second night with empty bellies, not even the British soldiers' great solace, a hot cup of sweet tea, was granted them and ammunition reserves were dwindling fast. It appeared that the brigade's situation was moving ominously from one of defence to one of survival; they were still some two thousand metres from the rest of the division in Oosterbeek and the noise from every direction of German activity during the night gave promise that there would be no lack of attention from the enemy when the brigade made its move in the morning.

So, in the event, it transpired. 156/Para set off in the lead at first light, with the intention of making a right-flanking attack on the Wolfheze-Oosterbeek road. Once clear of the woods and into an area of neat suburban houses, the battalion ran up against strong enemy fire from mortars, machine guns and armoured self-propelled guns, and were pinned down, extricating themselves with difficulty and at the expense of further casualties. This fatal haemorrhage was to continue unceasingly across the whole brigade and Division; the losses of the officer and non-commissioned officer leaders were grievous but most grievous of all to 156 Battalion was that its fine commanding officer, Dickie des Voeux, was among them. Buried in a field grave, probably by the Germans after the Battle of Oosterbeek was over, his body was re-interred in the British military cemetery the following year, but it was not until 1990 that men working in the area of his field grave found items of his personal belongings.

The two depleted companies that had been left to defend wooded areas north of the railway did not long survive the actions of the night. The 10/Para company held out until daybreak and the few survivors were sent away by the officer in command, Captain Lionel Queripel, who stayed to the end to cover their escape. He was awarded a posthumous VC.

B Company of 7/KOSB managed to extricate itself without serious loss and arrived at Wolfheze to find no British troops there. Unaware of 4 Parachute Brigade's movements and unsure of the location of the rest of the its own battalion, the company commander decided to move down towards the river in the hope of meeting other British forces. They had not gone far when they found themselves completely surrounded by German troops, who had astutely allowed the KOSB to walk deep into the net closing around them. Judging resistance to be futile, the order was given to surrender, an order obeyed by all except a group of Shan's 156th Battalion, which decided to take to the woods. Unfortunately, it was never able to rejoin its own unit. Faced with the blocking of his plan, Shan quickly revised it to put 10/Para in the lead along a new axis to the left of that first ordered. It moved off in some haste and contact was lost with the rest of the brigade, by now down to its headquarters troops and the few survivors of 156/Para. German pressure was intensifying and probing attacks were coming in from all quarters, the complete absence

110

of any anti-tank guns increasing their danger and demanding brisk counter-attacks to restore matters. Brigade headquarters in these circumstances was effectively an infantry unit, with every member fighting for his life. This included the brigade commander, who had armed himself with a captured German Mauser rifle that he records having used to good effect himself in maintaining the ascendancy that he felt had been established over the opposition, an ascendancy demonstrated by what Shan described as a most satisfactory ratio of German to British casualties. The scant comfort this gave him was circumscribed by his awareness that he was fighting an enemy that could replace its casualties and reinforce its strength while his own force was already almost eliminated. Shan was directly and personally involved in the fighting going on all around him and circumstances were about to give a particular demonstration of it. In the clearing which the force was occupying, Derick Heathcoat-Amory, the lieutenant-colonel from HQ First Airborne Army who had jumped with Shan as an extremely unofficial and somewhat unorthodox liaison officer (for his jump into Arnhem he had spurned the camouflage smock worn by all ranks of airborne forces and had insisted in strapping on his parachute over his officers' greatcoat), was lying wounded on a stretcher mounted on one of the few remaining jeeps in brigade transport. A German self-propelled gun appeared close by and fired three shells into the group, setting on fire one of the other jeeps and its trailer that were near at hand. There was a shout of warning that the burning jeep contained ammunition, followed by a rush of people dispersing and concealing themselves in self-protection. Shan, sizing up the situation with customary speed, dashed through the flames to the jeep where the wounded officer lay, jumped into the driving seat, started the engine and drove the casualty off to a safe distance. He was not to know then that the person who had been spared by that act of bravery on his part would, after his return to civilian life, eventually become Chancellor of the Exchequer.

The situation for Shan's dwindling band of survivors was growing more and more perilous. There had not for some time been any anti-tank guns with his force and the PIATs, the hand-held anti-tank weapon, were in short supply, as was their ammunition. Casualties were continuing to mount; Shan's brigade major, Bruce Dawson was wounded and dying, his own intelligence officer was already dead and it was reported to him that in 156/Para both the commanding officer, Sir Richard des Voeux and the second-in-command, Major Teddy Ritson, were among those who had been killed during the day. Ahead of them and in German hands Shan had observed a hollow in the woods that, if it could be seized, might provide some protection for his small surviving force. He called

Major Geoffrey Powell, the senior officer remaining in 156/Para, to him and ordered him to rush the position ahead of them. This officer, who had observed with admiration his Brigadier's courageous action in moving the jeep and casualty out of immediate danger and with an admiration mixed with anxiety that Shan was giving him orders while standing upright, which meant that he, a somewhat taller man, would have to be in the same exposed position while receiving them, must have revealed in his tired features something of his reaction to the order he had been given. As he had run over to join the Brigade Commander, what had been uppermost in his mind was how long could his handful of weary, hungry, outnumbered and outgunned soldiers go on holding out? Now he was being told to lead them into a suicidal attack.

The look Shan gave the officer told him that his mind had been clearly read and that the future of their beleaguered force lay in his resolve. The officer saluted and went back to his men, telling them that they might all as well die attacking the bastards as lying in a ditch being killed one by one. No one hesitated. Screaming and yelling, the men charged as fast as their physical state allowed towards the German position, scarcely conscious of the fire being directed at them, but slowly and bewilderingly aware that they had broken the enemy, that they were getting up and running away! The hollow, the Brigadier's objective that a glance from him had shown was within the British soldier's power to achieve, was theirs. The few brigade headquarters troops quickly joined the victorious soldiers of 156/Para and the defences of the hollow were set up around its entire perimeter. Shan noted with satisfaction and mentally recorded numerous acts of great personal gallantry, not only during the capture of the hollow but again and again during that long and demanding day.

The position they were occupying was roughly circular and about sixty metres across. It was not a single hollow but rather a series of hollows, probably remains of old excavations. There were by now barely more than eighty all ranks of assorted units present, with insufficient arms and dwindling supplies of ammunition. The Germans in their precipitate flight from the hollow had abandoned a fair number of hand weapons and ammunition to go with them and these were distributed to replace what had been lost, destroyed or gone missing. Geoffrey Powell, the officer commanding 156/Para's assault, had in the course of it thrown away his jammed and useless Sten gun and had equipped himself with a Mauser rifle for which its previous owner would have no further use. Shan was similarly armed, but, preferring the familiar, exchanged his German weapon for a British Lee-Enfield when one of his officers carrying the rifle became severely wounded during one of the enemy counter-attacks that continued without let-up for the whole of the afternoon. All of them were beaten back, notwithstanding frequent German penetration to within grenade-throwing range of the British slit trenches but the steady drain of casualties went on. One small comfort was that there appeared to be only one tank in support of the German infantry, the remainder seemingly fully engaged elsewhere.

Shan had not lost sight of the fact that his intention had been, and remained, to join up with the rest of the Division in the Oosterbeek perimeter. He was also doubtful of his force's ability to maintain their present position through the night. As ammunition was used up, ability to defend against German attacks was weakening and he sensed that the enemy was aware of it and becoming bolder. He had been out of wireless communication with divisional headquarters since the middle of the morning, his only knowledge of what might be going on coming from the noises of battle to the east, which rose and fell throughout the day. He judged from the map that the western edge of the divisional perimeter could not be very far away from them and decided that another concerted dash might take them within it at a lower cost than a night's constant enemy fire, even if they were able to survive until night fell. He could also hope to find food and water for his unfed men there, and perhaps a supply of replacement weapons and ammunition. He might also be reunited with his own 11/Para that had been taken from him just after landing two days before and of whose fate since their move to join 1 Parachute Brigade he had been told nothing. By now dusk was gathering and Shan was concerned that the enemy was likely to make one last major effort before dark to liquidate his position. Calling the few remaining officers and senior NCOs to him, he explained his intention that all those left who were physically capable of it were to rush the enemy and break through to join whatever might remain of the division. A quick question all round revealed that only a small number would be able to take part; the wounded and the German prisoners would have to be left behind. While the escape party was being hastily assembled, Shan just had time to go around the position to say goodbye to his wounded, assuring them of his confidence that the enemy would deal decently and properly with them when the time came.

Quietly checking that everyone was ready, he wasted no time in shouting the order to go. In a single group, screaming and yelling, the troops, with their Brigade commander in the lead and Geoffrey Powell bringing up the rear, burst over the lip of the hollow and made for the lane that led downhill towards Oosterbeek, bayonets fixed and weapons in hand. As usual, German reaction came quickly and they fired from all sides at the charging mass, but were unable to stop its frantic progress.

The first reaction among the British was that at least they had succeeded in breaking out of the hollow, then, as they got further away and the German fire began first to slacken and then die away completely, that their Brigadier's hope of getting themselves into the divisional position looked like happening. After about four hundred metres, when there was no more firing in their direction, they stopped running and broke into a sort of shambling walk that took them towards some suburban houses that lay on the outskirts of the town of Oosterbeek. This was confirmed when slit trenches manned by the air landing battalion of the Border Regiment could be made out around the buildings. As the parachutists came up to them, the Borders made quite plain their distaste at the sight of the dirty, unshaven and untidy warriors who had arrived in their midst, demanding a drink of water or a cigarette and giving accounts of what they had been through that day. They found themselves quickly hustled through and on into the divisional area, where Shan called a halt.

Giving a brief order to form a temporary defensive position and to check for numbers and for casualties, Shan went off to report to General Urquhart at divisional headquarters. The GOC expressed his surprise and pleasure at the return of his brigade commander and his concern at the cost to 4 Parachute Brigade of the day's actions. Bringing Shan quickly up to date with the state of the remains of 1st Airborne Division, he gave him responsibility for the eastern side of the perimeter, a line that ran roughly south from somewhere short of the railway line, where the White House position was held by a depleted 7/KOSB, down Stationweg and over the crossroads where the main dressing stations were, to join the river in the vicinity of Oosterbeek church. Shan made contact with what was left of 10/Para, now down to only some sixty-five all ranks, together with their wounded commanding officer, Colonel Smyth. They had been able a few hours earlier, in much the same battered condition as Shan's party, to get into the perimeter after their separation from the brigade during the morning's activities. There was also what was left of 11/Para, down to about eighty men under its second-in-command, Major Lonsdale, which had been pulled back into the perimeter after the failure of the last attempt to reach 2/Para at Arnhem Bridge.

This party was ordered to join a mixed group of divisional troops, glider pilots and survivors of 1 Parachute Brigade, under the command of Lieutenant-Colonel Sheriff Thompson, CO of the division's regiment of 75mm howitzers. Known as Thompson Force, its position was at the lower end of 4 Parachute Brigade's new responsibility, giving additionally, immediate protection to the guns of the light regiment, Royal Artillery.

Taking stock, Shan's own brigade units within the perimeter came in

1. John Winthrop Hackett, Shan's father, wearing Court Dress for his investiture in 1911.

(Battye Library)

2. *(below left)* Deborah Hackett, Shan's mother, before her Presentation at Court in 1910.

(Battye Library)

3. *(below)* SH in the Geelong football team, 1928. *(M.C. Persse)*

4. SH, when a lieutenant, with members of his victorious C Squadron cricket team in 193

5. SH at the head of his 8th Hussar troop in Palestine, 1936. *(Margaret Hackett)*

6. SH (*front*) with fellow officers of the Trans-Jordan Frontier Force outside the Cavalry Club in Piccadilly, 1938.
(*Margaret Hackett*)

7. SH on his horse when with the TJFF. (*Margaret Hackett*)

8. SH, now a major, in the Western Desert.
(Queen's Own Royal Hussars)

9. An 8th Hussar Honey Tank.
(Queen's Own Royal Hussa

10. SH receiving the DSO from the Duke of Gloucester.
(IWM E146

11. King George VI visits 4 Para Brigade in the UK. SH is on his left, with Lt. Col. Sir Richard des Voeux of 156 Para Battalion on his right. *(John Waddy)*

12. The battle in the woods at Oosterbeek: a jeep on fire. (IWM BU1140)

13. 4 Para Brigade defending a house at Oosterbeek. (IWM BU1122)

14. Dutch children laying flowers at the Military Cemetery at Oosterbeek.
(IWM BU10741)

15. After the war: SH with the TJFF at Burqa.
(Margaret Hackett)

16. SH in TJFF uniform, with Susan.
(Margaret Hackett)

17. SH and Susan at a meet of the Old Berkshire. *(Margaret Hackett)*

18. SH visits Berlin when C-in-C Northag. *(Army Public Relations)*

19. SH with his mother and his wife.
(Margaret Hackett)

20. SH, President Lubke of West Germany and General Sir John Mogg. Behind SH is Sir Frank Roberts, then British Ambassador in Bonn.   *(British Army Command)*

21. SH with 'Jumbo' Wilson at the Army Cadet Forces Association Dinner, 1963.

22. SH with Her Majesty the Queen and the Dean of King's College, London.

23. SH and
    Margaret in
    evening dress.
    *(Margaret
    Hackett)*

24. SH with the Queen at the opening of the new KCL building in the Strand. *(KCL)*

25. SH at home at
    Coberley.
    (Soldier Magazine)

26. SH fishing at Coberley Mill. *(Time-Life)*

27. SH with the many editions of his book *The Third World War*. *(Soldier Magazine)*

28. SH with Booty, Redman and US pilot Ulrich at a 4 Para Brigade dinner in 1990.
(John Waddy)

29. SH with HRH the Prince of Wales and Major General Johnny Frost *(far right)* at an Arnhem reunion.
(Margaret Hackett)

30. General Sir John Hackett in full dress.
(Margaret Hackett)

31. SH after lunch at the *Punch* table. (*Jane Bown*)

32. John Winthrop Hackett, SH's father, as First Chancellor of the University of Western Australia.
(St George's College, UWA)

33. SH as Principal of King's College, London. *(KCL)*

total, including stragglers and others who had found their way back separately, to some two hundred and fifty men, out of a total of some three thousand who had left England the previous Monday. Casualties during the dash from the hollow had been mercifully light. Counting them in with the various units from outside 4 Parachute Brigade that were already occupying defensive positions here and there on the eastern perimeter, Shan's total command came to no more than five hundred men.

A frugal but hot meal and rest overnight had transformed the men who had fought through the costly and wearying battles of Wednesday. Their clothing tidied up, some able to take the chance to shave and with ammunition replenished, they were ready to face whatever fresh German assaults would be mounted before the arrival of the by now overdue relieving forces of XXX Corps. The perimeter into which they had managed to get was, on its western side, the sector for which 1 Air Landing Brigade was responsible, largely wooded parkland. To the south lay the River Rhine and the flat water meadows that lined its banks. The eastern side, allotted to Shan's 4 Parachute Brigade, ran through the houses, villas and hotels of the little town that was to give its name to the final battle of Operation Market. Shan's men were no longer fighting in woods and on open heathland but in and around the solidly-built houses and wooded gardens of this prosperous suburb of Arnhem. The Nijmegen bridge was in Allied hands and the reinforcing brigade of Polish parachutists, after a twenty-four-hour postponement due to more bad weather in England, was due to land on a revised dropping zone around Driel, south of the river and opposite 1st Airborne Division's bridgehead, at some time during the day. Both ends of the Arnhem bridge, however, were now firmly under the control of the Germans and the resistance of 2/Para around its northern approaches was coming to an end.

The Oosterbeek perimeter now contained the whole of what remained of 1st Airborne Division as fighting units. With the Arnhem bridge firmly in their own hands and their north-south axis linking Arnhem with Nijmegen clear of Allied ground troops, the Germans were now free to throw their full weight on to Urqhuart's tightly restricted position. The enemy continued to combine his tactic of regular attacks during daylight of mixed groups of infantry and armour, the latter now reinforced by the latest mark of Tiger tank with its powerful 88mm gun, with a reluctance to continue to press attacks during the hours of darkness. What did go on unrelentingly into the perimeter during daylight was bombardment by artillery and mortars, although, to the relief of the airborne troops, it tended to diminish considerably at nightime. Adding to the torment were the multi-barrelled *minenwerfers*, or 'Moaning Minnies', their heavy rounds falling to the accompaniment of banshee shrieks from the sound devices attached to the fins. It was a noise that would remain irremovably fixed in the memory of anyone who had ever experienced it from the receiving end and no single living soldier within the airborne perimeter was out of earshot of its dreadful message.

The houses around the edge of the divisional position were the foundation of the defence. Solidly built and invariably with a cellar, they made sound strongpoints, although vulnerable to short-range fire from the main armament of the enemy tanks and self-propelled guns that had the temerity to approach within sighting distance.

The Germans had developed a healthy respect for such six-pounder anti-tank guns as remained useable and also for the PIATs, the infantry anti-tank weapon, whose lack of range was no disadvantage in the close-quarter fighting in which the defenders were now engaged. Consequently enemy armour that did venture forward tended to fire one round and then withdraw before it could be attacked in its turn.

One effective use by the Germans of the hours of darkness was the forward infiltration of snipers, who would take up station and wait for sufficient daylight to present them with the target of soldiers moving about the airborne position. There was, by the nature of things, considerable movement necessary within the perimeter; telephone cables cut by shellfire to be repaired, ammunition parties replenishing from the scanty reserves, runners carrying messages, perhaps even the transport of food and water, although food was for most of the siege lacking or in very short supply; in the case of the survivors of 156/Para, they received nothing between the meal they had been given on getting into the perimeter and being fed just before the evacuation the following Monday. The first task each morning for the defenders was to winkle out the snipers as they revealed their presence by causing the first British casualties of the day.

Thursday 21 September was a day of increasing German pressure on the sector that Shan was defending with the small force to which his command was now reduced. The enemy attacks were unceasing from the east and in 10/Para's area on that side of the perimeter line a particularly fierce assault succeeded, through heavy tank fire pressed home from close-range, in destroying and razing to the ground the houses the battalion was occupying. In this engagement the battalion's losses were extremely heavy, the commanding officer was again wounded and this time his injuries were to prove fatal; by the end of the day not a single officer of the battalion remained. Somehow the handful of survivors, now commanded by a subaltern from the Royal Artillery anti-tank battery, managed to maintain a position in the ruins of two of the houses, where they continued to hold off the enemy for another day.

This grinding battle produced an unceasing drip of casualties, among them Tiny Madden, Shan's second brigade major to be killed. This took place during yet another mortar attack in the vicinity of Oosterbeek Church, in the course of one of Shan's visits to the southern part of the perimeter. In the same attack Shan was slightly wounded and Sheriff Thompson more seriously, requiring him to hand over command of his sector to the 2i/c of 11/Para, it being renamed Lonsdale Force.

About the dead there was nothing to be done except a hasty burial where this was possible, but the growing number of wounded was a serious problem. The main dressing stations had been established during D+1 in two hotels at a main crossroads in Oosterbeek, in the confident expectation at the time of an early move to the main civilian hospital in Arnhem itself. The failure to secure the town made this move out of the question and other houses around the crossroads had to be pressed into service as the numbers of wounded rose. Not counting those being treated at regimental aid posts elsewhere within the perimeter and those who, despite their wounds, were able to continue to fight, there were by Thursday some one thousand two hundred casualties in the main dressing stations. Worse still, they and the medical staffs attending them were in the front line, the perimeter running through and around the two hotels pressed into service as hospitals. Generally the Red Cross seemed to have been respected and the officers and men of the RAMC went on doing their skilful duty with great efficiency in appalling conditions. There were, inevitably, casualties among those already wounded from the fighting going on all around them and all the time numbers were mounting. By Sunday 24 September the number of casualties being cared for had risen to over two thousand; medical supplies were almost at an end and the senior medical officer of the division, Colonel Graeme Warrack, realized that the dire situation in which the wounded of both sides now were could not be allowed to continue. Having received General Urquhart's authority, he was taken under a white flag to the headquarters of the SS Panzer Corps, where he was received with great courtesy and understanding by General Bittrich, its commander. A truce for the evacuation of the wounded was agreed and Warrack was even given a supply of captured British morphine capsules to take back with him. Breaking his return journey to Oosterbeek, he paid a short visit to the St Elizabeth Hospital, to where General Bittrich had directed that the evacuated wounded were to go and warned the authorities there of the early arrival of a considerable number of additional casualties. The medical teams he found working there were mixed between German and

British military and Dutch civilians and he was gratified to see for himself the quality of the attention and care being given to wounded British prisoners of war already in the hospital.

Throughout the battle Shan acted, very much in character, as a forward commander. Judging his main concern to lie in the southern part of the perimeter, he concentrated his visits there, confident that the last of his Brigade units in the line, the few men of 156/Para under Major Geoffrey Powell, would do their duty staunchly at the northern end. By this time 7/KOSB had been forced back from the White House position and the small group of 10/Para still alive was drawn back into divisional reserve. So 1st Airborne Division went on holding out through Friday and Saturday. The postponed drop of the Polish parachute brigade had come in late in the afternoon of Thursday 21 September, further delayed by the bad weather in England and with its strength reduced to two battalions through part of the airlift having been forced by the conditions to return to England. The pre-flight orders given to the Poles were to move from the dropping zone on arrival to the southern end of the Heveadorp ferry, which they were assured was in British hands. By the time the Poles landed the Border Regiment had been driven off the Westerbowing heights, the feature on the north bank of the river, in the south-western corner of the airborne perimeter that commanded the ferry, earlier in the day. Without the ferry, there were few resources available to 1st Airborne Division to bring Polish reinforcements across the Rhine; one Royal Engineer officer recalls being given a number of small inflatable dinghies and a liferaft taken from a shot-down Allied aircraft with which to improvise a crossing, with only signal wire as a line to haul the boats in a linked group across the fast-flowing river.

Eventually about fifty Poles, a grievously small number compared with the mass crossing that had been hoped for, were got across during Friday night by the tedious and time-expensive method of paddling one man across at a time, the maximum payload, in the handful of dinghies that were all there were available. The men were sent immediately to help strengthen Shan's sector of the eastern perimeter. A further crossing was made on Saturday night, 23 September, using the few canvas assault boats provided, without the crews to man them, by 43rd (Wessex) Infantry Division of XXX Corps, whose advanced elements had made contact with the Polish Brigade at Driel the previous evening. This time, again under appalling difficulties and heavy fire from Germans now alert to the danger of 1st Airborne Division being reinforced from the south bank of the Rhine, about one hundred and fifty Poles managed to get over, to be placed under the command of the Airlanding Brigade and to provide a welcome strengthening of parts of the western perimeter.

The indirect effect of these new arrivals was greater than their direct influence on the defence of the Oosterbeek perimeter, valuable as this was. The Germans interpreted the Polish drop south of the Rhine as being intended for an attack on the southern end of the road bridge and moved some armour and infantry from Oosterbeek to counter this new threat. To what extent this slight easing of the pressure on the perimeter increased the time the defenders were able to hold out can never be known but whatever it was, it served only to defer the inevitable, the next moves toward which were worked out during the morning of Sunday at a meeting between the commanders of XXX Corps and of I Airborne Corps, Generals Horrocks and Browning, and of 43rd Infantry Division and of the Polish Brigade, Generals Thomas and Sosabowski. Here orders were given to begin attempts to reinforce 1st Airborne Division by a crossing that night from Driel by 4/Dorsets, a battalion of 43rd Infantry Division and by the rest of the Polish parachute infantry not already in Oosterbeek. Sosabowski protested vigorously at the proposal to make the crossing at the ferry point, asserting that it would take place where German opposition was strongest and suggesting that a crossing further west in the area of Renkum would be likely to find much weaker defences on the north bank.

As the Polish General had foreseen, the attack that night was a failure. Because of a shortage of assault craft, there was no room to take the Poles and only the Dorsets and some attached troops landed, dispersed along the north bank and unable to collect together into a coherent fighting body. Part were pinned down on the river bank by the Germans defending the Westerbowing bluff above them, others in small groups penetrated into the surrounding woods and only a small party managed to make contact with the Borders and get into the airborne perimeter. Two-thirds of the approximately three hundred who got across ended up as prisoners of war and the only result of the gallant but misjudged operation was to make inevitable the abandonment of the Oosterbeek perimeter and the evacuation from it of the pitiful remnants of a fine airborne division that had landed with such great hopes and expectations only a week before.

During Monday night, in fittingly awful weather conditions, the survivors of the units forming the Oosterbeek garrison were brought back across the Rhine. Only one hundred and thirty-six men of Shan's 4 Parachute Brigade came back; the spirit of this gallant few typified by 156/Para's fifteen men under Major Geoffrey Powell, its only surviving company commander, who marched them the five miles back from the river bank to the reception area in a formed and disciplined body, their bayonets fixed and rifles at the slope.

119

Their Brigade Commander was not present among them. Shan had been wounded for a second time on Sunday, this time badly, while walking back from one of his visits of inspection to his units holding the perimeter, to the few slit trenches in the grounds of the Hartenstein Hotel that constituted his brigade headquarters. With the usual brief audible warning, a salvo of mortar bombs had arrived and splinters from the exploding projectiles had struck him in the left thigh and, potentially much more seriously, in the stomach. Once the particular salvo of which he had become the recipient had done its work and the German mortar batteries had moved on to other targets, he painfully dragged himself the few hundred yards that separated him from the cellar of the hotel where he knew that divisional headquarters maintained a medical aid post. Here he took his place among other wounded who had arrived before him, still believing his main wound to be the one in the thigh and that the aching stomach pain he felt might have been the result of a convulsive leap into the nearest slit trench after the bursting of the first bomb. Before long it was his turn for attention by the single and overworked young medical officer on duty. An orderly cut away the bloodstained leg of his battledress trousers, revealing the neat hole where the splinter had gone through the fleshy part of the thigh, although fortunately missing the bone. The leg wound was dressed, he was given a cup of tea and an injection of morphine; feeling sick and uncomfortable in his stomach, he sat on the floor with his back to the wall, thinking first of all about his brigade and the defence of its sector now that he was out of action. General Urquhart, the Divisional Commander, had been told of what had happened to Shan and came down to the cellar with Colonel Murray of the Glider Pilot Regiment. After enquiring kindly about his wounds and the circumstances in which Shan had got them, he ordered him to hand over his command to Murray, which was done to the best of his somewhat befuddled mind. After that he lay as quietly as he could, wary of making the inadvertent movements that sent a sharp pain through his stomach. Various visitors came and went, among them Colonel Warrack, the senior medical officer of the division, busy with the agreed evacuation of British wounded to the St Elizabeth Hospital in Arnhem, and Padre Harlow, the senior chaplain of the division.

Other wounded were coming in at disturbingly frequent intervals and one, who was placed next to him, he was particularly sorry to see. It was Pearson, his own brigade headquarters' staff-sergeant, who had splinter wounds in his back. Shan was distressed to observe how grey and drawn he looked, as if the high state of morale the sergeant had always shown throughout the six days of fighting had suddenly been drained from him.

Since Shan had entered the cellar the shelling and mortaring had gone on without pause, direct hits on the hotel being indicated by a shower of plaster from the ceiling above and the dull rumble of falling brickwork. An hour or two passed in this way, when the young medical officer approached him in what Shan felt to be an embarrassed manner, to explain about the truce that had been arranged and that the wounded were to be evacuated into other care, which would mean passing into German hands. He also asked if, given a shortage of stretchers and of bearers for them, the brigadier would be good enough to walk to the jeep taking him to the St Elizabeth Hospital. To all this Shan agreed, seeing no option and so, in a jeep marked with red crosses, he was driven over the perimeter line, past the positions where he knew his own troops were still holding out, through into the German lines, observing as he went some of the tanks and self-propelled guns that had wreaked such damage on the airborne soldiers. Eventually he arrived at the St Elizabeth Hospital, being driven for the last part of his journey, to his deep aversion, by an SS man who had stopped the jeep and evicted the British driver.

He was carried in on a stretcher with about a dozen others who had arrived at the same time, Staff-Sergeant Pearson among them, to a reception room where they were laid in rows waiting to be examined. Shan was almost the last to be seen, the doctor being an RAMC officer whose face he recognized but whose name he could not recall. He explained about his thigh wound and also about the discomfort in his stomach. The doctor opened Shan's smock and battledress jacket and remarked that he seemed to have found a hole there. Running his hands over Shan's bare stomach caused a sudden and excruciating pain, at which the doctor's demeanour changed abruptly from compassionate to urgent. Without delay Shan was taken to the operating theatre where the severe stomach wounds he had received from the same exploding mortar bomb that had injured his thigh (there were twelve perforations of his lower intestine) were brilliantly operated on by Captain Lipmann Kessel, a South African surgeon with 16 Parachute Field Ambulance, dropped with the first lift on the previous Sunday that had gone immediately to the St Elizabeth Hospital in the wake of 1 Parachute Brigade's early advance into Arnhem to set themselves up. With the failure to capture the bridge and to secure the town and the subsequent withdrawal of the Division into the Oosterbeek perimeter, the hospital had been occupied by the SS and most of the British medical personnel removed as prisoners of war, with only two RAMC surgical teams being allowed on humanitarian grounds to remain to carry out operations on their own casualties. This arrangement no doubt suited the Germans, as it lessened the demands on their own medical services.

Shan's life had undoubtedly been saved by the superb professional skill of Kessel, who, after leaving the Army at the end of the war, was to rise to great eminence and to achieve a world-wide reputation as an orthopaedic surgeon. While at the St Elizabeth Hospital, he performed similar operations on at least nine other casualties wounded in the stomach, operations he was later told by medical officers of the SS division were regarded in the German Army, together with serious head wounds, as not being worth the effort to carry out as, in the unlikely event of them being successful, the recovered soldier would probably be unfit to return to active service. For such casualties, he was told, the treatment was an injection of morphine. Some quick-thinking member of the RAMC had also concealed Shan's senior rank from the Germans and had entered him in the medical register at St Elizabeth's as a Corporal Hayter. No doubt against the possibility of further Allied attempts to capture Arnhem and its bridges, the wounded were being moved back to prisoner of war camps as soon as, in the judgment of their captors, they were able to make the journey.

From the moment it first arrived at the St Elizabeth Hospital, the Parachute Field Ambulance worked closely with the Dutch, who were stalwart in the way they helped give medical care to the flood of casualties from the battle going on around them. After the dashing of Dutch hopes that their day of liberation had finally arrived, members of the Resistance began to be seen more and more in the hospital wards, intent on seeing that the smallest possible number of British soldiers should remain in German hands and whispering quietly of plans to help some of the wounded to escape. Kessel, who was the last surgeon allowed to remain at St Elizabeth's, realized that escape was likely to be easier from Arnhem than from a POW camp, but that would-be escapers needed to have recovered a reasonable degree of personal mobility so did all he could to delay the removal of his remaining patients, by now numbering about forty. Shan was also promoted to major in the hospital records, in the hope that the treatment he received if he were to go back as a prisoner might be marginally better than that of a Corporal Hayter.

Shan's recovery from his operation was beginning as 1st Airborne Division's remnants were withdrawn across the Rhine. As soon as he was able to sit up he sent for pencil and paper and began to make notes recording the course of 4 Parachute Brigade's battle during the seven days in which he had been engaged as its commander and in writing citations for those of his officers and men he had observed as behaving in a particularly meritorious fashion. He managed to get from Colonel Ken Smyth, who was lying gravely ill in the hospital and was shortly to die of his severe wounds, his recommendations for gallantry awards for members of 10/ Para, the battalion of which he had been commanding officer. He also started to pick up smatterings of the Dutch language through question and answer with his nurses and other visitors, although Kessel's Afrikaans was of little use to him in language tuition, being almost as incomprehensible to the Dutch as it was to Shan himself. So he lay, recovering his strength, pondering on the disastrous turn of events that had befallen his proud brigade and waiting without perhaps realizing it, for the Dutch Resistance, who knew him to be a brigadier and therefore a considerable prize in German eyes, to contrive his escape from the hospital.

Chapter Eight

THE STRANGER

The story of Shan's extended period of convalescence and rehabilitation while being sheltered for four months over the autumn and winter of 1944/45 by a courageous Dutch family and his eventual escape back into British lines, was movingly described in his own book, I Was a Stranger, published in 1977. The author has an enigmatic note in the preliminary pages in which he says that his book, based on a narrative of the events that he set down within a few months of arriving back in England, was being published because references to some of the events he described had recently been made in what Shan thought to be an incomplete manner. The account given by his surgeon, Lipmann Kessel, in his own account of the Arnhem battle and its aftermath of Shan being spirited away from the Saint Elizabeth Hospital, differs in some respects from Shan's recollection, but his book had been published in 1958 and could not have been the recent publication to which Shan had apparently taken exception. In any case, the gratitude felt by Shan towards the remarkable South African surgeon made them, despite their marked differences in social and national background and in their political persuasions, firm friends for life and they continued to meet until Lipmann's death in 1986. Subsequently, Shan was much concerned with helping to set up a travelling professorship in memory of the man who in the middle of a battle had performed a particularly brilliant surgical operation on a badly-wounded airborne brigadier and had undoubtedly saved his life.

Whatever the circumstances and whoever published, in Shan's view, inaccuracies of unspecified events during or after the Battle of Arnhem, we must all be grateful if it provided the impetus for the publication of I Was a Stranger. The book is a tribute in the most heartfelt terms to the bravery of one Dutch family in particular and of many other recorded and unrecorded Dutchmen who gave him and other escaping Allied soldiers help and shelter when discovery by their German occupiers would have meant summary execution of the helpers themselves and severe punishment of their families. For those who, directly or indirectly, through these activities suffered incarceration in a concentration camp the end, almost invariably, was an extended and squalid death. What these courageous Dutch people did is a tribute to what a deeply held Christian faith can do to fortify the human spirit in times of great adversity and to what could be achieved by a steadfast application of Christian virtues in daily life, however dreadful the circumstances might be.

All battles tend to the chaotic and the one that raged in Arnhem and Oosterbeek in September 1944 was no exception. British and Germans were mixed up haphazardly with each other, the hospital to which the Allied casualties were taken was in German hands and both airborne medical staff and Dutch doctors and nurses attended to a flow of wounded that were not only military of both sides but also unfortunate civilians who had either been caught up in the ground fighting or who had been hit in the Allied shelling and air raids. These Allied attacks on German positions in and around Arnhem went on being made after 1st Airborne Division had been forced to withdraw the pitifully small fraction of the ten thousand men that had arrived from England back across the Rhine to the safety of the British Second Army.

For the Germans, their interest in the wounded lay in having them brought to a condition where they could be judged, in their eyes, fit enough to be transported to a prisoner-of-war camp. Lipmann Kessel, to his anger and despite fierce argument with the SS troops guarding the hospital, had to see desperately wounded men on whom he had performed near-miraculous surgery, removed peremptorily from their beds and sent off to the POW holding area at Apeldoorn. He became determined to deny to the enemy as many of his British charges as could be helped to escape and, by the random vagaries of war, the means to help him do so presented themselves. A young Dutchman, whose name was Jan but who quickly became known as Johnny, had come up to Kessel's group at the edge of the dropping zone, eager to take part in what he had imagined to be the imminent liberation of his country. He had started by helping to push the airborne trolleys on which the medical equipment was being transported to the St Elizabeth Hospital in Arnhem where the airborne surgical unit was to establish itself, but it was not long before he considered himself an unofficial member of the field ambulance, visiting the hospital daily and usually bringing with him such comforts in the form of fruit or the local cigarettes as he could beg, borrow or steal.

After the battle was over and the remnants of 1st Airborne Division had departed, Lipmann Kessel's work of operating on the wounded continued, but in slightly less hazardous conditions and at a slightly less frantic pace. Gradually, wounded who had been missed during the

Warrack truce were collected in and duties at the St Elizabeth Hospital turned more to the care of those recovering in the wards. In the aftermath of the battle, the German authorities ordered the evacuation of the entire civilian population of Arnhem and this prompted the visit of an old lady to the ward, asking to speak to a British officer. She wanted to report that four or five unwounded British soldiers, all anxious to escape, were hiding in her cellar and she was concerned that after she had been sent away from Arnhem they would be without any sort of help. The only possible link for Kessel with the outside world, he and all his colleagues being prevented by SS guards from leaving the hospital, was Johnny and it was to him that now he turned. The young Dutchman was certain that he could help and within a few hours he was back to say that he had made contact with the Resistance in the person of its local commander, by name Piet van Arnhem, and that a plan was being made to get the old lady's cellar guests away the following morning to join a considerable number of other British who had evaded capture and who were being assembled from their hiding places around the town and in the surrounding countryside. The old lady was to instruct the British soldiers to move into the hospital's mortuary during the night, which could be reached from a corridor inside the building but also had an outside door close to the edge of the hospital grounds. All went according to plan; bicycles and rough workmen's clothing had been surreptitiously brought into the mortuary and by six o'clock the party cycled away with Johnny as their guide, he keeping a discreet distance ahead of them.

After that, and in the short time that was still available to them, the mortuary proved invaluable as a transit post for other escapees and as somewhere that weapons collected from arriving casualties under the loose supervisory regime that existed in the early chaotic days could be placed and collected by the underground.

Piet van Arnhem had got to know of the existence of Shan, perhaps through Johnny, who knew that he was in the hospital and still in the early stages of his recovery from the operation through which Kessel's remarkable surgical skills had brought him. Kessel knew exactly how important it was that such a senior officer should not fall into German hands and, so that the least possible attention should fall on Shan, he had arranged for him to be put into a small basement room well away from the main part of the hospital and for him to be described on his medical records as Lance-Corporal Hayter. Piet was already planning the escape of the commander of 1 Parachute Brigade, Brigadier Gerald Lathbury, who was still at that time in hiding in a house outside Arnhem, from where with some one hundred and forty other evaders he would, before long, under the control of Piet's Resistance group, be successfully

126

ferried across the Rhine to safety. Although in Kessel's view Shan was far from being in any sort of state to cope with the strains and hazards of an escape attempt, being certainly unable to ride a bicycle and barely able to walk unaided, it was agreed that Piet would visit the supposed lance-corporal and have a preliminary discussion with him. By Shan's own account, despite Piet opening their conversation with the confident assertion that he could get him out of the hospital and into hiding, Shan's manner towards his Dutch visitor was cautious, bordering on the extremely suspicious. He refused to reveal his true identity, but did go so far as to say that he was a wounded British major and listened without response while Piet went about establishing his own credentials. Finally the Dutchman played his trump card and took from his wallet a folded piece of paper, asking Shan whether he would recognise Brigadier Lathbury's writing. The pencil-written note, which Shan saw at once was undoubtedly authentic, said that Piet was trustworthy and would help any British soldier in need.

Soon after this meeting Piet came to see Kessel again and told him that the remaining British personnel in the St Elizabeth Hospital, who by now had been reduced to his own small surgical team, a Roman Catholic padre and a number of badly wounded men, were to be taken away within a day or two as prisoners of war, whatever the condition of the wounded might be. Kessel's reaction was one of anger, realizing that some of his patients would be unlikely to survive the journey. Piet went on to say that his Resistance group had come to the firm decision that Shan had to be helped to escape and that they had contrived to lay their hands on a Red Cross car to get him away in, that it was waiting outside and the Brigadier was to go with them at once. They argued for a while, Kessel saying that Shan was not up to it physically and in any case would never agree to it. Urged on by Piet, the two of them went to Shan's small room, Kessel going in first for a quick assessment of the patient's condition, then calling Piet in to put his proposal to Shan. It was explained that he was to be got away in the car and, suitably dressed and bandaged, play the part of a civilian badly injured in the latest Allied air raid and being taken off for urgent treatment for his wounds.

Shan listened thoughtfully, rapidly weighing up the situation. He turned to Kessel. "Lippy, am I fit enough to do this?" The surgeon's reply was equivocal, pointing out that the alternative was to spend the rest of the war as a POW. Eventually Shan said he would need time to think it over, a suggestion that Piet said was impossible, that it was becoming dangerous for him to go on visiting the British in hospital and that there would not be another chance. All this interchange had to be laboriously translated from the Dutch through Kessel's Afrikaans to

127

English and back again, while time, particularly precious to Piet, was running away. Finally Shan said, "All right, I'll do it." In great haste he was dressed in civilian clothes and a bloodstained bandage wound round his head to lend credence to the cover story. In the meantime the padre had appeared to pack such small kit as Shan had with him and to put his uniform and parachute smock into a haversack, which was left for Johnny to take as soon as it was possible to the place where Shan was to go into hiding. Kessel handed Shan the Army medical card on which was recorded the extent of the wounds and the treatment he had received for them. "You ought to have this with you," he said. Shan put it in his pocket and went out into the corridor with the others, pausing only to look into the room where Kenneth Smyth, the badly-wounded and dying commanding officer of 10 Para, was lying in a comatose state from which he would not emerge. Saying his brief goodbyes, to which Smyth could not respond, Shan was led, supported by his companions and by the stick from which he would not be separated, out of the hospital and into the street. Piet was waiting there with the Red Cross car, the back seat already occupied by two silent civilians with a large bundle between them.

From somewhere not too far away came the noise of exploding bombs and, much closer, the sharp bark of German anti-aircraft fire. The street itself, lined with trees on either side, showed clear evidence of earlier battles. Slit trenches had been dug in the verges and abandoned equipment and fallen branches lay everywhere. After a delay while Piet, without assistance from the other civilians, struggled to move timber preventing movement of the car Shan was put aboard, Piet got back behind the wheel and they drove off. In his rôle as an injured civilian, Shan lay slumped in the front seat, his head down and his eyes closed, conscious mainly of the bumpy and uncomfortable passage the car made over the cobblestones. He became alert when, before long, the car came to a stop and a peremptory German voice fired a question at Piet. His answer, in German, repeated the cover plan that had been explained to Shan at his bedside. This seemed to satisfy the German, who indicated that they could proceed. The fact that the casualty was being taken away from the direction of the hospital rather than towards it did not appear to register with the sentry and there were no more alarms as they left Arnhem behind them. Soon they were making good speed across open heathland which Shan recognised as Ginkel Heath, or the *Groote Heide*, where he and the rest of his brigade had dropped three eventful weeks before. He gazed at it with a curious feeling of detachment as though the earlier events had no real connection with his new situation as a British officer on the run in German-occupied territory, with a totally uncertain future dependent on the barely known Dutchman driving the car. He now had one straightforward responsibility, to escape and to return as soon as he and the Dutch Resistance could contrive it, to his military duties.

Not much further on houses began to appear on either side of the road and Shan saw that they were coming into a town. Back in England, during the planning stages of the operation, he and his staff had carefully studied the maps and topographical models of the area around Arnhem and the dropping zones, and he now began to search his memory for place names. The town, he concluded, had to be Ede, some ten miles from the hospital from which he had been spirited away and the location, he remembered, of military barracks whose garrison Shan had seen as a possible threat to his brigade during the landings and which he had therefore asked should be one of the RAF targets during the preparatory bombardment. The car stopped and, with a few words of thanks, the couple in the back seat who had otherwise been silent for the entire journey, disembarked, taking their bundle with them. The car went on again and, after a short distance, turned into the yard of a house seemingly as neat and as well kept as others they had passed in that part of town. Piet turned off the engine, got out and came round to the passenger side of the car to help Shan out. "You cannot stay here but I am taking you first to see Brigadier Lathbury."

They entered the house through the kitchen door where two women were working. They greeted Piet and then, after a few words of conversation, turned to give Shan warm smiles of welcome. "Let's go through," said Piet and led him into a room with large windows giving out on to the street by which they had arrived. A startled Shan saw two German soldiers pass by outside, laughing and chatting, and felt himself sharply reminded that it was he who was the interloper in what was still their territory and that the environment was still very much one of enemy occupation. His thoughts were instantly interrupted by a call of "Shan!" and the tall and unmistakeable figure of Gerald Lathbury, his fellow parachute brigade commander, whose 2/Para had so gallantly held Arnhem bridge for three days and four nights against fierce and continual German tank and artillery attacks, rose from a chair in the corner. He was dressed in a dark civilian suit and appeared to Shan, in his own words, "like a somewhat seedy don about to give a tutorial". The two greeted each other affectionately, Lathbury showing his pleasure and surprise that someone he had thought to be dying in Arnhem should be in the same room with him, on his feet and very much in the land of the living. To Shan the normality of this social contact with his old colleague came as a great boost, as did his re-acquaintance shortly afterwards with another familiarity lately denied him, the use of a lavatory with a chain that pulled and assured him that his personal functions were as they should be.

The three men went back to the kitchen. Piet had urgent work to do and, while he was eating a quick meal, the two soldiers talked of the battle they had fought, the circumstances of their being wounded and the adventures they had had since. As Piet left the room, Lathbury explained what Shan had already learnt from Piet, that, as it was impossible for the family he was with to look after the two of them, he had gone off to arrange for another house where the new arrival could be hidden.

After Piet had gone, the members of Lathbury's household assembled for their evening meal, which Shan was invited to join. The party, including the Englishmen, made eleven in all, the householder with her four grown children, the two women whom Shan had met on coming into the house and a Dutch evacuee couple who had been billeted on the family. One of the two sons, who was addressed by Lathbury as Tony, seemed to be a Resistance colleague of Piet's. All the Dutch had a quiet and pre-occupied air, which Shan put down to the prudent reticence called for by the situation, or perhaps a natural shyness, rather than displaying any degree of discomfort in their enforced relationship. The simple meal of tea, bread and butter and a thin slice of cheese that followed a long grace by the male evacuee was soon over. Shan felt a wave of tiredness sweep through him, a reaction to the day's dramatic events, and was put to rest by himself in a chair in the corner of the room while they waited for Piet's return. He was also in some discomfort around the dressings that still covered his stomach wound and wondered whether the exercise he had been obliged to take during his escape from hospital had displaced something. For the time being, beyond mentioning his concern to Lathbury, there was nothing to be done about it.

When Piet came back into the house night was beginning to fall. Again, he had the brisk manner of a man whose time was fully occupied with many things and his stay was short. His message, however, was positive. Shan was to be lodged with other members of the same family (who, it was established, were also named de Nooij) at their place a few hundred yards away and, when it had got quite dark, two of the menfolk would come to escort Shan to his new billet. Tony introduced Shan to the two well-built figures who shortly came into the house as being his uncles. As Shan got up with some difficulty from his chair, it was obvious to the new arrivals that he would be hard put to make the journey under his own steam and so, making a sort of chair out of their linked arms, the wounded soldier sat between them, with his left arm around the shoulders of one of his supporters, the other hand clutching his beloved stick. With a large hat pulled down to conceal his face, the porters and their charge, fortunately a small and lean figure, made a laborious journey along the cobbled roads that separated the two houses.

They came at last to Torenstraat and to a white garden gate, behind which stood a house with its front door open and someone lit in silhouette by a lamp in the hall behind him. Shan was gently put on his feet, the two uncles left with expressions of good fortune and the door was closed behind them. Shan found himself with two young people, a tall fair-haired man and a pretty and much shorter girl, who introduced themselves as John and Mary, brother and sister. Mary, smiling warmly, said how very pleased they were to have an Englishman in the house. Behind them stood an older woman, Aunt Ann, who, like the two other members of the de Nooij family Shan had already met, addressed him in good English. Already he was beginning to sense a feeling of kind and gentle protection, brought about, as he came bit by bit to realize, by the obligations to their fellow human beings that his new hosts considered their simple but deeply-held Christian faith required of them. Shan recognized it because it was in complete sympathy with the way he saw his own beliefs and practices. He felt a sense of ease in his new surroundings.

Refusing the young people's offer to carry him upstairs, Shan hauled himself up by the banisters, closely followed by John and Mary in case he should slip. He was shown into a pleasant small white-painted bedroom, lit by a small oil lamp and with the bed already turned down. The family had been warned that their new charge was a wounded and convalescent officer and the first thing that Mary said to him when he had finished casting his eyes around the room was that a doctor would soon arrive to have a look at him. On being assured that he had no other immediate needs, brother and sister left him on his own.

In a short time a young doctor, whose name was Kraayenbrink, was looking gravely at the medical report that Kessel had given Shan before he left the hospital. He then asked Shan to lie on the bed and took off his bandages and dressings. To Shan's eyes, his stomach looked a mess, with a noticeable discharge from the line of stitches that ran across it. "This was brilliant surgery," the doctor said. He did not think that the discharge was too serious and that it was probably due to the natural decomposition of the stitches. He dressed the stomach and leg wounds, replaced the bandages, packed up his bag and turned to leave. "You will either die," he said, "or you will get better." Whether the stark inevitability of the prognosis was intended as a warning or a comfort Shan felt too tired to decide.

131

After the doctor had left Mary came back into the room and helped Shan to undress. She said goodnight and he turned to the comfort of prayers before retiring. In them he expressed his gratitude for all those who had helped him away from the hospital and into this place, where he was beginning to feel safe. All the companions of that eventful day were brought with fervent thanks to the attention of the Almighty and, this proper duty done, he got into his narrow bed with a feeling of great contentment.

The de Nooij family quickly established the simple daily routine that Shan was to follow while he was under their protection. He would always retain an abiding memory of it. It began early in the morning with Mary arriving with a waking-up cup of tea and a formal but sincere enquiry about how he had passed the night. Next Shan's breakfast was brought to him in his room, (on the first day and not infrequently afterwards there was a boiled egg. Shan wondered about the sacrifice and contrivance that the de Nooijs had certainly had to go to so that he might have this morning luxury). Breakfast over, Mary would skilfully wash the convalescent and, when Shan complimented her on her skill, she explained that she had trained as an emergency nurse so that her grandfather, who had died a few months previously, could be given the constant attention he needed during his last years. The bed having been made up, Mary would depart until she brought him lunch about midday. During the morning John would perhaps come in to play a game of chess, or Shan, once some books in English had been found for him, would read. After his midday meal, always proper hot food and, in the early days, more than Shan could possibly eat, he might doze until at four o'clock when Mary would come in with a cup of tea and some biscuits. She would then stay with her patient for a while and the two of them would carry on a conversation, mainly with her answering Shan's many questions about the family and their life in peace and war, about the neighbours and what went on in the town, about the Germans and their latest actions against the civilian population in the aftermath of 'Market Garden'.

Gradually, at intervals over a period of some days, Shan was to meet other members of the extended de Nooij family. It was explained to him that the introductions had been spread out so as to avoid overtiring him while he was adjusting to his new circumstances as a wounded fugitive. Aunt Ann, who Shan had met when he first arrived at the house with Piet, was one of three unmarried sisters who were permanent residents of the house in Torenstraat. Aunt Wilhemina, known as Mien, came in to see him on his second day and then came Aunt Cornelia, or Cor, a more highly strung person who suffered from occasional attacks of migraine. The last and fourth sister, Marie, was the mother of John and Mary and of another son, Wim, who had also been active in the Resistance movement but had been arrested by the Germans and taken away, as far as any of them knew, to a labour camp in Germany.

There were also three brothers of the older generation, Pieter, who had died, Zwerus, the present head of the family and Ko. Pieter's son Menno, (which was Tony's real name) led one of the Resistance networks in Ede and, much to Shan's benefit, was able to obtain not only extra ration cards but also the eggs, butter and other delicacies that Shan found so regularly on the trays brought up to his room. The de Nooij family, whose businesses were a paint factory and a pharmacy both in the town of Ede and sundry other enterprises elsewhere, was typical of the solid Dutch middle-classes of the time; prosperous, self-reliant, not extravagant but enjoying according to their lights a comfortable life style and conducting themselves in an altogether correct and disciplined manner. The war and the harsh constraints of the German occupation had come as a severe shock to the people of the Netherlands; to Shan the de Nooij family was an example of quiet determination to maintain their Christian principles, despite the conditions in which they were forced to carry on their lives.

It was mainly from John that Shan learnt of the complexities of the Dutch Resistance and the different movements of which it was formed. As in other countries in occupied Europe, political outlook, religious affiliation, peacetime background, all played their part in an atmosphere of fluctuating rivalries, jealousies and long-term and short-term aims. Shan learnt that in the view of his hosts, the most important of the different resistance groups in the Netherlands was the Land Organization, or LO, whose job it was to work to mitigate the effect of the German occupation and to go to the help of fellow citizens who had fallen foul of its many repressions, particularly those who had gone into hiding to escape compulsory labour service or who were suspected of having an active association with the Resistance. People who went underground to keep well away from the limelight were known as 'divers', either 'heavy' or 'light' according to the degree of risk they ran. For such people, and Shan realized that he and all the other British escaped from the Arnhem battle had become divers, false identity cards and forged ration documents had to be provided. It was of this organization that Tony was the local leader.

It was impossible to ignore or be unaware of the German occupation in Ede. The heathland surrounding the town had for many years been in use as a military training area and in consequence there were a number of pre-war Dutch Army barracks in the town. The Germans had taken over them all and this meant that there was a constant military presence locally, not only in the barracks but spilling over into requisitioned houses and in compulsory billeting on Dutch householders. Potentially more dangerous still to Shan, but not a matter that appeared to cause the de Nooijs any great concern, the house immediately next door to 5 Torenstraat was occupied by a detachment of the German Military Police.

The first important thing was to establish a Dutch identity for Shan, to give him at least a hope of protection were he to come to the attention of the German authorities, either from discovery during a house-to-house search or when he became fit enough to take exercise outside the house, through being caught in some routine German identity check. There were immediate problems to be tackled: Shan's military uniform and the personal possessions that would mark him out at once as a British Army evader were still with him in his room; apart from a few faltering words, he could not speak the Dutch language; he was without Dutch documents and he lacked a Dutch identity. This last problem was dealt with first. The family decided that, although within the house Shan would continue to be known and addressed as Mr Hackett, if it were necessary to refer to him to third parties he would become Mr van Dalen. John explained that the name had connotations of coming down from above to which Mary added that, since he had arrived with them from out of the clouds, it was most appropriate. So Mijnheer van Dalen Shan became. Next, anything that could identify him as a British officer would have to be hidden and so everything he had brought to the house, identity card, silver cigarette case and propelling pencil, papers and documents, military clothing and equipment, all were bundled together and carefully concealed beneath the floor boards, not to be brought out until that much desired day when he might be able to attempt to escape, or until, although this was not something that any longer seemed an early possibility, his liberation by the Second British Army, together with all the inhabitants of the town.

His inability to reply to a question addressed to him in Dutch was ingeniously overcome. A hospital for the treatment of tuberculosis at Renkum, a town on the north bank of the Rhine to the west of Arnhem, had recently been evacuated when the Germans had created a forbidden zone along the littoral. Cor had the brilliant notion that Shan should become one of the patients, billeted on the de Nooijs. John accordingly procured a paper, ostensibly signed by an official of the civilian administration of Renkum and stating that Mr van Dalen was suffering from tuberculosis of the throat, had lost his identity documents and had been placed in the care of the de Nooij family in Ede. Shan was given a thick woollen scarf which, as the occasion demanded, was to be soaked in a strong-smelling disinfectant and wound around his throat, a ruse that was judged to be proof against any German inquisitiveness short of a qualified medical examination.

During his time in hospital Shan had succeeded, while the memory was fresh in his mind, in putting on paper an account of the actions of 4 Parachute Brigade from the time of its landing outside Arnhem until he himself was wounded and taken to the St Elizabeth Hospital. He had brought this record with him to Torenstraat and, as soon as he was able, he also set himself to compiling citations for gallantry awards for those under his command who had particularly distinguished themselves during the fighting in and around Oosterbeek. He was not short of choice. He also wrote letters to his Divisional Commander, General Roy Urquhart, and of course, to Margaret. It was his hope that Gerald Lathbury would take them back with him, should Piet van Arnhem's escape plan have a successful outcome. These documents, too, found a hiding place with the rest of Shan's belongings.

Apart from Gerald Lathbury, Shan had another airborne visitor. Digby Tatham Warter, an officer of 3/Para, one of the units of Lathbury's 1 Parachute Brigade, and who had the reputation of being something of a character, was also on the run and hiding elsewhere in Ede. Finding out where Shan was living and the two having been well aware of each other during their time in England, he decided he would pay the Brigade Commander a courtesy visit and, to Ann's consternation, presented himself at the door one day, unannounced and unexpected, and asked to see the Brigadier. The visitor was so obviously a British officer that he was let in and the two of them spent an hour or so in cheerful gossip. It was then that Shan learnt something of Piet's plans for the mass escape across the Rhine opposite an area held by British forces. When Tatham Warter had gone, Ann went straight to Shan to express her concern for the danger the British officer had posed to them all, explaining that the arrival of a stranger at their door who was then let into the house could have aroused suspicion in the mind of some passer-by who might himself by chance have been a German or a German sympathizer. In future, she said, anyone who wished to see Shan had to be brought here by a member of the family, which would be much safer.

It was not long after that that Gerald Lathbury came to say goodbye to his fellow brigadier. The escape was fully planned, he said, and would take place as soon as conditions were right; he did not expect to see Shan again until they both met in England. Shan entrusted his letters and citations to Lathbury and wished him good luck. It was, in fact, a triumphant success. On 21 October more than eighty all ranks got safely away across the river, among them Gerald Lathbury, with his messages, and Digby Tatham Warter. It was to have an unfortunate consequence. One of the main reasons why it had been possible to organize the escape, depending as it did on close coordination with the British forces on the other side of the Rhine, was that, despite the division of the Netherlands between two opposing armies, the telephone system was still working throughout the country and so, by means of it, messages could be passed between the two zones of occupation without German interference. In broadcasting news of the great escape the BBC, with almost criminal foolishness, disclosed the part the Dutch telephone service had played in the achievement; the German monitoring service picked it up, with the result that the telephone service in the part of the country the enemy occupied was closed down. The removal from resistance groups of this effective means to communicate with each other seriously hampered their efforts against the Germans. It cannot have helped the organization of the next attempt at a mass escape in mid-November, which was, for a variety of reasons, a disastrous failure. That was the end of any further attempts at large-scale evasion.

It was now towards the end of October and Shan had been moved into Cor's room in the front of the house, while she took his place in the smaller one at the back. He was grateful for the exchange, as he not only had much more space but it was more lavishly furnished, with a sofa on which he could recline during the day. More important still, he could look out onto the road below and watch the traffic, both German and Dutch that passed continually along it. The wounds, both the serious one in his stomach and the other in his leg, were healing well, although he still felt weak and did not sleep comfortably. The single disadvantage of his move to the larger room was that he could now hear more clearly the activities of the German military police in their billet next door. In particular, one of the dogs belonging to the police had the nightly habit of long periods of conversation by deep barking with another, smaller yapping dog somewhere in the vicinity, seriously interfering with Shan's sleep. It was unlikely that even the de Nooij pharmacy would, in this fifth winter of German occupation, have a source of sleeping pills to protect Shan against the noisy irritation. Ann noticed one morning that he was in a low mood and enquired anxiously as to his state of health. He mentioned the cause of his problem and asked whether any sleeping pills could possibly be found to relieve the distress this enforced lack of sleep was causing him. Ann had another and more practical idea. She deduced that the deeper-voiced dog was an Alsatian belonging to the German police, while the other was a small terrier from the local butcher's shop. It was obvious to her that the correct solution was to eliminate the source of Shan's problem, rather than to try to alleviate it through taking pills that, even if they could be found, would certainly be in short supply. First she went to the butcher and threatening him with the loss of the custom of the de Nooijs and all her friends, if ever the shop had meat again to sell, if he did not silence his dog at night. She got from him a promise that it would be kept inside the house and not be tempted into a barking competition. The other side of the problem seemed on the face of it to be more difficult, if not downright dangerous, but Ann was undaunted. Presenting herself at the door of the police billet and demanding to see the officer in charge, she refused his invitation to go inside and enquired, in peremptory tones from the doorstep, whether he kept a dog. He said that he had a fine German shepherd and indeed there it was in the corridor behind him. The determined Dutchwoman wasted no time on compliments or civilities. She sharply told the German officer that someone in her house was very unwell, that the poor fellow could not sleep for the racket made by his dog barking at night and would he make it his business to see that in future it was kept indoors. Too astounded do anything other than comply, the officer agreed that he would do so. From then on Shan's nights were more comfortable.

His strength was slowly returning, although the immediate area of the stitches in his abdominal wound went on being uncomfortable. The visits of the Dutch doctor, overburdened by the never lessening demands of his own practice, became of necessity infrequent, although when he did come he continued to marvel at the quality of the surgery that Lipmann Kessel had performed on him and to reassure Shan that every-thing was progressing very satisfactorily. The passing weeks were filled with reading the books that he was brought by Ann, the sister who before the war had gone to England to study and whose ambition to become a teacher of English had still not been realized. There were among them some Dickens, Wordsworth and Scott, but particularly precious to him, apart from the authorized version of the Bible, on which Shan had been brought up, were a complete Shakespeare and an anthology of English verse. To these he returned over and over again. A Greek language Gospel according to St Matthew had been found for him by the local pastor and this also was a source of great comfort.

Thoughts of freedom had been seriously aroused in him some time earlier when a Dutch SOE agent with the codename of Bat, who had been dropped in Holland after the Arnhem operation with a colleague (called Ball), with the job of finding out how many British soldiers there might be on the run in the general area of the battlefield and of working out with local Resistance groups how they could be got back, came to the house to talk to him. Encouraged by the discussion, he had even

137

allowed himself to contemplate the thought that he might be in England, and reunited with Margaret, in time for his thirty-fourth birthday. Reality would decide otherwise.

By the time in early November when his birthday did come round Shan, being deeply touched to have it marked by a party at which his favourite hymn and the entire four verses of 'God Save The King' were sung, his state of health had progressed to the point where he could get in and out of bed unaided and wash and dress himself. He began to spend a short time each day in exercise, walking up and down his room, but the effort made him realize how weak he had become and how much more would be required to make him fit enough for an attempt at escape.

The next marker on the road to rehabilitation was a decision by the sisters that he had become well enough to spend the evenings downstairs with the family, although he was not permitted to join them until after the hour of curfew, then eight o'clock in the evening. This was to ensure that no unexpected visitor would arrive to find a stranger in the house and, however unwittingly, mention it outside to the danger of them all. On these evenings Shan would feel himself cocooned in domestic tranquillity, each family member occupied in their separate tasks of sewing or mending; last of all, before retiring there would be a reading in Dutch from the Bible, which Shan would follow in the English Bible provided for him as part of his library. Sometimes, before the Bible was opened, the others would lay aside their different occupations and ask Shan to talk about his life before he had come to Holland. They were particularly struck by his service in the Middle East and his knowledge of Palestine and thought it marvellous that in their house they had a man who had travelled in the land where Christ had lived and died. The Bible reading was followed by the distribution of an apple to each one of them, to be taken to bed, and so the end of the day was signalled.

After a little while, as the days grew shorter, the Germans advanced the hour of curfew to six in the evening, which allowed Shan to go downstairs in time to share the simple evening meal. More significant in Shan's progress was Ann's decision one day, stated as a simple fact not requiring discussion or consent, that he should begin to take daily walks. His military boots were retrieved from their hiding place, he was given a warm overcoat to wear and, with Ann and John to support him and with his stick in his hand, they set off one evening into the night, with just enough time left before curfew to manage a short trip of a few hundred yards. Shan returned tired but well pleased with his first excursion outside No 5 Torenstraat.

It was about this time that the second attempt at a mass escape across the Rhine failed. Kessel, the surgeon who had saved Shan's life, had been

138

successful, with a number of other members of the RAMC, in getting away from the medical POW barracks at Apeldoorn and had gone into hiding. He was one of the second group attempting to get back over the river and was fortunate to have managed to avoid recapture in the general melée and more fortunate still to have been able to make his way back to the house where he and three others from the Parachute Field Ambulance had previously been hidden and to be taken in again. The event had considerably raised German awareness and they began a drive against the Dutch Resistance. Bat, the SOE agent, was cornered in his hideout, wounded and captured; cousin Memmo had a fortuitous escape from capture in the same place and had to go into hiding.

There was an emergency family conference, at which they concluded that, because of their connection with Memmo, they were likely to come under the close attention of the German security services and it was decided that it would be better for Shan to be moved to another refuge until matters quietened down. There were family friends, a married couple called Boeree, the husband up until the occupation a colonel in the Dutch regular army, who lived a sufficient distance away in Ede and they willingly agreed to take Shan in.

Shan found his sojourn in the Boeree household agreeable; the two men, both sharing a common calling, found much to discuss, including the events of the German invasion of the Netherlands in 1940, which up to then were largely unknown to Shan. As had been the case at the de Nooijs, he found that considerable sacrifices were being made to provide comforts and treats for their English visitor. He continued to take the regular exercise that was essential in the build-up to a level of fitness that would give him the ability to withstand the exertions an escape attempt would demand. His companion on these walks through the wooded outskirts of Ede was Mrs Boeree who, like her husband, spoke excellent English, which they used with great caution outside the house in case they were overheard. It pleased Shan to feel that his presence in another place might give some degree of peace of mind to the de Nooijs, who had risked so much for him. The Boeree's house on Station Road was much more in the centre of things than No 5 Torenstraat and from his window Shan could observe a great deal more of the comings and goings of the Germans. It interested him to see what a heterogeneous lot they were and that even in the formed bodies that passed up and down units of all sorts were mixed up together. He also observed that a major mode of transport for them was the bicycle, all too frequently one that gave every indication of having been requisitioned from some unfortunate Dutch person, to whom the loss of the means to get about for any distance was serious.

Unfortunately, he was not to be long in his new billet. Colonel Boeree occupied most of his time with work for the organization concerned with looking after, as well as they were able, the welfare of Dutch people forcibly evacuated by the occupation authorities and who were now swelling the population and making more demands on the resources of the township of Ede. Engaged one day in the mundane but necessary task of finding straw for mattresses, he had the misfortune to call on the farm where Bat had been arrested and where the Germans had left an armed party to seize any of the agent's accomplices who might turn up. He was arrested and taken away for interrogation. The first inkling that something might be amiss was the Colonel's failure to return in time for supper. It was not until late that same night that he reappeared, shaken by his experience and certain that he had fallen under suspicion of taking part in Resistance activities. He thought, therefore, that to have an escaped Allied soldier in his house was too great a danger for them all and he had decided that the following morning some other hiding place would have to be found for Shan. This news soon found its way round to Torenstraat and, as was their practice, a family discussion was called to decide what was to be done. The option of finding some third house was quickly discarded and it was firmly agreed that Shan's place was with the de Nooijs and it was to them that he should return and that he should stay until, in whatever circumstances, the time came for him to leave.

When Shan got back to the de Nooijs, Ann, in her usual open way, gave him a full account of how the family had reached its decision, in terms that gave him no chance of dissent or reservation. For his part, he was happy to be back in the emotional security of what he would always see as his other family.

The German drive against Dutch Resistance groups was beginning to have its successes and there was some anxious conversation at No 5 Torenstraat about how long it might be before it too was the object of a German raid that could result in the capture of Shan. As his health and fitness were progressively restored, thoughts turned again to ideas of escape and of resolving their other serious concern, the safety of Memmo. It was decided that, if an escape could be organized, the two men would go together. Memmo got in touch with Sam, another parachuted agent, to see what possibilities there might be make an attempt. The agent, whose instinct for self-preservation was, not unnaturally, well developed, in the first stages communicated with Memmo and Shan only through messages from his undisclosed hiding place. Various possibilities were passed back and forth between the three of them: that Shan might be lifted out by air, with a Lysander or some similar aircraft collecting the fugitive, or that he might be got down to a rendezvous on the north bank of the Rhine where a ferrying craft from the Allied side could be waiting to collect him. When consulted, the British authorities' objection to the first suggestion was that the heavy autumn and early winter rains had made the ground so soft that it would be impossible to select a suitable landing place where there was not the unacceptable risk of the rescuing aircraft being bogged down. The difficulties of the second idea were that, since the end of the Arnhem battle and particularly after the failure of the second escape attempt, the Germans had done considerable work, using forced labour from the local population, in extending their defences on the north bank of the Rhine. They had also created a forbidden zone along the river from which all civilians, including even the farmers, had been compulsorily evacuated, which effectively eliminated any possibility of help or shelter to an escaping party attempting to make its way to the rendezvous point with a ferry craft. Furthermore, only certain parts of the south bank were in Allied hands with any real degree of solid occupation, so the rescue attempt, if it were to take place along such lines, would demand great precision both in planning and in execution. Nevertheless, Sam and Shan were made aware that active steps were being taken on the British side to extract the brigadier, perhaps towards the end of the year, and with that news hopes rose.

It was now December. As best they could, the family celebrated the Feast of St Nicolas on the fifth, this being the traditional day in the Netherlands for the exchange of Christmas presents. Shan was deeply touched to see how closely he was brought into the family's celebration and how ingeniously small and attractive gifts had been found for everyone. He was rigorously following his fitness routine with the goal of an attempt at escape always before him. He and Memmo went steadily ahead with the planning, with Sam in his secret location the vital link with the other side. Maps were found and studied and what seemed to be a suitable crossing point chosen, a large brick factory connected by a foot causeway to a great river dyke on the north bank of the Rhine. The plan that was put together was for the two would-be escapees to bicycle to the edge of the forbidden zone, four kilometres from the ferry rendezvous that would be arranged, leave their transport at the last farm still in occupation and then go by foot to lie up in an abandoned farm they had identified, where Shan would change into his uniform. Memmo had made a reconnaissance of their route as far as the edge of the forbidden zone and they carefully planned their move to the brick factory beyond that point on a large-scale local government land use map. This showed in meticulous detail every building, path, ditch and dyke and the two set themselves the job of visualizing and committing to memory every step of the way they would follow. The escape would take place on or immediately before Christmas Day and, on the date fixed, a British patrol was to pass through the German outpost line on the south side of the river, bringing a boat to carry them back to freedom.

The weather had become clear, sunny and bitterly cold, with a hard frost coating the ground in white. At night the waxing moon shone brightly from a clear sky. The crossing, it was decided, would take place on Christmas Day, when it was known that work on the fortifications would end early during the afternoon and when it was hoped that the sentimental Germans would be less attentive to their duties and less likely to expect any hostile activity. Preparations for the two to leave were made, the airborne escape kit brought out, checked and stowed where it could easily be retrieved, clothing and food for the journey selected and put readily to hand. All that was needed was the confirming message from the other side that they were ready and would cross to the brick factory on the chosen night. From Sam there was silence and by the early afternoon of Christmas Day, Shan was forced to conclude that there would be no attempt to cross that night and that there was unlikely to be another during that moon. Reluctantly, stores and equipment were unpacked and put back into their hiding places. The decision not to move down to the rendezvous turned out to have been absolutely correct when, a day or two later, a note arrived from Sam telling them that, in the conditions of extraordinary visibility on Christmas night, it had been decided not to risk sending a patrol across the river and that he would inform them when or if another attempt would be made.

There were some small changes to Shan's daily life after his return to the de Nooijs. During his absence with Colonel and Mrs Boeree, Aunt Cor had reoccupied her own room and so Shan had found himself back in his small back bedroom. A second wireless set seemed to have been acquired and Shan was shown its hiding place and told that it was for his use. When the family assembled together after supper, it was to discuss what the de Nooijs had heard from the broadcasts in Dutch from the BBC's Radio Orange and what the BBC's English transmissions had told Shan. Outside, the activities of the Allied air forces continued unabated; there were frequent attacks by fighter-bombers on the German road and rail communications passing through Ede, while at night Shan would listen to the steady drone of the RAF bombers crossing Holland on their way to targets in Germany. Other manifestations of air warfare were less agreeable. One day there was a loud, low-altitude roar and a V1 passed over the town, the first the Dutch had seen and, by its direction, headed for Antwerp, the port now a vital part of the Allied supply chain since the expulsion of the German garrisons from the Scheldt approaches during the previous month. From then on a steady stream of these pilotless aircraft passed over Ede, which lay directly under the flight path from launching site to target. Not all the weapons went on their way without incident. The unreliability of the V1s was regularly demonstrated by the numbers that fell in and around Ede, three of them on one particularly bad day causing considerable casualties. Shan would watch all this during his evening walks, when the steady progression of the fiery tail from the weapon's motor would suddenly change into sudden and erratic perambulations around the sky, followed by a plunge to the ground. Shan speculated that the cause of this high failure rate was not so much something inherent in the V1 but more probably due to icing-up of the wings and control surfaces in the bitter weather. Sometimes, but less frequently, the walkers would see a vapour trail rising vertically into the clear sky and then gradually curve over into the trajectory that would carry it to its target, the V2 rocket disappearing before the dull rumble of its motor was audible to them.

Shan was becoming increasingly concerned about the harsh weather conditions and their effect on the chances of he and Memmo getting away; there was no let-up in the severe cold and by now the whole landscape was covered in a layer of snow that it seemed would never thaw. The trials of occupation life also began to bear even more heavily on the occupied. Street controls of identity documents became more frequent and the pace of German requisitions was speeded up. It was as if they had become more conscious how close an inevitable German defeat was and that they had little time left to them to deprive the Dutch of everything they might still have of value or usefulness. On one bad day the two uncles were rounded in a *rafle*, Ko, the younger during the morning and Zwerus an hour or two later; both were taken off with a large group of other unfortunates to be interrogated at the barracks of the Dutch SS in a nearby town. Anxious hours followed until eventually Zwerus appeared, dishevelled but defiant, to give an account of the misdeeds of the day. What had transpired was hostile questioning of those taken, with, as an act of humiliation, head-shaving of each suspect before he was taken before his inquisitors. Many had suffered severe beating during the interrogation, but this Zwerus, perhaps because of the dignified demeanour with which he had faced the interrogators, was spared and released. Ko was less fortunate and, although he too, a frail and not a fit man, had escaped a beating, he was sent to a labour camp to join those working on the German defences.

These events brought an increased tension at 5 Torenstraat and the realization that further precautions might have to be taken to keep their guest secure. Because he went on taking as much daily exercise as possible, Shan's strength was steadily growing, but now the risk of being stopped and questioned during his walks in the street had grown enormously. Ann managed to get hold of one of the official badges given to deaf people and from then on, inside and outside the house Shan wore it prominently. This, it was hoped would be some protection, were he to be stopped in the street, against some security official or soldier asking a question to which any reply he made would have destroyed his cover and revealed him as a 'diver'. It was this device that successfully protected him when it was agreed that his hair was so long that not to have it cut could draw unnecessary attention to himself. Uncle Ko, who up to now had performed the duty, was, because of his conscription by the Germans, no longer able to do it and so the barber, a man not totally trusted by the aunts, would have to be summoned to the de Nooij's factory and given the impression that he was attending to a deaf Jew who, by reason of his circumstances, required to have his hair cut discreetly. In the event all went, in Ann's presence, without incident. She said during the walk back to the house that she had detected nothing particularly suspicious on the barber's part, who had gossiped incessantly with her during the session but seemed to have accepted Shan's assumed status without question.

The New Year came and went, celebrated by the German troops in Ede loosing off their small arms at midnight, and elsewhere in the Allied-held area of Holland and Belgium by the *Luftwaffe*, which carried out widespread night and early morning attacks in unusual strength, no doubt in the well-founded belief that those responsible for air defence would probably be otherwise occupied. By then, too, the German offensive in the Ardennes had run its course and the Allied lines restabilized, but, if these events had been a cause of concern to those around him, Shan, in the tradition of Jane Austen and the Battle of Waterloo, did not record it. There was no let-up in the cold weather and maintaining supplies of fuel became a constant preoccupation. Shan went one day to the barn and, finding John sawing up some timber that had somehow been acquired, took one end of a two-handed saw. He was pleased that he seemed to be able to undertake this new exercise without any discomfort to his stomach wounds and, when Mary later changed his dressings, a daily task she would let no one else perform, no damage seemed to have been done. Shan thereafter relieved John of his share of the duty, glad not only of a new way of increasing his strength and fitness but also getting pleasure from the contribution it was making to the well-being of the family. So well did he develop his new skills as a woodman that when he had sawn and split the timber available to his own household, he was asked to perform the same service for other members of the de Nooij family. This he did with great pleasure and to the considerable benefit of his own fitness.

He lived in the daily hope of being given news that new plans were being made to get him away. Sam sent a note which spoke of the possibility of a small party of two or three being got across somewhere well to the west of Ede. Another visitor at about this time was Piet, moving about with reasonable freedom under the cover of an official of the food control authority. He brought news that Graeme Warrack, the senior medical officer of 1st Airborne Division and a particular friend of Shan's, had, like Kessel, avoided capture at the disaster of the failed escape attempt in November and was also back in hiding with the same family that had first sheltered him. Memmo had by now firmly concluded that his duty lay in staying in Holland where he could continue his Resistance work and also be able, he hoped, to keep a watchful eye on the family and so said that he would not take part in any attempted crossing. Shan immediately decided that Warrack should keep him company in Memmo's place and asked Sam to make sure the doctor was included in the plan. The real purpose of Piet's visit was, in his position as military commander of the whole province, to ask Shan to take with him an up-to-date picture of the state of the Resistance organization of the area, together with Piet's proposals for cooperation with Allied forces when, as he confidently expected would soon be the case, they moved to complete the liberation of the Netherlands. All this he asked Shan to put across to the British Second Army as soon as he was safely with them.

Shan listened carefully to what Piet had to say, conscious of the Dutchman's hope that liberation would soon come to him and his brave countrymen and women but also sadly aware that the picture Piet had composed in his mind of the way freedom would arrive and normality be re-established in life could well be somewhere ahead of the likely reality. He gently attempted to downplay some of what he felt were the more fanciful hopes and to give his own careful description of how things might turn out, including the very real possibility that the Allied line of advance might not resume along the Eindhoven-Arnhem axis of the September offensive but aim itself more directly towards the Ruhr, at some point where the Rhine ran north-south. (Such a plan had been suggested to Montgomery before the decision to proceed with Market Garden was made final, but was rejected by him in favour of his vision of the airborne carpet over the three river obstacles.) It was clear from Piet's reaction when Shan had finished speaking that he was being warned, in as kind a way as such unpalatable facts could be imparted, that liberation of the northern and western Netherlands might have to wait until Allied business across the Rhine and into the main German territory had successfully been accomplished.

Shan took the letters and papers the Dutchmen entrusted to him and gave a promise that they would be put into the right hands as soon as he was in a position to do so. Piet said goodbye with the thought that the two of them were unlikely to meet again in their present roles as evader and Resistance leader; Shan attempted to explain to the man to whom he owed so much something of the gratitude and admiration that he felt, but as usual the Dutchman made his feelings clear that he was only doing what he freely accepted as his duty and that Shan, like everyone else, was only one factor in the exercise of that duty.

Through January Shan's impatience to be away continued to grow in the awareness that, although the determination of the de Nooij family to keep their charge secure was as resolute as ever (they let nothing show in their normal daily contacts with Shan), the worsening circumstances of their life under occupation and the seemingly endless extension of Shan's stay under their roof were greatly increasing the strain they all in their different degrees were suffering. He spoke more than once to Ann, putting it to her that in the family's interest he should be found some other hiding place until his escape could be arranged. Each time she listened carefully and each time replied that he was and would remain welcome in their family and that it was a situation with which they were completely content. He was their guest, this was his house and would remain so until God, if he so willed, allowed Shan to return to his own family. With this he had to be satisfied.

Then came disturbing news from Memmo. The rumour was, he said, that Sam had left Holland, a rumour confirmed almost at once by a note from Sam saying that his headquarters in London had ordered him home without delay and that he was to leave almost at once by a series of complicated and difficult river crossings well to the west of Ede, a journey he doubted Shan, in the prevailing weather conditions, was yet fit enough to undertake. Shan immediately sent a reply saying that he felt quite up to making an attempt now and asking in strong terms to be taken out with Sam. Over the next few days nothing was heard and Shan had to accept that Sam had left without him.

Hope was almost immediately revived by a letter that arrived from another agent who went by the name of Vandyck. Memmo, who had not met him, had once or twice mentioned the high reputation he had gained through his success in organizing the escape of Allied soldiers. Vandyck had said in his letter that he was prepared to take on a new client, so Shan wrote in the first instance asking to be given names of such members of 1st Airborne Division as Vandyck knew were still in hiding somewhere in the area. The list arrived quickly and Shan searched it for those members of his own brigade of whom he had had no news since he left St Elizabeth Hospital. To his intense regret none of those he had hoped to learn were still alive were on the list. It would be a long time before he was able to learn the fates of the missing men; in almost every case the news was as bad as could be feared.

John's impatience was grower faster and more fiercely even than Shan's, not for any desire to see the back of their guest but because he felt the authorities, both the Allies across the Rhine and the Resistance who had taken responsibility for him were not doing anything like enough to secure the escape of such an important senior British officer. John had been giving the matter much serious thought and proposed to make his own plan by calling on the help of the Resistance further downstream of which his brother Wim, now a prisoner of the Germans, had been the highly respected leader. He was sure that they would do all they could to help an Englishman who was in the care of Wim's brother. The family conferred to approve the suggestion and John prepared himself for a journey to people of whom he only knew some by name, of whose whereabouts he was only roughly aware and who did not know him. As proof of his standing, he took with him a family group photograph showing John, his mother and sister and his brother Wim.

During John's absence Vandyck, who had not waited long in making the acquaintance of the officer he had taken on, presented himself at 5 Torenstraat, telling Aunt Ann that his name was Jan and he had come to see the British general. The first impression he made was, to Shan, very favourable and they turned at once to practical concerns. Vandyck confirmed that Sam had indeed been recalled and declared himself doubtful about following a similar route to the one he had taken. He thought it better to think of going upstream, passing round to the north of Arnhem and attempting a crossing of the Rhine further to the south. Shan then spoke of John's plan, of which Vandyck had immediate reservations. He pointed out that when told to take on Shan, he had been enjoined to take particular care of him and he was concerned that he knew nothing of the people John had gone to visit. On that cautious note he left, promising to be in touch as soon as he had something to propose.

John came back the following day, his face showing that he felt his journey had been worthwhile. Nothing could be revealed, however, until the usual family meeting in the evening and Shan's curiosity had till then to be held in check. What John had to say was indeed encouraging. His brother's photograph had opened the right doors, to reveal the existence of a regular canoe service down the lower Waal, through the great marshes known as the Biesboch that lay at the confluence of the Rhine and the Waal. It was the means by which the Dutch government-in-exile in London moved people and papers between it and its agencies in occupied Holland. Because of the nature of its cargoes, it had kept well away from escaping prisoners but John's contacts thought that an exception would be made for an officer as senior as Shan.

Suddenly it seemed as if the ideal solution had been found. John was urged to go to meet Vandyck and to put the plan to him, and arrangements to do this were quickly made through Memmo. Another visit to Torenstraat by Vandyck followed shortly, when he made a whole series of objections. He knew nothing of the canoes but had painful memories of having been involved in an escape route for Allied aircrew that in its Belgian sector was found to be delivering the escapees directly into German hands. He would require a great deal more information before agreeing to John's proposal and, for Shan's own security, it might be best perhaps to make a trial run with a couple of others first. John was indignant at Vandyck's reaction, pointing out that it was as a personal favour through his brother's friends that he had secured a promise of a passage for Shan. In the end the two agreed that John would try to get fuller information to help allay some of Vandyck's doubts, while he for his part offered the use of a good staging post near Utrecht, where, as it happened, a party of British officers in his care was even then being hidden.

Preparations for Shan's departure now went briskly ahead. Dr Kraayenbrink came for his last examination of Shan's stomach and pronounced it satisfactory for the exertions of the long bicycle rides in winter weather that would have to be made. They talked while the doctor was there of the sad condition of the undernourished and poorly-clad men he had seen engaged in forced labour on German defensive works and of the impossibility of giving them adequate medical care. Uncle Zwerus and his wife and most of the other members of the extended de Nooij family who, in their different and deeply appreciated ways, had contributed to their visitor's well-being, came to say their goodbyes, all of them dismissing as unnecessary Shan's efforts to express his gratitude for all that had been done for him. Shan was photographed for false identity documents; warm underclothing and provisions for the journey, including two bottles of brandy obtained by barter by Uncle Zwerus, were got together; arrangements made to borrow a bicycle for Shan and his personal gear and the torn and bloodstained uniform in which he had fought the Battle of Oosterbeek were taken from their hiding place, made ready and packed in a couple of haversacks. On the last evening Shan sat with the family for their final gathering, talking together of their hopes for the future, of when the war would be over and how and when they would all meet again. Finally, Shan promised to let them know through a clandestine message broadcast by the BBC in its Dutch language service that he had arrived safely back in England. The message was to be, 'The Grey Goose has gone'.

In the morning, after a good breakfast, the woman courier arrived who was to guide them to Vandyck's hiding place. It seemed to be the customary Resistance practice for women to be used for this duty, experience having shown that they tended to pass more easily through German check points and questioning and verification of their documents was less rigorous. For this reason any of the men's belongings that, if opened, might prove suspicious or incriminating were carried on the woman's bicycle. Their courier, who seemed to speak no English and whose name Shan did not learn, was someone in early middle age; she drank a cup of tea in the kitchen and then went to wait outside, taking Shan's large pack with her. Then came the last fond farewells, Shan hugging and kissing each of the de Nooij women and, with a check to see that Shan's pack was securely strapped to the courier's bicycle, the two men set off in the pre-dawn gloom, keeping a discreet thirty yards or so between themselves and their guide.

The first objective was a village some twenty kilometres further on, where a friend of John's was in hiding and where they could take their first rest. They bicycled into a stiff wind, the sky above them dark and threatening and it seemed that it could not be long before it would begin to snow. They left the town behind and made a good pace along the road that ran straight and flat ahead of them. John pointed out the burnt-out ruins of what must have been a substantial farm, explaining that it was where Bat had been betrayed by an informer and where the unwitting Colonel Boeree had been arrested during his search for straw. Soon the conditions worsened as snow began to fall heavily and large wind-driven flakes were flung into their faces. At least, said John, in this weather there should be fewer German checkpoints to worry about. There was also little evidence of the occupation, apart from the rare German military vehicle passing them and in the one village where the sight of a marching file of forced labourers under German guard came as a sharp reminder of it.

They came to the outskirts of another village and John announced that it was the one where they were to rest. Shan let his companion go on ahead and then followed him behind a row of houses. They knocked and were let into the farm, being taken straightway to the cow byre, which, in the fashion of the Dutch farms of the time, was a section of the main building. In the heavy snow they had lost touch with the woman courier and John decided that he would have to go back to look for her, that Shan was to wait in the kitchen and that he would explain to the woman there that Shan was deaf, to avoid any need for conversation. The wait after John left seemed interminable and Shan began to be afraid that some misfortune had struck and that he would find himself alone with strangers and with no means of locating Vandyck's hideout. After an hour the door opened and John came in, covered in snow. The two of them went into the cow byre so that the 'deaf man' could be told of the situation. John recounted how he had come upon the courier a considerable way back, finding it very difficult in making progress in the appalling conditions and he had decided that, if she were to have any chance of returning to Ede before curfew, she should, despite her protests, turn back at once. He had not forgotten to transfer Shan's big pack to his own bicycle. They went back to the kitchen, ate the sandwiches they had brought with them, thanked the woman of the house and set off once more. The snow had stopped, although a thick coating lay on the ground and the wind was as strong as ever. The road surface was treacherous and slippery and they had thirty kilometres more to go to reach their rendezvous under a railway bridge at a village called Maarn, not far from Doorn. Sometimes the bicycle would skid from under him and Shan would push it for a while before attempting to remount. He blessed the fact that at least there were no hills on their route. Eventually they arrived in Maarn and, after an enquiry in the village, they reached the planned spot under the railway bridge a few minutes before the appointed time, to find not the expected Dutchman who would be able to tell them the whereabouts of the hideout but a parked military truck full of German soldiers, the NCO in charge standing by the driver's cab. The soldiers showed no interest in the new arrivals, so, whatever they were waiting for, it was clearly not John and Shan. Trying to look like two men with nothing on their consciences, they dismounted and moved a little way off, hoping that their contact had only been delayed. A number of civilians passed by, but each enquiry drew a blank, as did a visit to the bleak and almost bare village shop. By now they were half an hour beyond the time set for the rendezvous. There was nothing for it but to go back past the bridge and the German soldiers and find someone with whom to make the more precise enquiry that John was under the strictest of instructions not to use except in emergency. It was to ask for directions to a particular village and to go along the road to it until they saw an entrance to a drive flanked by two stone lions. This time they had better fortune and were soon bicycling along the right road, slower now because Shan was tiring and the road led up a steep hill. The gate at last came into view and they turned in and went along the drive, apparently in the grounds of a large property. They arrived at what seemed to be an outbuilding to the big house and as they did so the door opened and to their relief and delight, they saw the familiar and welcoming face of Vandyck.

The kitchen into which they were led was large and, at first glance, full of people. Some were sitting at a central table, typing or dealing with papers and there seemed to be others further back. A figure detached itself and with one other man, came over with hand outstretched to greet Shan. It was Kessel, in whose debt Shan considered himself very much to be. The second man was another airborne doctor, Theo Redman, who had been with 4 Parachute Brigade since its formation and who had become a great friend of Shan. They fell to talking about their different adventures on the run and what news there was. Sadly, it transpired, very little of those who had not been heard of since the battle. Then in came Graeme Warrack, the Division's senior airborne doctor, together with another doctor from 1 Parachute Brigade and the conversation opened up further. In the meantime John had established that there were two railway bridges at Maarn and that the guide had waited, and was still waiting, at the other one. Someone was sent to bring him in and he was back in time to share the evening meal. After supper there was chess and a tot each of Uncle Zwerus's brandy and Shan was then shown to his bed, happy with the way things had gone since leaving Ede but too weary to sleep properly.

The following morning John went off to try to get the information that would persuade the cautious Vandyck that the Waal route was a safe and acceptable one to pass Shan. Before he left, Shan made a plea that perhaps the other airborne evaders they had found at Vandyck's hiding place could be got out by the same means and John promised to do his best. Vandyck also left to look further at the possibilities of escaping to the east, the plan he had at first proposed to Shan. The five airborne colleagues were left in what they learned was the headquarters of the local Resistance group. The place was very secluded and surrounded by woods; the main house, a short distance away, was a home for the elderly infirm and, despite the considerable comings and goings of Resistance people, they had managed not to attract the attention of the occupying authorities. Kessel at once suggested an examination of his handiwork and was disappointed to find that the hairline scar he had so profession-ally achieved had been distorted by festering around some of the stitches. With borrowed medical equipment and a makeshift operating table in Shan's bedroom, he and the others did what was described as a tidying-up job. They were all delighted to be trying their professional hands again and Shan was declared to be quite fit to travel.

In John's first plan, it had been hoped to get Shan across the Waal and into the British lines on 5 February and the ferry had been warned accordingly. That was six days ahead and there was still the Rhine to be crossed, and no final decision about going ahead was possible until both John and Vandyck were back in the house at Maarn. It was agreeable for Shan to have companions once more with whom he could talk freely but he could not conceal his impatience for the return of the two Dutchmen. They both got back on the third day, Vandyck with disappointing news about the eastern route, which would only work, apparently, if the escapees were able to make their way right up the Rhine and get into Switzerland. In contrast, John came back full of enthusiasm and hope. What further details he had been given of the Waal canoe service seemed to satisfy Vandyck of the route's bona fides, but, better still, the organizers were prepared to take two more on Shan's trip, with the other two following later. Shan proposed that one of them should be Warrack, because of what he would be able to report back in England of the medical lessons of the airborne battle and the other Kessel, in recognition of the immense personal debt owed to him by Shan. So it was agreed to leave early the following morning, with Shan and John going one way to the next rendezvous and Vandyck leading the two doctors separately. With good luck, Shan was coming to the last stages of his journey home.

Chapter Nine

ACROSS THE RIVERS

Shan was called and dressed before it was light, putting on his warm underwear and the shirt, jacket and trousers belonging to John that were to be returned when, on the very last leg, he was once again wearing his military uniform. Over everything else went the thin black overcoat with its badge proclaiming his inability to hear a word spoken to him. Taking a final affectionate look around the higgledy-piggledy store room that had been used as a dormitory during his stay in Maarn, he picked up his baggage and went through the coach house and into the kitchen, warm and well lit and already full of activity. There was a young and pretty girl he had not seen before, who came up to him and introduced herself as Elsa and asked if he was the General she was to conduct over the Rhine. He enquired about Kessel and Warrack and John told him that they had already left with Vandyck, taking the other doctors with them to wait in a different hiding place. After a breakfast of porridge they went outside, strapped their luggage to the bicycles and moved off, again with the woman courier some way ahead. The change in the weather over the previous two days had caused most of the snow to disappear; the wind had dropped and lost its harsh edge and there was almost a feeling of spring in the air. They went on at a good pace into the outskirts of Utrecht when disaster struck; a flapping noise announced that the rear tyre of the bicycle John was riding had disintegrated. Elsa had been keeping a regular watch on her charges and, when she saw that the men had stopped, came back to them and inspected the damage. It was agreed that it was impossible for John to continue and it looked as if that day's enterprise was over and they would have to return to the coach house and think again. Elsa however, took a determined view of the situation and, pushing their bicycles, the men followed her to a yard in a back street where a carpenter was busy in a workshop. Elsa spoke quietly to him in rapid Dutch, the man looked briefly at John and Shan, nodded his head and, taking John's bicycle into the back of the workshop, produced a replacement and, with a smile, handed it over. The whole transaction had barely delayed them and soon they were riding through the centre of the city surrounded by other cyclists going about their daily business. Shan had plenty of time to admire the great church and its tower as they cycled past and then they were beyond the city and beginning what to Shan was to be the worst part of the day, the long and seemingly interminable journey on the road that ran along the top of the Rhine dyke and which led to Schoonhoven, where it was intended that they would be ferried across the Rhine. The front line was much further away than it had been at Ede and German troops, once they were outside the city, less in evidence. In their open and exposed position the wind, blowing in their faces, seemed a great deal stronger than it had when they left the coach house. Shan began to cycle like an automaton; only the next thrust on the pedals counted, first the left leg, then the right, then the left again in an interminable repetition. It was late afternoon before they got to Schoonhoven and with the light already beginning to fade, they carried on to the next village, where Elsa said the boat would be found.

There was indeed a boat, a fair-sized rowing boat, pulled up in the mud and clear of the water's edge. Thankfully Shan dismounted and sat down with Elsa beside the bicycles, while John went off to find the boatman. Shan had been told that it was strictly forbidden to take a boat out without authority and did not dare speculate on the chances of the boatman being persuaded to ferry them across. It was with some relief that they saw John return with another man who was carrying a pair of rowlocks. Shan was later told by John that the ferryman had consented to the offer of two pounds of knitting wool as payment for the journey, the last wool to be found in his mother's shop in Renkum that had been brought with him against just such a need. The small activity of the boatman putting the rowlocks in place did not go unnoticed and soon a group of four people had assembled, also with bicycles, begging to be taken over to the other side. The boatman looked enquiringly at John, who without any hesitation nodded his head in agreement. All the bicycles were stowed in the bow, the boat was pushed down to the water's edge and in no time they were being rowed diagonally across the river. Shan looked back from his seat on one of the thwarts to the town through which they had so recently passed and saw the last rays of evening sunshine light up the domes and spires of Schoonhoven. The sight was so lovely that he persuaded himself that it was a good augury for the rest of his escape.

In twenty minutes they had reached the far shore, the boatman skilfully guiding them through the broken ice that edged the bank. They disembarked, the bicycles were handed up to them and they were on their way. John said that in thirty minutes they should be at the village of Groot Ammers, where they would find the next hiding place and where Kars, John's old school friend and now the district Resistance leader through whom the escape arrangements had been made, should be waiting. He was not in fact there but did not keep them waiting long. Kars and his son Klaas quickly brought them up to date. The good news was that a party was expected that very Saturday evening from Sliedrecht on the Waal, where the canoe service was based, to brief the escapers. The bad news was that the strong winds had created a poor sea state and it was not certain how soon it would be possible for a canoe to make a crossing through the Biesbosch marshes to the south side of the river.

While they waited, they chatted together. John and Kars had much to talk about so Shan went across to where Klaas's father was sitting in the corner to practice his rudimentary Dutch. This was abandoned when Shan found the pronunciation of the local dialect beyond his limited abilities and so turned to Klaas and to speaking English. The young man, who like so many of the younger Dutch people Shan had been in contact with, already spoke the language well. He explained to Shan how essential it was in his country to reach a very high standard, as fluency in English was an important part of the civil service examination, which he had determined to take as soon as the war was over and normal life resumed. They were interrupted by the arrival of two messengers from Sliedrecht, a young man and a girl dressed in the uniform of a nurse. The manner of their greeting showed how excited they were to have a General, as they described Shan, put into their care. They also confirmed what Kars had said, that the weather was unsuitable for risking the river crossing. No boat would go that evening nor on Sunday, the following day, either, but there was a strong possibility that one would cross on Monday. They would send guides the next day to bring the General to Sliedrecht and, furthermore, this announced with an air of great pride, they had acquired the use of a motor car, had obtained petrol and would be able to drive him there in a style befitting his rank. It also meant that John need go no further and was free to make his own way back to Ede.

This did not have the effect anticipated. John and Kars saw at once the dangers of transporting Shan in such a conspicuous manner, when the civilian car had for everyone, apart from doctors and officials, all but disappeared from the roads of Holland. Shan, buoyed up by the thought that, if all went well, he would find himself back in three days behind British lines, had no wish to part company with John, his companion ever since he had been spirited out of St Elizabeth Hospital, until the last possible moment. There was also the question of returning John's clothes, which Shan had on at that moment and, more important still, there was the bicycle to be handed over to John for safe return to Uncle Zwerus. After a great deal of argument, the visitors conceded and it was settled that, under Kars' guidance, John and Shan would bicycle the relatively few miles to Sliedrecht on Monday, to a house where they could wait until it was time for Shan to embark.

Three nights now lay between him and what it seemed he could almost touch, his liberty – two of them there in the farmhouse at Groot Ammers and the last one, he fervently hoped, making the crossing. That Saturday night he said his farewells to Elsa, who would have left on her return journey before he was awake the following morning. He, and he knew John as well, had grown especially fond of the lively and engaging girl who had led them on their second leg. On Sunday he was taken to see Graeme Warrack at the house where he was being hidden and the two of them had a chance to talk together before the doctor moved on.

Shan did not find much comfort in the small, unlit room in an outhouse where he had been lodged; it had been particularly cold at night and the scrabbling noise of rats had not helped him to sleep. He was anxious to be on his way and on Monday morning, after a good breakfast of porridge and his goodbyes said to Klaas and his parents, they set off, the guide as usual riding some distance ahead of them. By the early afternoon they had arrived without incident in Sliedrecht to be shown into a house of a doctor that looked out over the water. Here Shan changed out of the clothes he had worn since Ede, back into his uniform, the British Army identity card in one pocket of his battledress jacket, his silver pencil and cigarette case in another. He ran his hands down the khaki serge of his trousers with a feeling close to disbelief that it could at last be happening and, distressingly, that the time had come to say goodbye to John. The parting happened in a manner that seemed to come naturally to them after their long saga together in quest of Shan's freedom, simply and unemotionally. With handshakes and wishes one to the other of good luck, John took his belongings and, wheeling both bicycles, went through the garden gate and out of sight.

There was nothing now for Shan to do except wait until the evening arrival of his next guide. He was given a bowl of soup and sat watching the light fade over the water. At last he was told it was time to go and, greeting the burly man who had come for him with a shake of his hand, set off thirty paces in rear through the narrow streets of Sliedrecht. To conceal his military uniform, he carried on wearing the thin black overcoat and thought to himself that it could well be needed when they were out on the water. From time to time they passed other pedestrians, absorbed in their unhappy situation, and Shan allowed himself occasionally to think that, God willing, he would soon be elsewhere but that they would still be in Sliedrecht under a harsh occupation and with no indication when it might end. They came to a street where once more they were in sight of water and waited at a factory gate while the Dutchman went off to get the keys of the boathouse from the night watchman. He was soon back and before long Shan found himself on a jetty next to the boathouse, looking down river to where a single red beacon flashed monotonously, somewhere in the distance. The night watchman helped him into the stern of the boat and, as soon as he and the oarsman were settled, the head was pushed off and they were away. There was little to be seen except the red beacon and the occasional distant flashing line of machine-gun tracer curling across the darkening sky, which by its random intervals he took to be firing from German posts along the bank to discourage any nocturnal voyagers.

Shan, his eyes by now accustomed to the darkness, became aware of a looming black shape ahead. The boat came alongside where people were waiting to lift him and his luggage on to the jetty. The oarsman spoke for the first time since they had left Sliedrecht and told Shan that he would be looked after, but that he had to return without delay. In a few moments he had disappeared into the darkness and Shan was being led towards what appeared to be a cottage standing on a low mound. The room into which he was taken was well lit and full of activity. Men dressed as fishermen were sitting at one table cleaning and assembling automatic weapons and loading magazines, the brass cartridge cases shining in the lamplight. At another, men were packing letters and envelopes into transit cases. The man who seemed to be in charge came and shook his hand and led him to a chair; a woman brought him a hot cup of cocoa and someone else poured him a stiff whisky from a bottle that seemed thoroughly genuine and offered him a cigarette from one of those round tins of fifty that were such a welcome part of the regular rations of the British Army. A young girl, perhaps the leader's daughter, came up to give him biscuits and chocolate and to ask whether he was really a General; their very first, she said. All the time the activity around him went on unabated.

It had puzzled Shan at the Sliedrecht jetty to find himself being put into a rowing boat and not the canoe he had been led to expect, but the picture now became clear. The courier service was not, of course, based on the town riverbank where there would have been the unacceptable risk of discovery or betrayal but out in the seclusion of the Biesbosch marshes, much less accessible and difficult for any German parties to approach without giving themselves away. The comforts that had been pressed upon him as soon as he arrived had obviously been brought back on the return journeys from the British-held end and this tangible evidence of a link with his own people gave him more hope and comfort on what he was now sure was to be the last leg.

The leader came over to him to say that it was time to go. The girl took Shan's luggage and, with others carrying the official packages and bundles that were the principal purpose of the journey, they set off on foot across the Biesboch, along a winding path that ran sometimes through fields and sometimes by the edge of the marshes. At last they came to a solitary tree on the bank of a channel, where the party waited while the leader went forward. The girl handed Shan his haversacks and whispered goodbye, slipping back the way she had come. The only noise came from his own breathing, the gentle lapping of the water and the occasional cry of a sea bird. The leader returned, complaining that the canoe was late; the party sat down and talked quietly and smoked, secure in the belief that there could not be a German for miles around. Shan was told about the craft he would travel in, a Canadian canoe driven by an electric motor that could move it silently through the water, but sometimes the battery did not last for the whole journey. He was also told that the river was very wide below the marshes and that the German defence posts on either bank were well spread out and did not seem to be sited so that they could support each other across the water. In any case, a few miles downstream the left bank was in Allied hands and that was where he would shortly be taken.

Time was again running with paralyzing slowness for Shan. It seemed an age before the sound of a paddle was heard and then the shape of the canoe made out. It was soon alongside and loading began at once. The single crew-member got out, explaining that he had had problems with the engine. He shook Shan's hand, introduced himself as Piet and then Shan was being urged aboard, wedged in by his own packs and still with his faithful stick in his hand. He felt hands arranging a blanket around him and covering him with a waterproof sheet. As they pushed off a pistol was put into the canoe beside him; 'in case', he was told. Piet had paddled for what must have been over an hour through channels that grew broader and the surface of the water more agitated, until again Shan could see that they were nosing into a high bank. The boat pulled up against a stone wall and hands reached down to grasp the gunwales. They had arrived at the great dyke bordering the main channel of the Waal and from this point would no longer have the protection of the Biesboch islands against the elements. Shan got stiffly out of the canoe; Piet told him that the people on the dyke were waiting for other boats they hoped would carry them across the main river. The two climbed up to the top of the dyke and Shan suddenly felt the full force of the wind. Below him, on the river side, the sound of breaking waves could be clearly heard.

Piet said they would wait and Shan sensed that he was trying to decide whether, in the conditions, it was possible to go on and wondered if that would mean having to paddle back through the marshes and make another attempt when things got calmer. Then Piet turned and they went back down to the canoe, which, with the help of the others waiting in patient hopefulness, was lifted over the dyke and put afloat in the main river. There were quiet goodbyes and a small packet of biscuits was pressed into Shan's hand. As Piet once more took up the paddling, the canoe seemed to lift and crash from wave to wave, the noise of the wind rose higher and spray dashed itself in their faces. There was nothing Shan could do but keep his head down, grit his teeth and trust in his companion's strong arms to get them over the main stream where the wind, blowing against the river current, was creating atrocious conditions. Gradually he thought he detected the wind easing and the motion of the boat becoming less violent. Piet had now by his own efforts been driving the boat along for what must have been three hours and, with smoother water under them Shan took up a paddle on the opposite side of the boat. This activity brought a welcome warmness back to his body but before long he again had the realization he had experienced while cycling, that his stamina was still low and such reserves of energy as did build up inside him could be quickly exhausted. Thankfully he heard Piet give the order to stop paddling and on a smooth surface and with stars beginning to break through the clouds, the engine was restarted and they went ahead on what remained in the battery. As the sky cleared Shan saw Sirius high in the sky, the same star that had watched over him during his night marches with the TJFF. This seemed a good opportunity to reach into his haversack for the bottle of brandy and the two of them took a good pull; Shan could feel its warmth as it found its way down into his stomach. Light started to appear in the sky and he saw that they were again running among small islands and beds of reeds, the channels between them marked with perches driven in to show direction.

When the motor cut out they took up paddling again until the battery had recovered sufficiently to give them a short respite from their efforts. Finally they arrived at the entrance to an inlet into which Piet turned, paddling now as strongly as at any time through the night. Soon Shan was aware of other boats and of a number of figures standing about on a quayside, against which they pulled alongside. Piet shouted out to identify himself and two of the men came down and lifted the stiff and tired Shan from the canoe. He was led to the foot of a flight of stone steps, with at their top a tall figure clutching a bottle. Wearily Shan climbed up towards him. "Shan, we've been expecting you!" There was something familiar in the voice but Shan was beyond making the effort to search for the name. "Tony Crankshaw, 11th Hussars. You must be ready for some brandy."

Shan was back, not only in British hands but also among old friends from the Desert war, the armoured car reconnaissance regiment of 7th Armoured Division, now holding part of the bank of the Waal and the country behind it. He felt he could not have had a happier arrival, other than the improbable coincidence of having an officer of his own regiment, 8H, to greet him, and his happiness was compounded when Crankshaw told him, as they walked towards a house, that a friend of his had also arrived just a few minutes before him. This was Graeme Warrack who welcomed the arrival of 'the little man at last' with a rib-crushing hug. Shan took in the familiar sight of a British Army billet, with its hot stove in the middle of the room, soldiers in battledress, weapons, equipment and all the paraphernalia that goes with the military. Piet had come in too and for the first time Shan got a proper look at this stalwart man who had brought him safely across the last great river. But Piet could not stay; another boat, with Kessel as its passenger, had also set out, but was overdue and he had to take his canoe and go to look for it.

The airborne surgeon did get through, but not on that night. The craft on which he had embarked in the Biesbosch was not one of the sleek, modern Canadian canoes with electric motors but a Dutch canoe that had been for a long time stored away from the eyes of the Germans. In its dried-out state it was far from seaworthy and, while still among the marshes, the craft sank and they were just able to stagger ashore. Somehow they managed to make their way back to their safe haven in Sliedrecht, where they slept and set off again in a stouter craft. This time the crossing went smoothly but the South African Marxist medical officer captain was not to have quite the same reception as the Anglo-Irish cavalry brigadier who had preceded him. As Kessel went up the stone steps from the quayside, the figure at the top was not an old friend equipped with a bottle of brandy but a British soldier carrying a rifle. As Kessel records in his own book, not only was he not challenged but the man did not even say good morning.

For Shan things from the time of his arrival went smoothly. After a comfortable night, or rather first part of the day, in the bed of the absent commanding officer of 11H, he was taken to the reception centre for escaped prisoners and on the journey marvelled at the contrast between where he had been until a day or two before and where he was now. It was not just the military differences in the scale of resources that he could see on every side but more particularly what he was able to observe in the civilian population, the cheerful and decently fed children clustering around the British soldiers, grown-ups with heads held up, their faces not grey and their cheeks less hollow. At the centre, his worn and soiled uniform was taken from him and replaced with a new one. Here his wounds were looked at by a Canadian surgeon who studied, with an interest equal to that shown by each Dutch doctor who had seen it, the medical card Kessel had given Shan to carry as he left the hospital in Arnhem. The Canadian removed the filthy bandages that had served their wearer for so long and replaced them with a broad strip of elasto-plast. The next day Shan was summoned to the headquarters of Twenty-First Army Group to be given by the abstemious Field Marshal Montgomery 'a very decent dinner', such as he had not had for a long time, including, he recalled, oysters. Monty seemed extremely pleased that Shan was back and, recalling with more good humour than Shan could remember him exhibiting at the time, referred to the famous recruiting interview that he and David Stirling of the SAS had had with the then Eighth Army commander while Shan was GSO1 Raiding Forces.

Next morning Shan did his serious business at the headquarters, putting over Piet van Arnhem's proposals for close cooperation between the Dutch Resistance and the liberating forces and giving the intelligence staff his observations on both the civilian and military situations in the part of Holland in which he had passed the previous four months. He spent much time enquiring the whereabouts of those he believed to have survived the Battle of Oosterbeek and those of whose fates he was still uncertain and grieved to learn how many members of his airborne family had been killed and how severe had been the eventual tally of casualties in 4 Parachute Brigade. He got a message that greatly pleased him, that Major Joel Crouch, who had been the pilot of the American squadron's Dakota from which Shan had parachuted on numerous occasions, had heard of his return and offered to come with his Dakota anywhere in Europe to bring him home.

Monty had already offered his personal aircraft to take Shan back to England and the following morning he was flown to Northolt. There he made two telephone calls, the first to Margaret to say how soon they would be together and the other to Colin Harkess, one of the only two officers on Shan's brigade staff to survive the Battle of Oosterbeek and return safely home. He was charged with alerting Joel Crouch to Shan's arrival at Northolt. Within the hour a US Dakota had landed and taxied over to the control tower where Shan was waiting for them. Crouch had brought with him another of Shan's favourite American pilots and the greeting they gave him was tumultuous. They took off within a few minutes, to be met by Margaret on the airfield at Cottesmore. Only one thing remained before he could return, if only briefly, to his own family and that was a telephone call to the number he had been given at the BBC. That very evening the message that 'the Grey Goose had gone' was broadcast to Ede and to the rest of occupied Holland.

Shan had still not fully recovered from his wounds and would have to return to hospital under observation. Before that there were important things to be done; a full de-briefing at the War Office about the work of resistance groups in Holland and of those such as Bat and Vandyck who had been sent to operate with them. The citations for awards for gallantry that Shan had written out in Holland and sent back by the hand of Gerald Lathbury had been rejected on the grounds that they had not been submitted on the proper forms. All these had to be recalled and re-submitted. There was the domestic matter of attempting to persuade the Army branch of Lloyds Bank, Messrs Cox & Kings, that whatever officialdom might think, he was no longer a missing officer, as the bank official on the other side of the counter could clearly see, and was therefore entitled to draw his back pay from the middle of the previous September. It was arranged that his further medical treatment would be at the Radcliffe Infirmary in Oxford and for the latter part of his time there under observation he was to be allowed to live in his old college as an outpatient, an arrangement that gave him great pleasure, as well as access to some particularly fine port.

After the crossing of the Rhine in late March, the war moved on apace and in mid-April Shan got the news he had been waiting for, that the Germans were being driven out of Holland and that the liberation of Ede had taken place. He put in hand at once the plans he had been making ever since he arrived back in England; within a day or two he flew to Holland with as much in the way of tea and coffee and tinned foods and clothing and personal gifts and letters of gratitude and thanks as could be put together. His welcome was warm and his reunions with the de Nooijs and all the others in the town who had befriended and assisted him were both to him and to his Dutch family joyous and deeply affecting.

The stock pronouncement to a newly captured British soldier by a German officer, at least those who had sufficient English, was that 'for you, Tommy, the War is over'. For Shan it certainly was. The end had been marked by two events of the deepest significance to him. The first was the destruction at Oosterbeek of his airborne family, 4 Parachute Brigade, which he had raised, trained and moulded in his own fashion, become deeply devoted to, given it and received from it great loyalty and made from all its constituent parts a very fine brigade in a very fine division. To quote his own much-quoted words, 'He had been the Brigade's midwife and had then become its sexton'. The second followed directly upon the first, the finding of his Dutch family, formed of those, beginning with Piet, the resistance leader in the St Elizabeth Hospital in Arnhem, through the never-to-be-forgotten de Nooij family in Ede, through many known briefly and ending with the other Piet, his canoe coxswain on the last journey across the Waal, who all had, by selfless and almost transcendent devotion to a common humanity, restored a wounded officer back safely to his own people. To both his airborne and his Dutch families he felt and exhibited a deep affection and loyalty that remained undiminished to the end of his life.

Chapter Ten

DOWN TO EARTH

The Shan who had returned to England was thinner and weaker than the fit and youthful parachute brigadier to whom Margaret had said goodbye the previous autumn. The two stepdaughters were at school in Devon, while Margaret was pregnant with what was to be the only child of the marriage, Susan Veronica, born on 20 May 1945. There was no question of Shan being able to return to active duty until his physical condition had been considerably restored and so the summer and autumn of the last year of the war was spent peacefully at the Oakham house the Hacketts had bought during the training and preparation of 4 Parachute Brigade for the campaigns in North-West Europe. There was the new addition to the family to be cherished and when Bridget and Elizabeth were home from school, outings in the pony and trap to be undertaken. These expeditions invariably included a picnic and these and riding lessons for the two older girls contributed to the first settled period of family life the Hacketts had been able to enjoy since their marriage in the Middle East three years before.

The United Kingdom had endured almost exactly six years of war and the whole country, exhausted and impoverished, was beginning to try to come to terms with its future. There was a universal pride in the achievements and sacrifices that had been made in overcoming the enemy, but there was also a feeling that the future did not require a return to the past. The Beveridge report, the foundation of the welfare state, had been published the previous year while the armed forces had, by deliberate Government policy, been given regular periods of instruction in social and economic matters; some believed this had been the principal factor in the defeat of Winston Churchill in the General Election, called in perhaps precipitate haste in July 1945, before hostilities with Japan had ended. The contemporary quip was that if the Royal Army Educational Corps were to be granted colours and be allowed to troop them before His Majesty, they would be proudly emblazoned with their single battle honour, 'General Election 1945'. It was an election in which, understandably enough, a considerable proportion of the parliamentary candidates were serving members of the Forces. Shan, now that he was undertaking the full responsibilities for a young family, had been giving some thought to the idea of leaving the Army. He had no great material ambition, not having, perhaps, inherited the strong entrepreneurial instincts of both his parents. Quintin Hogg (later Viscount Hailsham) was among those who tried to get him to contest the 1945 General Election in the Conservative interest, but since Shan was well aware that such a step would mean him resigning his commission, a course it was by no means certain that he wished to take, a parliamentary career was rejected, a shrewd decision in what turned out to be a landslide victory for the Labour Party under Clement Attlee.

Another course of action that Shan spent some time pondering during his convalescence was a return to academic life, but this, too, was rejected. His mind finally made up, he was to devote himself to his military career until his retirement and it was not until after that came about that he published his account of his months in the occupied Netherlands and his escape to the Allied lines.

By the end of the year he was fit to return to duty and in January 1946 was posted to the headquarters staff of 6th Armoured Division, then stationed in Padua. In common with many others whose abilities in wartime had been rewarded with rapid but temporary promotion, in a shrinking army he too had to step backwards and so it was in the rank of lieutenant-colonel that he took up his duties in Italy as the Division's principal general staff officer. The wartime rule forbidding the presence of wives on station was still in force and Margaret had to remain behind in the Oakham house.

The appointment in Padua was to be a short one and two months later Shan, not entirely certain that it was a job he really wanted, arrived in Vienna on 8 March 1946 to assume the appointment of head of the intelligence branch of the Allied Commission for Austria (British Element) (or BGS(I) ACABE). This was the formal title for the British part of one of the Allied counter-intelligence organizations operating in the occupied countries of Germany and Austria in the aftermath of what had been a long and extremely destructive war. What had been a brigadier's appointment was downgraded to Colonel (General Staff) and it was in this rank that Shan was to spend the next eighteen months of his military career.

Europe at the time of Shan's arrival in Vienna was a place of ruined towns and cities, of a severely damaged transport system, grave shortages of food, fuel and electricity (the civilian ration was for long periods barely over one thousand calories a day), of thousands of people

165

displaced from their pre-war homes in their own countries and held in refugee camps until politics and the physical means allowed those willing to return to their native lands to do so. It was also the time of the beginnings of the Cold War and the Iron Curtain, when ideological differences would sweep away the coalition that had won the war and when Soviet suspicion of the West and its desire to protect its western boundaries from the capitalist world would lead it to set up in Europe a defensive barrier of states under communist governments subordinate to Moscow. Within the Allied zones of Germany and Austria there was ample work to keep counter-intelligence busy. Their duties included denazification and demilitarization, surveillance of political movements sympathetic to or supportive of the Soviet Union, control of movements between and within the zones of occupation. There was also the flourishing black market, assessment of civilian morale and attitudes towards the occupying forces, intelligence-gathering on activities in the Soviet zones and of particular interest to the British authorities, the development of organisations with the purpose of facilitating the movement of Jews from European countries into Palestine. The basic intelligence-gathering work was carried out by Field Security sections, small specialist teams usually commanded by a warrant officer or senior NCO. During Shan's period of stewardship of counter-intelligence in Austria, there were some fifteen of these sections stationed in different parts of the British zone of occupation, reporting regularly through subordinate headquarters to the BGS(I)'s office in the Schoenbrunn Palace in Vienna. They informed on the state of civilian morale in their areas, of relations with the occupying forces, of infractions against military government regulations, of the activities of pro-Soviet communist organizations and their attempts to infiltrate the civilian administrations, of illegal crossings of inter-zonal borders and, sometimes, of rumours of some political uprising or *putsch* being planned by groups to whom the developing scene was uncongenial. It also seemed customary to include accounts of the civilian population's views of the Soviet occupation forces, usually making unfavourable comparisons between life under them and that in the zones controlled by the three Western allies. Shan was, at Commission level, dealing with the consequences of the increasing freedom of action of the Austrian Government in the years leading up to the peace treaty and with the demands from London for financial economies and increased civilianization of the organization he commanded. He was concerned about the activities of the government of Yugoslavia under Tito, a hostile neighbour of the British zone of Austria, as well as how a proposal to lift postal censorship within the Allied zones would remove the source of a considerable amount of intelligence information, although, in this last matter, his own libertarian instincts welcomed the modest increase in individual freedom that the abolition would bring about.

In May 1946, as a consequence of the decision to let wives join their military husbands on stations where suitable living conditions existed, Margaret was at last allowed to be with Shan in Vienna. The country she had left in 1931 to go to Palestine seemed to her drab and unhappy, with little yet done to restore war-damaged buildings and with rations small and food of poor quality. She was, however, heartened by the resurgence of cultural life in the capital and took great pleasure in the theatre and the concerts. Her parents, who had spent the war in their native country, had fled from Graz to Innsbruck to escape the Soviet advance into Austria, but, by the time of Margaret's arrival, were back in Graz, their house vandalized by the Russian Army before it withdrew to its own designated zone of occupation. It gave great pleasure to Margaret to be able to see something of her own family and it was also possible for her own two daughters to spend part of their summer holidays in Vienna. But, all in all, Margaret no longer felt at home in Austria and it was with little sense of regret that she learnt that in September 1947 Shan was to hand over as the British counter-intelligence chief and to return to command the Trans-Jordan Frontier Force in the rank of full colonel.

Within two months Margaret, with their young daughter Susan, was able to rejoin her husband in the commanding officer's house at the TJFF base cantonment in Zerka. One of her early concerns was to discover the fate of the Tiberias hotel that had belonged to her in-laws and where, as a young widow in 1937, she had first met Shan. A day visit was arranged for her, but it yielded only the information that it was still in the hands of the Custodian of Enemy Property.

As Shan returned to the TJFF as its commander, Palestine was in turmoil. The Jewish revolt and the campaign of terrorism through which it was conducted was by then two years old. The Labour Government had come to the decision that the only way forward lay in the partition of Palestine into separate, self-governing Arab and Jewish territories and it drew up plans to this end. Realizing that the devil lay in the detail, the Jewish Council, the negotiating body for their side, felt itself to be acting from a position of strength. It was fully aware that in Washington sympathies were firmly on the Zionist side and additionally that the US Government had never shed its policy of opposition to what it saw as the lingering colonial practices of certain European powers, the United Kingdom by no means excepted. The realization took hold in Downing Street that continuing to fulfil the duties and responsibilities that the Palestine mandate imposed on the British people was no longer possible and that it would have to be surrendered and the problem of the future of Palestine placed firmly in the lap of the United Nations Organization.

On 26 September 1947 the British Government formally notified the UN of its decision to surrender its Palestine mandate. Almost exactly two months later the UN resolution to partition Palestine between the Jews and the Arabs was passed and the following day hostilities broke out between the two sides. At first the Zionists adopted a policy of what they described as 'aggressive defence', going over to the offensive the following spring. By that time the remaining British armed forces were withdrawing into the Haifa enclave before their complete evacuation on the formal expiry of the mandate on 25 May 1948.

Shan took over in September, just before the surrender of the mandate by the British Government. At the time the TJFF, as part of the British armed forces, was fully occupied with its internal security duties in Palestine and was under the command of 6th Airborne Division, with Galilee its operational area. The wartime transfer of control of the TJFF in 1941 from the Colonial Office to the War Office meant that its future was from that moment firmly bound up with that of the British Army in Palestine. This was in contrast with the position of the Arab Legion under Glubb Pasha. No longer, as it had been before the war, a gendarmerie responsible for maintaining law and order in the Bedouin areas of Trans-Jordan, it had become the regular army of the Kingdom of Jordan.

Once Shan learnt at the end of September that the mandate was to be surrendered, he began to think seriously about what this boded for the future for his force. One possible outcome was that it would not survive partition and would have to disband. Unlike the Arab Legion, it was politically impossible for the TJFF, as a formed body within the British Army, to take sides, yet there were many Palestinians in its ranks whose loyalty would be expected to go naturally to their fellow-countrymen once partition became certain and if, as seemed inevitable, Palestinian Jew and Palestinian Arab began to struggle for territorial dominance. On the other hand, if an ordered and negotiated partition were to come about and some sort of Palestine state be set up and begin an independent and peaceful existence, there could be an important place within it for the sort of organized, disciplined and well-trained force that the TJFF represented. Although his close involvement with Palestine affairs during the previous ten years and his knowledge of the personalities on both sides gave him little hope that a peaceful partition, even if desired by a majority of the population, could ever come about, Shan's first instincts were to work for the continued existence of the force in which he had served for so long and that he held in such affection and regard. Although at the beginning there were expressions of support from higher headquarters, the UN resolution to impose partition and the outbreak of hostilities that followed immediately after ruled out any further consideration of it and disbandment of the force became the only course possible. Shan's main concern now became one of maintaining cohesion and discipline in deteriorating military and political circumstances and in this he was extraordinarily successful, the greater majority of the force obeying their commander's special order of the day appealing for soldierly good order and it continued to carry out its duties loyally and with the strong sense of duty that had been its hallmark. Only a few of his Palestinian soldiers succumbed to the calls made to their patriotic feelings and deserted, when they could with their weapons, to go immediately to bring their soldierly qualities to one of the untrained and ill-organized bodies that were being put together in an attempt to maintain the integrity of the lands allotted to the Palestinian Arabs under the UN plan.

Early in the New Year the TJFF was withdrawn into Jordan so that its disbandment could take place in an orderly and peaceful manner. It was a time of great difficulties and high emotion for Shan, faced as he was with the unenviable job of presiding over the destruction of a formation that had given much to him and to which he had given, as was his nature wherever in command of troops, an unswerving devotion. It would be the second time in little more than three years; with 4 Parachute Brigade at Oosterbeek in Operation Market Garden it had been in battle, fighting against heavy odds. Now it was to be an administrative act, made in response to international political decisions and the disappearance would be total; all would have to be dispersed, broken up and got rid of, the units with their weapons, their equipment and their cantonments, their support units and the civilian element. The horses had to be parted with, the records preserved and most importantly, the future welfare of the locally-recruited officers and men and of their families to be provided for and just compensation paid to those who had so loyally served the interests of the imperial power. This last matter was the cause of much anxiety and effort for Shan. The first proposals for severance pay and pensions for his men would have seen them treated significantly less generously than the Palestine Police and Shan fought a tenacious battle to achieve a degree of parity of treatment that would represent an honourable discharge of its obligations by the sovereign power. He found himself less than entirely satisfied that it had been achieved in the final arrangements and, long after he had left the Middle East, continued to intercede vigorously and effectively on behalf of old members of the force whose treatment might reasonably be thought unjust or whose circumstances gave them genuine grievances. The

169

proposals he made for the use of the various regimental funds existing on the date of disbandment were accepted and the money was devoted to a good cause, the extension of the ophthalmic hospital in Arab East Jerusalem.

Shan resolved that the TJFF should go out with a bang and not a whimper. He was determined that before his troops were discharged, they should have a farewell parade to show what the Force had been and to allow all ranks to express their pride in their achievements in the quarter century or so of the TJFF's existence. This took place with great ceremony at the end of February 1948 in the presence of His Excellency the High Commissioner, the GOC in C Middle East, senior representatives of the other services and officials of the civilian administration. The cavalry regiment marched past accompanied by a guard of honour from the mechanized regiment, there was a last reception in the officers' mess, after which the regimental silver was packed and despatched to London for safe keeping and the melancholy business of discharge of the officers and men begun.

For the last tidying-up actions and final formalities, Shan moved his small residual HQ first to GHQ Middle East Command in Egypt and then, when GHQ began its own move out of Cairo and the Delta and down to the Canal Zone, to HQ British Troops Cyprus. Last rites completed, it was time for Shan, in accordance with his firmly held military principles, to calculate the amount of leave due to him and to decide how the time might most usefully be employed.

Chapter Eleven

THE YEARS OF PROGRESSION

With the sad but inevitable business of the disbandment of the TJFF, it may be said that Shan, from his point of view, had closed the books on his involvement in the Second World War. Immediately ahead lay the Berlin blockade, effectively the formal declaration of the Cold War by the USSR and its satellites, and it was within this state of world affairs that Shan entered what were to be the final two decades of an exemplary military career. In his first fifteen years of regular soldiering he had demonstrated beyond doubt his courage and leadership under fire and the depth and breadth of the intellectual strengths he could bring to the problems of soldiering. What was to come would take him almost, but not quite, to the pinnacle of his profession and bring him an international reputation as a military thinker who could speak and write with clarity and authority, particularly in his views on the relationship of the soldier with the State and on his place in society. Here Shan was fortunate in serving within the British tradition, which holds that a military man is nothing 'but a civilian clothed in a particular way'. He relished the easy intermingling of civilian and military in everyday life, the way the off-duty soldier would change naturally into civilian clothes and the fact that the Army was able to function, outside the exigencies of wartime, without the need for conscript services. Shan was particularly fortunate in that his remarkable facility for languages made him a ready inter-locutor wherever he went.

He believed strongly that leave of absence that had been earned should, when the situation allowed, be taken in full. He had by now accumulated a sufficient amount to allow him to revive what had been one of his particular interests when he first went up to Oxford, the study of mediæval history. This he decided to do by enrolling for a term at Graz University during the first half of 1949, a move which not only offered him a wider perspective in his chosen subject but which gave Margaret the opportunity for some months of close contact with her ageing family and for daughter Susan to imbibe something of her mother's background.

In the context of Shan's failure to cap his career by becoming head neither of the Army as Chief of Staff nor of the armed forces as a whole as Chief of the Defence Staff, it is an interesting fact that after the disbandment of the TJFF and his return from the Middle East he was never again to serve outside Europe. Whether by accident or design, he was denied what was given to most of his peers, the direct experience of post-imperial developments in South-East Asia and the Far East. He also escaped any involvement in the Suez affair of 1956. The extent to which such relative narrowness of career was to weigh in the minds of those concerned in choosing candidates for the highest military offices may be impossible to know with any accuracy, without access to the relevant files, although Healey rather more than hints in his autobiography that aspects of personality could have played a large part in Shan's falling just short of the top. The old Army saying that it is affability and not ability that counts the most may be relevant, but it cannot be denied that, whether as a soldier or an academic, Shan gave unreservedly of his great and many abilities to the service of the country he had adopted.

Graz was not to be merely an interlude in Shan's re-involvement with the academic life. He returned to England to be appointed, in August 1949, as the senior Army instructor at the Royal Naval College, Greenwich, followed in 1951 by a year as a student at the Imperial Defence College, as it was still then known, in London. Attendance on this course, which numbered among the student body senior Whitehall civil servants, military officers of all three services and from the Commonwealth and from Allied nations, could be taken as intention to consider the individual destined for progression to the highest levels of his profession. It was perhaps inevitable that, on graduating from the IDC, Shan, happiest when leading or close to fighting troops, would be given an administrative post and so it turned out. His new appointment was with the headquarters of the British Army of the Rhine (BAOR), as deputy quartermaster- general, where his duties would be concerned with matters of supply. BAOR was and remains one of the major constituent parts of NATO and Shan was thus, for the first time, brought into close contact with this Allied organization. It was of a different order of things from his service in counter-intelligence with the Allied Commission for Austria.

His services during the two-year appointment were rewarded with a Companionship of the Most Excellent Order of the British Empire (CBE), to go with the gallantry medals of DSO and bar and Military Cross that he had gained in action during the War. Then, in January

1954, he was able once more to do what he so much enjoyed, to lead troops. He became commander of 20 Armoured Brigade, part of BAOR, in the rank of brigadier, followed in January 1956 by promotion to major-general and command of the Desert Rats, the 7th Armoured Division. In these two jobs he was able to apply, throughout, all the intensive training programmes, his strong views on mobile warfare and the use of armour that were the practical results of a great part of his past service in peace and war. Invited to the American zone while GOC of 7th Armoured Division to be the observer of large-scale exercises, he returned to say that he wished he had been able to take all his commanding officers with him, as they would have been given perfect examples of what not to do. His two years of successful command of this front-line formation of BAOR was recognized in the Birthday Honours of 1958 with a Companionship in the Order of the Bath (CB).

Shrivenham

Shan then returned to the United Kingdom and, once more, to the academic side of soldiering with his appointment in March 1958 as Commandant of the Royal Military College of Science (RMCS) at Shrivenham, a military educational establishment of staff college rank. At that time and, unlike the present day, it was still comparatively rare for the average regimental officer to have a university degree, other than for those officers of the Royal Engineers and the Royal Corps of Signals who had graduated at Cambridge; entrance through the academic route, which was how Shan had been commissioned into 8H, having practically dried up after the war. There were, however, signs that the situation was beginning to improve.

The RMCS, or Military College of Science, to give it its pre-1939 title, had been divided by the exigencies of war into three specialist schools in Bury, Stoke-on-Trent and Chobham, dealing with artillery equipment, gunner fire control and tank technology respectively. Its main pre-war site at Lydd in Kent, which would have lain in the path of any German invasion that might have been mounted, was closed in 1940. In 1944 an Army Council committee laid down the post-war pattern for the technical training of army officers, leading directly to the establishment of the RMCS (still the MCS) at Shrivenham. Before the war the War Office had bought Beckett Hall near Swindon, a large late-Georgian mansion with extensive grounds, which had been used as a training establishment first by the British Army and from 1942, following the decision to give first place in the south of the country to American forces, by the US Army. Interestingly, its last use by the Americans was, briefly, as a university college for American troops awaiting demobilization. It received the distinction of becoming a Royal college in 1953, when the newly-crowned Queen conferred the accolade upon it.

The first of Shrivenham's three main tasks, when Shan arrived to take command, was to provide facilities for about one third of its students, all young officers of the technical arms who had not been to Cambridge, to read for external BSc degrees at London University in engineering or another science subject. A considerable number of other students followed what might be regarded as post-graduate courses in disciplines such as nuclear science and technology, and guided missile systems. The remainder trained as technical staff officers in a course lasting two and a quarter years, taking in officers largely, but not entirely, from the technical arms; military staff work was also taught to this group, taking up rather less than half the curriculum. The educational standards reached on this latter course were at least equal to a first degree at a leading university. Students who successfully completed the technical staff officers' course were awarded with the letters *ptsc* (passed technical staff college) after their names in the Army List, the official record of serving officers and were regarded as being on a par with graduates of the Staff Colleges at Camberley and in the Commonwealth, who were *psc* and had sometimes a snobbish tendency to regard the general staff, despite the lessons of history and the evidently broader and arguably better academic attainments of the *ptsc*, as being inherently superior beings.

The post of Commandant at Shrivenham was of particular and growing significance in the military world and Shan had his own clear ideas on how he intended to fill it. He was well aware of the rapid pace of scientific development, especially in communications and electronic guidance systems and saw that an essential skill of the successful future commander would be a proper understanding of the application of technology on the battlefield. He knew this would not be adequately realized by bolting a short specialist course on to an officer trained as a generalist and that what was required was a considerable upgrading in the educational qualifications of the whole of the officer corps, beginning the requirements for entry as a cadet into training for commissioned rank.

Shan's own academic achievements as a classical scholar were valuable in helping to establishing a good relationship with the professorial staff, but they in no way prevented him from a thorough understanding of the increasing importance of science in the contemporary world. As the possessor of a fine brain and a decisive and enquiring mind, he was to be quick in unravelling the mysteries of technology and their application to the needs of the military and, in jest, he would sometimes remark that his particular suitability for the post of commandant of the

RMCS lay in possessing more degrees than the teaching staff and more medals than the soldiers. To underline the personal commitment he brought to his new responsibilities, he set himself to the part-time study for an A-level in mathematics, which he passed without difficulty, sitting in the examination room alongside sixth-form schoolboys.

It was a source of great pleasure to Shan and Margaret to be back in England after more than six years in Germany. They were delighted with the Commandant's splendid old house and its lovely garden and described the move as being like a breath of fresh air, and his new responsibilities, too, appealed to Shan in all their aspects. Susan, now thirteen, was sent to school in nearby Lechlade, while of the two other girls, Bridget was studying at Edinburgh University and Elizabeth, now working in London, was a regular weekend visitor. The interest in nature and in country life that Shan, enthusiastically supported by Margaret, had always vigorously encouraged in their children, was carried on and the possibilities presented by their new surroundings exploited to the full. Apart from fattening a pig, two cages of rare poultry breeds, including Indian gamecocks, were maintained in the garden and there were other chickens to provide eggs and food for the table and a well-stocked pigeon loft, an activity that gained Shan an honorary membership of the Little Cotswell Pigeon Fanciers' Guild. Benedict, the rough-haired dachshund brought back from Germany, had to be exercised and Shan and Susan went fox-hunting with the Old Berkshire. Shan's restless spirit of enquiry into everything that came to his attention became the mainspring of their family life, happily entered into by them all. Margaret, as wherever she went, was a charming and generous hostess and took pains to see that as many of the staff and students as was physically possible were entertained at one time or another in the Commandant's house and, in the traditions of the British Army, she was active in the welfare of the families.

Shan the countryman took great pleasure in his immediate surroundings, in particular the fine trees that grew in the College grounds. He continued his predecessor's work in the preservation of the trees and the maintenance of the estate, calling the Forestry Commission into aid and setting up internally a tree committee to oversee the carrying-on of sound environmental practices in the future and in a properly recorded way. He also had to become concerned with the maintenance of the fabric of the main building of the College, Beckett Hall. This stone-built nineteenth-century Gothic pile had not during the war received the degree of attention that its age and somewhat extravagant architecture demanded and Shan had to nag and cajole a reluctant and straitened Ministry into providing the funds for a restoration of the roof. In this task he was successful and the work was put in hand before the end of his time as commandant. The enterprise had also given Shan another opportunity for the deployment of his restless intellectual curiosity and in the course of his battle with the establishment over the roof he thoroughly researched not only the history of the building of the present Hall but also discovered much about its predecessors on the same site. His findings were recorded in the four-page illustrated article he wrote for the 1960 edition of the RMCS journal.

A peripheral involvement, with which Shan was much concerned, was the future of his own regiment. It was a time of disbandment and amalgamation in the British Army and 8H were to merge with 4H, their old companions-in-arms from the days of the war in the Desert, to form a combined regiment under the title of the Queen's Royal Irish Hussars. One consequence would be that the affiliation that had been enjoyed by 8th Hussars with an Ulster territorial regiment, the North Irish Horse, and which provided a suitably Irish recruiting area, would be lost and substituted for by the Shropshire Yeomanry, which recruited in North Wales. This Shan took as a thoroughly unsuitable proposition, although he had no argument with the main amalgamation with 4H, and he set about trying to influence those with the power to change things. The two regiments formally became the Queen's Royal Irish Hussars in October 1958, with Shan being successful in the matter of the affiliated yeomanry regiment, the final choice settling on the North Irish Horse.

Time was always found for Shan to give to regimental matters, among the first being the selection of the first commanding officer for the new combined regiment.

He went on being much involved in the affairs of the disbanded TJFF and, as was to be the pattern of the rest of his life, willingly gave his help in realizing the hopes and attempting to solve the problems of an enormous number of those who had served with him and who saw in Shan a source of aid and comfort.

While he was at Shrivenham Shan had a letter from Colonel Boeree, the retired Dutch artillery officer who had been one of those who helped and, for a time, sheltered him during the winter of 1944/45. He had written a critical account of Operation Market Garden that he was anxious to see published, but felt he could not do so without knowing Shan's view of some of the opinions he had expressed in the book on the planning and conduct of the airborne battle at Arnhem. A lengthy correspondence was entered into between them, into which Brian Urquhart, the intelligence officer whose warnings about the presence of German armour in the proposed dropping and landing zones around Arnhem had been disregarded and who by now was a senior member of the headquarters staff of the United Nations in New York, was drawn. This was another example of the scale of the involvement in other people's concerns that Shan, always willingly and always helpfully, accepted as being part of his full and busy life.

Despite it all, family life continued in its happy and contented way. Shan organized a sailing holiday for the summer of 1959, when Ragged Robin III was chartered from its British owner in St-Jean Cap Ferrat. Somehow, he contrived to squeeze the five of them into the small four-berth sailing yacht for their Mediterranean cruise, which included finding themselves in Monte Carlo harbour moored alongside *Christina*, the enormous Onassis yacht. At the casino, Margaret took particular pleasure in playing roulette, which she dubbed her favourite ball game.

As a result of an article that Shan published in the September 1958 issue of the British Army Review, a correspondence began with Basil Liddell Hart, then probably at the height of his international reputation as a thinker and writer on military matters. It was his pre-war work on the strategy of the indirect approach that was widely believed to be the inspiration for the German Army's development of the *blitzkrieg* and its extraordinarily successful employment of armoured forces in the great offensive campaigns against Poland, France and the Low Countries, culminating in the invasion of the Soviet Union. At the time Liddell Hart was engaged in the preparation of a paper entitled 'The problems of European defence' and in evolving theories on the relationship between military force and the space in which it operates, and he sought Shan's reaction to the lines on which he was working. This developed first into an active dialogue and then into a friendship that was to last until Liddell Hart's death in 1970. Since both were publishing articles and lecturing with fair regularity, Shan found the candid commentary that flowed between them a stimulus to his work; it also brought him membership of the Military Commentators' Circle, of which Liddell Hart was president in 1959 and where military and political thinkers of established reputation took part in a regular programme of discussions. While commandant of RCMS, Shan also lectured widely and on a number of subjects, giving while he was there, some thirteen speeches to different audiences and usually stressing in some way his belief in the values of sound leadership and broad learning. Two of the more important were his talk to the Imperial Defence College in July 1960 on the lessons to be drawn from the land battles of the first and second world wars and his lecture at the Royal United Services Institution the following November on the education of the officer. Early in 1962 he followed up the theme of the second lecture when he spoke to an extended paper on the technical training of the professional officer at a NATO conference on military education.

In his IDC paper Shan's opening statement was that it would in any case be foolish to have a third world war. He foresaw clearly that in conditions of nuclear stalemate there could be a proliferation of localized non-nuclear conflicts and then went on in the body of his paper to deal with the failures of command that had resulted in what he saw as the lost opportunities of the two world wars. He described the first war as an artillery and machine-gun affair and contrasted the ineffectiveness of the mobile arm, horsed cavalry, insufficiently protected and weak in firepower, with the dominance of the tank in the second, where the most successful exponents of its use were the German and Russian forces. He stressed how logistics would usually determine what could be attempted tactically and queried whether Operation Market Garden should have been launched before the Scheldt estuary had been opened to Allied supplies by sea. Mainly, he deplored the inability of commanders and staffs to recognize opportunities when they presented themselves, irresolution when they were recognized and slow response when action was finally taken. He concluded with a quotation from Hanson Baldwin, the eminent American military historian, with his universally recognized but almost universally disregarded truth, that war is futile without a clear political aim.

The Commandant of the IDC had been unavoidably absent when Shan gave his paper, which perhaps explains a less than fulsome letter of thanks a few days later. His important RUSI paper of November 1960 on the theme of the education of the officer and on which he was warmly congratulated by his constant correspondent, Liddell Hart, set out the beliefs that had governed the conduct of the affairs of the RMCS during Shan's stewardship and the value that he felt his own background as a classical scholar had brought to his career in war as well as in peace. As much of what he then proposed has since come to pass, it is well worth restating the main planks of his argument. First, he was insistent that, for the officer and leader, a training merely in the vocational aspects of the military trade was not enough and that the first requirement was for the strong foundation of a liberal education. Without it, the individual was less prepared mentally for what should be the principal task of the commander, the bringing of a disorderly situation into a state of order. He went on to say that those to whom a liberal education had given a greater mental capacity would more easily acquire the professional skills necessary in military life. He did not draw the conclusion from this that every British regular army officer should necessarily be educated up to at least first-degree standard, but welcomed the various schemes in place, or about to be put in place, for selected regular officers to read for either arts or science degrees at one or another of the major universities. He felt confident that in the future all those chosen for the higher command and staff appointments would be drawn from those officers educated to degree standard and that they should be soundly grounded in the sciences and technologies that would have major influences in the outcome of future wars. He hoped that the number of university entrants to the armed forces would increase and those who did not obtain their commissions by this route would have at least two A-level passes on entry to cadet training.

He went deeply into the history and current practice of the education of the officer in the British armed forces, dealing mainly with the Army, but describing the different ways in which the other two services dealt with their own particular requirements. He also made comparisons with training in the other countries of NATO and the Commonwealth and with the Soviet Union, covering the standard of their cadets at entry, their education up to the time they were commissioned and the advanced command and staff training during their subsequent careers. He hoped that encouragement would be given to officers to develop and retain a lifelong enthusiasm for learning, to travel widely to increase their knowledge of the world and that the study of languages would always remain important. In this respect he included the effective use of English, something he found strikingly absent in much of the military communication of the day. His profound reverence for the English language was, of course, a lifelong passion.

He did not fail to remind his audience that the officer also required qualities other than brainpower. Drawing on the somewhat archaic to make his point in a paper that made firm recommendations for the future, he found it unfortunate that an officer was no longer expected to ride, saying that any occupation where incompetence, idleness or timidity gets one into trouble must be useful and that equitation, mountaineering and sailing all fell into that category.

The case his lecture had so persuasively made was extended and put into a wider context in his next paper, given to a NATO conference on military education fourteen months later on the subject of the technical education of the professional officer. To stress that the emphasis was on the technical, he reminded his international audience that the duty of the officer in the field in relation to his weapons and equipment was to be able to organize and direct their use and maintenance in an efficient manner and to organize and direct the training of others in this use and maintenance. Furthermore, he had to be able to advise on their design and development.

His legacy on leaving Shrivenham in February 1961 was an increase in the number of specialist courses of particular relevance to the armed forces, an augmentation of its academic staff and the adoption of a policy that all students at the general staff colleges should first have attended the RCMS for an immediately prior term of three months, although this fell considerably short of his own recommendation that the period should be a full year. He instituted an annual conference of major-generals to further their awareness of the importance of scientific and technological developments to military affairs and caused a regular visit to Shrivenham to be included in the syllabus of the Imperial Defence College. He also did much to make the work of the RCMS known in the outside world, and by the time his appointment ended the reputation of the college had been enhanced not only within the armed forces but in academic circles as well. There is no doubt that the personal kudos Shan earned while at Shrivenham was a significant factor in his becoming Principal of King's College London, some six years later.

In July 1961 Shan moved to succeed Lieutenant-General Sir Douglas Packard as GOC in C Northern Ireland, being promoted to the same rank on taking up the appointment. An IRA insurrection that had begun in December 1956, presumably in the expectation of gaining some sort of advantage from the British Government's preoccupation with the fall-out from its disastrous Suez adventure, was still taking place, but was losing both momentum and public support in Eire. This was brought home in the Irish general elections of October 1961, when not one of the twenty-one Sinn Fein candidates was elected and the incoming admin-istration responded to the public mood to increase the pressure on the IRA by setting-up special military courts. In January 1962 HQ 39 Infantry Brigade, the formation responsible for the internal security of Northern Ireland, was able to report that the month was the first since November 1960 to pass without a single IRA incident. A long commu-niqué issued by the Army Council of the IRA on 26 February decreed the end of what it called 'the campaign of resistance to British occu-pation' and set out what it saw as the achievements of over five years of effort. The campaign had been largely directed towards the disruption of communications between Ulster and the Republic through the blowing-up of bridges and railway tracks, and the murder of members of the Royal Ulster Constabulary and of the British Army. Compared with what was to follow after 1969 the affair had been low-key, with the IRA claiming to have killed six and wounded twenty-eight soldiers and policemen during the whole time.

It is an encouraging aspect of human nature that it should seek to maintain, during what might seem to the outsider fraught and difficult situations, the greatest possible degree of normality in daily life. The British Army has seemed to be adept at it, perhaps helped by *le sang-froid habituel* of the English. This was certainly Shan and Margaret's attitude during their time in Northern Ireland and so on 25 November 1961 Bridget Hackett was married to Tim Hope, of the Tenth Hussars, in Lisburn Cathedral. To Shan it was thoroughly appropriate that the wedding should take place in the country of his ancestors and that a wartime padre in the Parachute Regiment who had become the Bishop of Clogher should perform the ceremony.

The rest of 1962 and the remainder of Shan's appointment passed fairly peaceably. The Emergency had not stemmed the flow of official visitors; both Her Majesty and Lord Louis Mountbatten, the Chief of the Defence Staff and a guest of Shan's family in Adelaide forty-two years before, had come to Northern Ireland during 1961. The Queen Mother followed at the beginning of April 1962 and the director of the Women's Royal Army Corps later the same month. A regular flow of others during the rest of the year included the CDS again and General Gerald Lathbury, his old colleague-in-arms at Arnhem, now Quartermaster-General to the Army. He was certainly not so occupied with his duties and the entertainment of his visitors as to be unable to prepare and to give at Trinity College, Cambridge, the influential three Lees-Knowles lectures of 1962. The important lecture on the technical education of the professional officer at a NATO conference earlier the same year has already been mentioned and there were others that dealt with the subject of leadership. The Cambridge lectures covered, across a broad historical canvas, the profession of arms since its first origins and were later re-published under that title. The quality of Shan's thought, the sheer scholarship in the papers and the depth of his conclusions, particularly in the matter of the relationship of the soldier to society, a favourite theme of his, made a deep impression and widened still further his reputation as a profound military thinker. He was made Knight Commander of the Order of the Bath during his time in Northern Ireland.

Shan had thought to revive his Irish roots as early as 1947, his first intention being to buy an ancestral property in Tipperary, where the Hakets had been granted land after the Norman invasion of Ireland. He approached his mother for the loan of ten thousand pounds, the asking price of the property, but she was unwilling to advance what was a very considerable sum for the time and the project lapsed. After returning to Ireland as GOC in C, his interest revived and in 1962 a cottage was built at Loughros, near Killibegs, on Donegal Bay. It was here that Margaret caught her first salmon and where happy family holidays went on being enjoyed for some years after the Hacketts' tour of duty in Northern Ireland had ended.

He handed over on 31 December 1962 and early in the New Year

Shan, Lieutenant-General Sir John Hackett, KCB, CBE, DSO, MC, moved to the War Office in London to take up one of the most senior staff posts in the British Army, that of Deputy-Chief of the Imperial General Staff (DCIGS). At that time the broad organization of the armed forces of the United Kingdom was as it had been for generations. The three services, the Royal Navy, the Army and the Royal Air Force were to all intents and purposes organized as separate entities, each with its own government ministry and chief of staff and its own distinct command and administrative structures. During the late war the Prime Minister, Winston Churchill, on the grounds that it was generally accepted that he was responsible for the overall conduct of hostilities, added to his description the title of Minister of Defence. There was not a formally organized department of defence in his administration, Churchill finding it sufficient to be supported in the performance of the office by a small secretariat under General Ismay. Another innovation, which was to survive into the post-war period, was to have the Chiefs of Staff Committee report direct to the War Cabinet and to the Minister of Defence, by-passing the three defence ministers to whom, strictly speaking, the chiefs of staff were subordinate. The position of Minister of Defence was maintained in the post-war Labour government but not combined with that of Prime Minister. In successive governments the minister continued to sit in the Cabinet and to represent, and occasionally adjudicate between, the three service ministers who were outside the Cabinet. Each of the three services themselves were governed by what was in effect the equivalent of a company board of directors, with the minister its chairman, supported by his senior civil servants and with its service members being its chief of staff and those responsible for the operational and organizational functions and for the administration of personnel and supply. In the case of the Army, the body was known as the Army Council and its senior military member was the Chief of the Imperial General Staff with his two immediate subordinates being the Vice-Chief, who had control of operational matters and the Deputy-Chief, whose responsibilities were broadly organisational.

In 1962 the Conservative government of Harold Macmillan revived its interest in the centralization of the three services, something that had always been one of the Prime Minister's hobby-horses. Admiral Lord Louis Mountbatten, both as First Sea Lord and later from 1959, as the Chief of the Defence Staff, had been a strong advocate of such a move, not the least of its attractions being the extent to which his own power would be augmented. It also had the merit in political eyes of appearing to offer considerable financial savings through simpler organization and a degree of common procurement of equipment and supplies. The minister and the CDS between them, knowing they had the full support of the Prime Minister, succeeded, not without some modification to their original plans, in overcoming the resistance of the Service ministers and the three chiefs of staff and by the end of July 1963 the proposals had passed through Parliament. The minister was confirmed as a secretary of state with a seat, as hitherto, in the Cabinet, while each of the three services was to be headed by a minister of state reporting to the MOD. The new ministry set up shop in the post-war group of buildings that had been built to house the Air Ministry and began the long task of reducing overlap and duplication and achieving the savings that the protagonists of the reorganization had promised. Mountbatten, an ambition at least partially gratified and with the powers of the CDS substantially enhanced, was to continue in the senior post for two more years, when the incoming Labour minister of defence, Denis Healey, would take the decision not to extend the incumbent's term of office further.

In the meantime the Army's business had to be carried on. Shan's public reputation and his exceptional skills as a speaker, combined with his enlightened views on public duty and public service, set out with such admirable clarity in his Lees-Knowles lectures, made him much in demand for school speech days and other educational occasions. Civil honours began to come his way, beginning with an honorary LLD from his father's Western Australian endowment in 1963, followed by a similar award from Queen's College, Belfast, two years later. He also made official visits of inspection abroad, during one of which, in attendance in May 1965 at one of the frequent but unproductive conferences on the standardization of Allied weapons and equipment, he was in Australia when his beloved mother Deborah died.

Some few months after Shan's arrival in the War Office, in September 1963, there was a change in appointment of the Director of Staff Duties, that part of Shan's empire having responsibility for Army organization. The new arrival was Major-General Michael Carver, a tall, forceful and ambitious Wykehamist some five years younger than Shan and who had been given command of an armoured brigade in Normandy in 1944 at the age of twenty-eight. Healey was later to describe Carver as the ablest intellectual in any of the three services and the possessor of one of the finest brains he had encountered in public life. Those who served under him admired particularly his ability to reach a swift and binding decision and had confidence that, the decision made, he would support his subordinates to the limit.

It was inevitable that Healey, who on the Labour Government taking office a year later became the political master of these two senior soldiers, would make a judgement about the relative esteem he gave each man.

To Healey, despite their difference in age and seniority that were such important factors in the matter of advancement to higher office, Shan and Carver were rivals for preferment to the highest appointments in the services; to Carver, Shan's opponent was George Baker, a tall and amiable gunner whose wife had the engaging habit of smoking a good cigar after dinner and, as VCIGS, was Shan's counterpart and colleague and the other member of the CIGS's senior triumvirate. He was two years younger than Shan and had served under him as CRA of 7th Armoured Division in BAOR, when Shan was its GOC. In the event, both Baker and Carver were to go on to be promoted field-marshal and in their turn both to be CGS, with Carver also serving as CDS, while Shan would retire as a general from being C in C BAOR and from his last command of fighting troops, the type of appointment that had been his dearest wish and preference throughout his career.

When Shan took over as DCIGS, the reserve forces of the Army in the United Kingdom consisted of the Territorial Army and the Army Emergency Reserve. The latter was the pool into which all those regulars whose period of active service had ended were placed under the terms of their engagement and required to be ready to rejoin their units as reinforcements on the declaration of an emergency. The Territorials saw themselves as a reserve to the Regular Army, to be mobilized and deployed in time of war in the service of the country. They were organized, exactly as the Regular Army, into divisions, brigades, regiments and battalions and, at unit level, were based on the county regiment or its equivalent in other arms and drew on regular units for training and other types of support. The TA's local loyalties were fierce and jealously guarded and was closely interwoven at all levels into the social fabric of its area.

While some may have considered that the department of staff duties at the War Office did not quite have the social cachet of, say, the department of military operations, it did tend to contain the brighter element within the officers of the Army posted to Whitehall duties. One of the staff officers serving under Carver as GSO1 of SD5 was Lieutenant-Colonel Hugh Beach, a sapper and another Wykehamist. The soundly argued paper he produced in May 1965, in response to a request from the Treasury to the War Office to look at the military command structure in the United Kingdom and at the role of the reserve forces, proposed a radical reorganization of both the TA and the AER. It aimed to combine them both into a single force and remove the previous distinction between them by creating not a reserve army in its own right but a reserve for the regular army and particularly for that part of it stationed, in the circumstances of the Cold War, facing the powerful Warsaw Pact armies in Germany. The title of the proposed force was to be the Army Volunteer Reserve. It would be based on local and regional centres, with the regular army units that would receive the reinforcements from that centre providing its permanent staffs. Its order of battle would be based not on the production of whole formations in time of war but upon the needs of the regular forces in the field and in consequence considerable changes were contemplated to the TA as it then existed, including the disappearance of a large number of volunteer battalions and regiments with their proud histories and strong local connections.

In the eyes of the TA the proposed cull was murderous. Seventy-three infantry battalions would be disbanded, together with nineteen armoured regiments and forty-one regiments of artillery. Out would go any home defence role and the balance of the new TA would swing towards a formation of logistic and support units.

Carver saw at once the sense and logic of Beach's paper and hastened to bring its merits to the attention of Shan, his immediate master. (He was later to complain that he felt Shan did not give it the degree of support he might have done, but if the DCIGS expressed any reservations, it was likely that they were political rather than organisational.) Beach had got to know Shan at the time he took command of 7th Armoured Division in 1956 and had quickly come to appreciate and respect the intellectual powers of his new GOC. He had his thoughts, however, about other character traits and felt uncomfortable about what he saw as Shan's inability to resist taking others down a peg.

The full backing of the Secretary of State was swiftly given to the paper and by the end of July Healey was ready to make a detailed statement to the House, with the intention of presenting a reserve forces bill in the autumn. In the Lords, the Duke of Norfolk, as chairman of the Council of Territorial and Auxiliary Forces Associations, made plain his hostility to the whole idea.

A joint working party of MOD officials and representatives of the TA Council was proposed to be set up to consider the scope and implementation of the proposals, with its first meeting to be held during August. Despite including a place for modified local TA associations in the proposed control and administrative arrangements for the new reserve force, it was soon clear that the scheme in its entirety was unacceptable to the territorial establishment. Before the working party had even met, the TA Council, made up of two hundred and fifty delegates from associations all over the country, produced a strongly worded resolution in protest, which was sent to the Secretary of State. It asserted that the plan was manifestly against the national interest and in any case unworkable and went further to say that the Council would participate only if the whole scheme were open to negotiation with its representatives. The formidably influential Duke of Norfolk followed up the resolution with a meeting with Denis Healey the following day. His concerns were many: the abolition of the TA's divisional structure, the alterations in its make-up away from the teeth arms of the old reserve army to a preponderance of logistic and service units capable of giving rapid support to the regular army, the elimination of its role as a home defence force, the weakening of the whole national framework of the TA and the effect on the recruitment of volunteers of the disappearance from the order of battle of so many proud units and famous regiments. There were those in the War Office who suspected that the parallel disappearance of the jobs of many association secretaries, the great majority of them retired officers of middle rank, was also not too far from the minds of the Council. This became evident in later meetings of the working party.

To Shan and his staff the planned reorganization was a long-overdue attempt to relate the reserve forces realistically to the present needs of the regular army. To the Secretary of State, a wartime soldier who had seen active service, it was additionally an annual cost saving of £20,000,000 for a government in urgent need of economies wherever they might be found.

The TA element of the working party was led by Lord Clydesmuir, a doughty champion for the integrity of the TA as he conceived it to be. To reach conclusions on the various strands of the plan, sub-committees were set up and early in September the CBI and TUC representatives demanded, and got, membership of the main working party. The wrangling continued throughout that month and, as modifications and differences emerged, so Carver's department assiduously prepared revised papers for consideration at following meetings. The Home Commands of the Army, of which there were eight at that time, were all consulted and kept informed and before the end of the year matters had proceeded to the point where the results of a great deal of consultation could be incorporated into a White Paper. This was duly debated in both Houses and in December in the Commons the Opposition motion to reject the proposals was defeated by only one vote. In February of the following year the concept of a Home Defence Force had been reinstated as one of the three principal elements of the reorganized reserve forces and the word 'Territorial' had come back into their title, which was now to be the 'Territorial and Army Reserve'.

For Shan and his team it had been a long and sometimes bitter struggle, disappointing in its outcome. He and his director of staff duties were considered to be the villains of the piece and a quip went the rounds that Hackett and Carver were ideal names for the two men intent on the butchery of the Territorial Army. There is a story, no doubt apocryphal, that together they sent a request to a Jermyn Street emporium for the production of a limited edition of a silk tie bearing, on a blood-red background, crossed symbols of a hatchet and a carving knife. There is no doubt that feelings ran high.

With the reorganization of the Ministry of Defence in 1964, the word 'Imperial' was dropped from the titles of the Army chiefs of staff and Shan became Deputy Chief of the General Staff, with otherwise no perceptible changes in his responsibilities. In 1966 his four-year tour of duty in London came to an end and in mid-April he moved to Germany to succeed General Sir William Stirling as Commander-in-Chief of the British Army of the Rhine and Commander of the Northern Army Group of NATO (NORTHAG). With his new post came promotion to the rank of general; apart from the British forces of BAOR, he now also had under his command troops of Federal Germany and of the Netherlands and Belgium.

Shan Hackett had arrived when the involvement of the United States with its war in Vietnam was becoming a matter of preoccupation and when France under de Gaulle was about to make the decision to withdraw from membership of NATO. In Germany the Berlin Wall was only five years old, while memories of Hitler and the Nazi regime still influenced perceptions of the Federal Republic of West Germany. That the soldier chosen to take over command of a major part of NATO forces in Germany at that time not only had an Austrian wife but was himself a fluent speaker of the language would prove to be one of the inspired elements of the appointment.

Hackett found himself responsible for the control of four Army corps, one from each of the countries making up NORTHAG. Of these, only those from Great Britain and from Germany could be regarded as approaching full battle strength, those from the two smaller countries of Belgium and the Netherlands having to rely heavily on reinforcement by reserve forces, were a major crisis with the Warsaw Pact countries to erupt. It was clear from the beginning that the task would be almost as much diplomatic as military and here Shan found himself very fortunate in HBM Ambassador to Bonn, Sir Frank Roberts, another man of small stature but formidable intellectual energy and with a razor-sharp mind. Healey saw the two of them, not altogether unflatteringly, as very similar characters: 'Two waltzing electronic mice with sharp teeth and powerful muscles'. They would come to work very closely together over the coming two years.

The cause that came close to the top of Hackett's list of priorities was the strengthening of relationships with the German elements within the Western civil and military communities, of which they were so vital a part. The Americans had formulated and NATO had adopted a policy that took account of the major power's present commitments in South-East Asia and the limitations this could in the event place upon its ability and its willingness to reinforce the European theatre swiftly in the event of a major war. This policy involved the concept of the nuclear trip wire, in which a Soviet incursion into Western Europe, were it to come about, would be met first by the use of tactical battlefield nuclear weapons and, after what was seen as an inevitable raising of the stakes, the deployment of the strategic nuclear arm. The West Germans for their part were naturally and understandably reluctant to contemplate the transformation of their country into a nuclear battlefield. Shan saw that NATO could only be strengthened if the Bundeswehr, the German armed forces, could be brought to see itself as a true and integral part of the Western Alliance that had the full confidence of the Allied commanders. This was a job to which Shan set himself with a will. He made certain that both the German General Graf von Kielmannsegg, his superior as the C in C of the central region of NATO, and General Bennecke, GOC of the German corps under Shan's command, understood that they were engaged in a full partnership with their British colleagues. This was never better exemplified than when Bennecke was chosen to succeed Kielmannsegg at Central Region on the latter's retirement. Shan's demeanour on his rapid transition from superior to subordinate and his subsequent comportment were to every observer impeccable. He also made certain that his own headquarters fully reflected the multi-national nature of the forces under his command and that key appointments were shared between the different nationalities on the basis of ability and not quota.

Hackett saw too that, following the French withdrawal from NATO and the consequent severing of the formal and obligatory relations that had been in place, the consequence of the major supply lines for the Allied forces, including the most important fuel pipeline, running through France, would require that informal relationships needed to be as strong as possible. General Massu, a much decorated and highly capable French parachutist and someone with a great deal of political weight, was in command of the French forces in what had been, before the sovereign independence of Western Germany, their zone of occupation. Shan felt that the similarities between their military experiences and background justified an informal approach to his opposite number. This was done and a meeting arranged at the Frenchman's headquarters, Hackett returning after two days secure in the belief that a solid understanding existed between them.

With the Americans his relationship was less close, possibly because there was not the same need for it. He had had plenty of experience during his military career of both the strengths and the weaknesses of the United States military machine and maintained a somewhat distant respect for the strengths. He felt a cultural gap between himself and many of his transatlantic colleagues and was undoubtedly happier in his relationships with the members of the European component of his command, in particular the Germans, for whose professionalism he continued to retain an unreserved respect. This respect did not indicate any automatic acceptance of German practices at tactical level. The infantry component of the armoured divisions of NATO was by now transported in armoured personnel carriers (APCs); American policy was that the infantry would fight from the APC and the German Army was showing signs of following suit. Shan's every instinct and all his experience of armoured warfare told him that to be effective in their role the infantry, having been brought to the scene of action, had to dismount and fight on foot. Within his command, Shan's views in this respect were obeyed.

Shan was now fifty-five years old and considering his future. From the time of the appointment of Dick Hull as CIGS, someone with whom Shan's relationship was cool, he had had the growing conviction that he was no longer part of the order of succession to the top. Just before leaving London to go to BAOR, he went to see Sam Way, the recently retired PUS at the War Office and a close friend and colleague during Shan's previous appointment. He told Shan to expect that the succession would go to George Baker and not to himself. After the first disappointment, this confirmation came as a lightening of heart to Shan, who now knew that after BAOR, the biggest active military command the country had to offer, he and Margaret could begin to plan on retirement from the Army and the consideration of a new direction in their lives. They were soon to receive indicators. At the end of June the suggestion was first made to him that he might be prepared to succeed Sir Peter Noble on his retirement in the middle of the following year, as principal of King's College London. Shan's first reaction was not whole-heartedly enthusiastic. It would be too soon after his arrival in BAOR (a view strongly urged by Roberts, the Ambassador), it was an administrative and not an academic post and it was not Oxford. The idea had its attractions; the salary offered was good and the principal's lodgings that came with it was a comfortable house in Kensington. His late mother's estate had recently been settled and with what had come to him, he and Margaret would be reasonably comfortable and could perhaps start to look for the house in the country they had both looked forward to for their later years.

Shan flew to London to talk to Jim Cassells, the CIGS, on BAOR matters and, while he was there, mentioned the soundings he had had from King's College. He was not surprised to have it confirmed that after BAOR, the Army would have nothing more to offer him. King's College were able to agree to defer Sir Peter Noble's departure until 1968 and, provided all the necessary consents were obtained, Shan's life was now determined up to the normal age of retirement at sixty-five.

During Shan's time in command, there was one brief and localised flare-up of temperature in the Cold War. The River Elbe formed a considerable part of the border between the two parts into which Germany was divided and the Federal Government maintained a survey ship, the *Kuchelbacker*, whose task it was to keep under surveillance the build-up of any sandbanks along the river that might come to impede navigation and to chart them for dredging. For some reason, one day in 1967 the East German border police stationed along their bank of the Elbe fired on the *Kuchelbacker* while it was carrying out its lawful and authorized surveying work. The action caused outrage in Bonn and there were threats of heavy West German retaliation. Alerted by the British ambassador, Hackett went at once to Bonn where together they succeeded in persuading an angry German government that the incident was properly the duty of NATO to solve, and specifically the British part of it whose responsibility it was to safeguard that particular area of German territory. As a precaution, Hackett, before leaving for the West German capital, had prudently 'stood to' the British 7 Armoured Brigade. With the German acquiescence obtained to the joint Roberts/Hackett approach, he ordered the brigade commander to deploy his tanks along the west bank in the area where the *Kuchelbacker* was operating and, if the East Germans were to fire on her again, to retaliate in kind. This show of force proved to be an effective deterrent and there was no further hostile action from across the Elbe. The survey work continued unmolested and Hackett was justifiably able to point to another success for the doctrine of the use of minimum force.

A circumstance during 1967 that helped to redress Shan's apparent imbalance in his attitudes towards his different allies was an invitation to go to the States and give that year's Kermit Roosevelt lecture. This he did very successfully, making through the scholarship that informed his paper and the intellectual rigour of his arguments, many new friends and admirers and gaining fresh insights into the nature of the most powerful member of the NATO Alliance.

During an important NATO exercise held that year in Luxembourg, a small interlude showed that Hackett's military duties were not being allowed to stifle his intellectual and scholastic curiosity. There was a short period of time before the exercise proper took off and it had to be spent usefully. Hackett's new MA, Ted Burgess, a gunner lately passed out of the JSSC and who would also eventually retire with the rank of General, happened to remark that the body of the blind King of Bohemia, killed fighting on the French side at the Battle of Crecy, lay in Luxembourg Cathedral. On the way to inspect the tomb, the two of them speculated on the manner of the King's death. Shan asserted that an English knight could not under the rules of chivalry have killed a monarch and that he must have died by being struck by an arrow from a Welsh longbowman. Burgess argued that it was more likely that in close-quarter fighting a foot-soldier armed with a short stabbing sword had first brought down the horse to unseat the rider and had then despatched the helpless king. Enquiries of an official revealed that the cause of the king's death was indeed a deep wound in the groin. The triumphant Burgess then made the error of wondering out loud why the body lay in that particular cathedral, to which Hackett sharply replied that his MA should have known that the king had also been Count of Luxembourg. The visit ended with the laying on the tomb of a saltire composed of a red rose and a leek. Hackett remarked to his MA that that there might not be many other visitors who would understand the significance of the gesture, an observation that brings to mind his small teenage prank, on board the ship taking him and his stepfather to Europe, to stir the memories of his fellow-passengers towards Hymns Ancient and Modern.

The exercise in Luxembourg was conducted without any actual movement of troops on the ground, (a TEWT, or tactical exercise without troops, in military parlance) and was a victory for C in C NORTHAG. Hackett, playing the role of commander of the invading Warsaw Pact forces, announced his intention of penetrating the defending American armies and getting across the Rhine within three days. This he succeeded in doing. It may be supposed that these few days in Luxembourg raised a thought in his mind that would lead on to the collaborative effort of the publication, some ten years later, under the title The Third World War, of the fictionalized account of just such an invasion, how it could have developed and its eventual outcome.

Hackett saw with total clarity the function of himself and the forces he commanded and, going beyond it, the reason for the existence of NATO. He was less certain that this clear vision was widely shared and understood within the broad community of nations that made up the Alliance. He therefore felt it his duty to set down on paper a statement on the true present purposes of NATO as he conceived them to be, as clearly expressed and as cogently argued as lay within his powers. To have the effect of stimulating debate and focusing minds on essentials, it was necessary that the statement be given the widest possible publicity. Accordingly, having received permission for its publication from Central Region of Allied Command Europe, to whom he reported, it was sent off to the London Times where it appeared on 6 February 1968, spread over three columns, as the principal item on the letters page. In it he cast doubt on whether a massive invasion of Western Europe by Warsaw Pact forces was a major policy objective of the Soviet Union, certainly since the death of Stalin. He was concerned that a general perception that the risk of a Soviet invasion was slight could lead to a belief that NATO had lost its *raison d'etre* and that consequently its forces could be run down. He pointed out that the USSR and its satellites continued to maintain very substantial forces close to the Iron Curtain and that a weak NATO might provide a temptation towards what he described as military adventurism from the other side. His answers to this proposition were that NATO should always possess sufficient strength to ensure that the USSR would be unable to control events in their own interests and that the legitimate defensive requirements of West Germany were met by a military system not dominated by the Germans themselves. He concluded that NATO was the instrument of a military alliance and that its purpose was primarily military; to carry out that purpose a sufficient military strength was essential and any suggested broadening of the activities of NATO into fields outside the military had to recognize that basic fact.

The reactions to Shan's letter were swift and predictable. They at first centred around his right to publish the letter at all and whether a British General was not straying dangerously on to political ground, this despite his clear statement in his second paragraph that he wrote as a NATO commander with the full authority of his superior headquarters. Tam Dalyell MP put down a question asking whether the authority of the Ministry of Defence had been sought for the letter's publication and The Times, having sounded out the temperature in Whitehall, wrote a leader on 8 February expressing sympathy for Shan's actions and support for his arguments. The following day the Minister, Denis Healey, whose views on Shan Hackett had crystallized during the affair of the reorganization of the Territorial Army four years previously, answered the question by drawing attention to Queen's Regulation and to C in C NORTHAG's position as a commander under NATO control. Nevertheless, he sent for the General and, from beginning by being indignant and accusatory, moved to a situation of understanding and they parted on good terms.

The correspondence carried on for some little while, meandering here and there into backwaters. Whatever weight Hackett's action carried across the Alliance, the historical facts are that NATO was not run down and there was not a Soviet invasion of Western Europe.

Shan's two-year appointment was coming to its end and with it, at the age of fifty-seven, his military career. During his tour of duty in BAOR, he had been raised to Knight Grand Cross of the Order of the Bath, the most senior and the last honour bestowed on him in recognition of the great contributions he had made to the armed forces of his country. The succession to the post of chief of the general staff had been decided and it was not to be offered to the gallant survivor of Arnhem. In any case, his future had been determined by his enthusiastic response to the offer to become principal of King's College, London, and the appointment was in fact announced officially while he was still wearing his NATO hat and before his successor had arrived to take over. In a gesture typical of the man, Shan had discovered in his early correspondence with King's that the president of the students' union and his girlfriend were on a walking tour somewhere in Germany. The couple were located, an official car sent to fetch them and they spent the weekend in the C in C's house as the guests of Shan and Margaret. The new principal had well learnt the value of early reconnaissance during his Army years.

Chapter Twelve

THE ACADEMIC

In early July 1968 Shan handed over his appointments as Commander-in-Chief of the British Army of the Rhine and commander of the Northern Army Group of NATO to General Sir Desmond Fitzpatrick and flew home. His first duty as an officer newly retired after thirty-five years' service (thirty-seven if the date of his taking up a commission while an undergraduate at New College is taken into account) was to go to Queen's College, Belfast, on 9 July to receive an honorary doctorate of letters. From there the family went on to the cottage at Loughros to take a well-earned holiday and to put in hand the building of a small extension. They had barely arrived and settled in before the local newspaper, in its edition of 12 July, informed its readers that General Sir John Hackett, 'formerly commander of the British occupation forces in the Six Counties', had taken up residence at his holiday home. The paper's political allegiance was as unmistakeable as it was, perhaps, understandable in the developing situation that was to lead to a renewed outbreak of the Troubles in 1969. The realities of the Hacketts' position became increasingly evident; they were aware that there was always a discreet but permanent police presence in the vicinity of the cottage and that if they wished to travel to Dublin, an escort had to be provided for them. After a year or two the general atmosphere became more tense and the noise of IRA firing practice down by the shore beginning to be heard from the cottage, which Margaret found slightly disturbing, was an indication that Loughros might not be the best place for a retired British officer who had been GOC Northern Ireland to spend his leisure hours. In the deteriorating situation it seemed less and less prudent to go on using the place and it was finally sold, with great regret, in 1976. It was somewhere they had been very happy, where they had both worked hard to built a nice garden and where, on the whole, they found themselves accepted by the greater part of the local population. They were, in fact, to keep in touch with a number of them for a good many more years. They had both greatly enjoyed the fishing even when they caught nothing and after they gave the cottage up and left Ireland it was, in Shan's own words, with their zeal for salmon fishing, as distinct from catching salmon, quite undiminished.

When they first went to live at Loughros Shan convinced himself that, if there were to be trouble, it would come from individuals brought in from elsewhere and that any hostility would be directed against their property, rather than their persons. If that was a sound judgement at the time it was made, the outbreak of the Troubles changed matters for the worse. Earl Mountbatten continued to take holidays regularly with his family at his Irish castle, not a long way from the Hackett house, for some years and it was there in 1979 that he was brutally murdered when his fishing boat was blown up by the IRA, together with a grandson, his daughter's mother-in-law and the young local boatman. On the same August day, at Warrenpoint on the far side of Ulster, IRA explosions killed eighteen British soldiers, among them the commanding officer of the Queen's Own Highlanders.

These events were still far in the future when Shan, with any earlier reservations now entirely removed, began to look forward with growing enthusiasm to taking up his new appointment as Principal of King's College, London, due to begin officially on 31 July 1968. Sir Peter Noble, who he was to succeed, was a benign and imperturbable Scottish professor, who had completed sixteen years as the College's head. He had been a kind and approachable principal and an efficient administrator, with an attitude towards the professorial body and their departments of awareness bordering on interest but not extending to undue interference. One of his disappointments as principal was that his long efforts to acquire the use for the College of Somerset House, largely occupied at the time by the Inland Revenue, had been unsuccessful. One thing he had done immediately on taking up his post in 1952, in which Shan would have found an echo of his own soldierly practices had he come to know of it, was that before going into his own office for the first time he did a complete tour of King's College, during which he visited every room in each of its buildings.

To the Delegacy, as the governing body of KCL was then known, Noble lacked the political skills in Whitehall and other seats of power that could help to further the aims and ambitions of their college and they had decided that, when the time came to choose a successor, they would look for someone who was able to show firm evidence of such abilities.

The process that was to make Shan the new principal was begun by the setting up of a search committee in 1966 under the chairmanship of Canon Sidney Evans, Dean of the College and a man of powerful personality and considerable influence within KCL. One of its members was the Professor of War Studies, Michael Howard, a decorated officer of the Second World War. He had come to know Shan during advisory work he had done for the Ministry of Defence during the 1960s and knew that the serving General harboured ambitions of a return to academic life after retirement, possibly as master of an Oxbridge college. It was Howard who, at one of the committee's meetings, put forward Shan's name as a candidate and the proposal struck a chord in the mind of another professorial member who was aware of the success Shan had made as Commandant of the RMCS at Shrivenham. Soundings taken and the initial difficulties cleared up, a firm decision was made to offer the appointment to Shan. The Dean, having first made enquiries of the College chaplain, a graduate of the University of Western Australia, who reported favourably on the legacy left there by the proposed principal's family, travelled to Shan's headquarters in Germany to put the offer directly to him.

The offer, to which Shan readily consented, had first to get the support of Harold Wilson, the Prime Minister, who had the responsibility of approving that the recommendation be forwarded to Her Majesty for the Royal seal to be set on the Crown appointment. For whatever reasons, his approval was not forthcoming. Shan's letter on the future of NATO was written to The Times in February 1968, well into the future and therefore could not possibly have had an influence, but the Prime Minister would also certainly have known of the guarded views on the candidate held by Denis Healey, his Minister of Defence. It may just have been that he thought it inappropriate to appoint a soldier, against all precedent, to such an important academic post. The search for an alternative candidate came to nothing and Shan's name was put up a second time and, helped by the influence wielded in high places by the chairman of the University Grants Committee, Sir John Wolfenden, went through without further difficulty. It was agreed that the handover as Commander-in-Chief in Germany would take place during July and that Shan would take charge of the affairs of the university college from the beginning of its Michaelmas term, 1968.

Inevitably as the outgoing principal approached the end of his own term of office, rumour and counter-rumour circulated within the college as to the identity of his successor. It was not long before it could be whispered with some certainty that the new incumbent would come from the armed forces and this refined itself into a certain fact that he was a General and that his name began with H. The man best-known to the general public at the time and who fitted that very sketchy description was General Horrocks, who made frequent appearances on television and who had been, of course, commander of XXX Corps with its pivotal role in Market Garden. What on earth qualities, wondered members of the faculty who were not in the know, could that particular soldier bring to the problems of running our college? When the real choice was finally announced, there was relief tempered here and there with feelings of uncertainty and unease, for there had been academic principals since time immemorial and a soldier, any soldier, in the post was an unknown quantity.

Shan's view of the demands his new appointment would make upon his time and capabilities may have been influenced by his predecessor, who told him that being Principal was 'a three-day-a-week job', which, after some sixteen years as an esteemed head of college with a hands-off philosophy, it may well have been. Discussing his future life with friends, it seems that Shan saw his task as that of an administrator who would also have the opportunity to carry out his own studies on such subjects as he might choose to pursue – the student reborn, spending long days in the reading room of the British Museum and other sources of enlightenment, giving and publishing papers to learned societies. The leaning he had always had for the academic life and the attractions of its almost monastic nature that he remembered from New College were about to be gratified and to him becoming Principal of KCL was a move into the sort of career he had seriously considered while an undergraduate and which perhaps his second class degrees had persuaded him was not to be the purpose of his life's work. There was also the satisfaction in prospect of adding to what had been without argument a highly distinguished military career new successes in the academic world.

The times, however, were turbulent. In Czechoslovakia, the Prague Spring had blossomed and was being snuffed out and in South-East Asia America was dangerously deepening its involvement in the Vietnam War. In this latter imbroglio students all across Europe found another cause to add to those of nuclear disarmament and the growth of global capitalism, and unrest, much of it severe, broke out widely. In Paris the student revolt was particularly violent, to the point that the government of General de Gaulle felt itself under direct threat and used extreme measures to suppress the uprisings, which had also involved, with a fervour comparable to that of the students, the trades union movement. What may have saved the situation there was the failure of the parallel revolts to make common cause, something greatly desired and confidently expected by the students, but rejected out of hand by the workers. London was not immune from the contagion sweeping across Europe, with the London School of Economics its main engine of dissent.

International politics aside, it was also a time when the place of the university graduate in society was undergoing change. The establishment of new universities in considerable numbers all across Europe had greatly enlarged the student population and had broadened the areas of society from which it was drawn and the graduate was moving away from being part of a small and privileged section of society, enjoying the almost automatic expectation of achieving in their adult life the higher and more responsible positions available in the state. An era was opening, in England at least, where people rising to prominence and gaining reputations in politics, in business and in the arts would say, with increasing frequency and openness and no little sense of pride, that they were the first person in their family ever to go to university.

The state of affairs in the United Kingdom during that year provided the undergraduate throughout the universities with fertile ground for dissent. Unhappy about a faltering domestic economy that seemed to be increasingly riven between lacklustre management and assertive trades unionism, perturbed about much that was happening overseas and uncertain as to how with such gloomy prospects they would make their various ways through life, meetings and protests unauthorized by college authorities were held and here and there boiled over into violent demonstration. It was into this bubbling cauldron that Shan dipped his toe at the beginning of the 68/69 academic year at King's College, London. It may have been some help to him that KCL had a long and rigidly observed tradition of being resolutely opposed to whatever the LSE was engaged in and so there was no automatic predisposition to join the riotous mobs from close at hand in Kingsway on their sit-ins and marches on the American Embassy. Nevertheless, it could not be certain that the contagion would not worsen and spread and Shan set himself to tackle what might be a potential problem in the way he knew best from his years in command of troops in peace and war, by addressing the matter of man management. To prepare himself, he studied all the available accounts of the student revolts that had taken place during the year and he also read regularly the more inflammatory of the periodicals subscribed to by the activists in the College. Armed, as he himself described it, with powers as a principal to impose discipline on students far greater than those he had wielded over soldiers as a commander-in-chief, he first gave the students his attention. A member of the staff at KCL said later that he always seemed fonder of the other ranks (this category included junior academic staff in addition to the students and College staff) than of the officers and some of his actions seemed to confirm this and to reflect the feelings of reserve, to put it at its mildest, he sensed he felt from some members of the faculty. The student union was the first organized body within King's to have a formal meeting with its new principal and, with a distant echo of Montgomery's arrival in the Western Desert to assume command of the Eighth Army perhaps at the back of his mind and with his own ingrained practice of making himself highly visible to the troops under his command, he felt it his proper duty to show himself to the students at the earliest possible opportunity and to impress his personality upon them. National Service having been long abolished and such knowledge of military matters as most undergraduates might have had probably being limited to hearing about their fathers' wartime experiences, they were unlikely to have been overly impressed even by the courageous conduct of their new principal during his military career. In his first term, he therefore proposed himself as the commemoration orator, normally the task of some distinguished person from outside the College. Presented to the entire membership of the union assembled for its annual general meeting, it was for the great majority of students their first opportunity to learn something of their new principal and his attractive speaking voice and the fluent delivery of his speech made a strongly positive impression on his audience, while its content was designed to indicate to them how Shan saw the task ahead.

Put together with his customary lucidity and balance of argument, the paper intertwined many of the tenets of his basic philosophy with his views on the purposes of a university education and he indicated clearly the direction in which he intended his leadership would take the College. He described the choices open to man in society as acceptance, withdrawal, replacement and improvement and making direct reference to feelings of unrest among the students, drew distinctions between the activists who took the replacement view, which meant destruction and reconstruction, and the reformers, who sought improvement within existing structures. He made his own preference very plain.

Shan came early to the decision that the governing body of King's College, the Delegacy, ought to be broadened and got agreement that it should include student representatives. In future the president of the student union would join the governors by right of office, together with three student members, elected at their annual general meeting. At this point it appears that Shan's judgment may have somewhat faltered. Perhaps with the intention of protecting the Delegacy from some of the wilder spirits among the activists, he seems to have made some attempt to guide the union in its selection of suitable candidates for the three elected places. The reception given to this was hostile and Shan wisely withdrew; the election went through perfectly properly and the students could feel that they were playing a useful part in the governance of the College.

The Principal had a strong personality and he knew how to project it.

One member of the faculty during Shan's time recalls how she would go into a crowded room where he might have been present. 'Because he was such a short man,' she said, 'one could never see him, but somehow I was always acutely conscious that he was there.' She also remembers being taken to be formally introduced to him for the very first time, the only woman among a considerable body of the faculty. Shan was in the middle of an animated conversation with a number of other men and, as she came up to his elbow, he half turned and, giving her a quick glance out of the corner of his eye, handed her his empty coffee cup without a word and turned away again. 'It was the spirit of the age,' she said with no trace of rancour. Something very similar happened on Shan's arrival at the main building on his very first day in office. The head porter, the holder of a university post carrying with it a measure of self-esteem, opened the door on Shan's approach and thrust forward his right hand in greeting, to have put into it the new Principal's rolled umbrella and bowler hat.

Shan Hackett immersed himself in the job and in the daily life of the college, judging that the behaviour of an enlightened commanding officer would be perfectly suitable comportment for a university college principal. His office, hung with portraits of his own ancestors, opened directly off the main corridor but he invariably reached it through the outer office so that he might greet and briefly chat with the staff, at first only a single private secretary, the efficient and experienced Mollie Butcher. Shan soon came to the conclusion that there was a need for a rather larger staff and that the administrative side of his responsibilities would be better discharged were he to have an able assistant at his right hand, someone not already immersed in the ways of KCL. Neil Somerton, a highly intelligent civil servant who had done the post-graduate course in War Studies at KCL, was recruited from the Ministry of Transport as the assistant administrator reporting direct to Shan and not to his notional superior, the College registrar. This worked very well, Somerton acting in the post of what Shan would, in his previous career, have seen as that of his chief of staff. His immediate entourage was completed by the arrival of a second secretary, allowing his faithful private secretary to be upgraded to the role of personal assistant. Although a small number by the standard of the various military headquarters in which Shan had served, it was exactly right for his present purposes and the team functioned together in an efficient and contented way.

The appointment of a soldier as Principal of King's College had set a precedent, as had the provision for him of a car and driver; Sir Peter Noble had been content to use public transport to go between the principal's lodgings in Campden Hill and the Strand. Another aspect of

Shan's management style was his infrequent use of the senior common room, preferring to lunch at his club or to eat a piece of fruit at his desk. From time to time either some of the faculty or students would be taken, in separate parties, to the Cavalry Club for lunch or dinner, certain of the freer spirits among the students being persuaded to overcome their reluctance to wear jacket and tie for those occasions. Shan and Margaret also gave sherry parties and dinner parties in the principal's lodgings and whenever the arrangements permitted it, Margaret would attend faculty and student events at the college.

Generally, relationships within the College during Shan's period of office grew out of the way he felt he could best carry out his job. It would have been unlikely for the principal to have much contact with individual students but he did keep closely in touch with the successive presidents of the student union (each of whom held office for one year) and the chairmen of other organized clubs and bodies, attending their meetings and taking part in their entertainments and sporting activities. The riding club was predictably a special favourite of his and he introduced its members to eventing, an activity that did not long survive his period of office. As might be expected, he showed great interest in the annual Greek play and he also went to one party given by the Gay Club, remarking afterwards that he had never seen a more miserable collection of b*****s in his life.

His concern for the junior end of the academic staff was warm and genuine. As if they had been younger officers in his regiment, he encouraged them in their work and research and identified particularly with those whose efforts looked like taking them to higher things. This was the point at which for Shan the other ranks ended and the professors, the officers, began. Here, with a few of them, relationships were more guarded. Many among them had reached what they felt to be a satisfactory level in their particular disciplines, they had tenure and were happy to combine their academic work with research or writing. All this tended towards a state of mind of dignified independence and the feeling, however unjustified, that with the arrival of Shan they had somehow been placed under command and were now expected to obey orders caused unease among some of them. The procedures of College governance brought all of them together twice each term in meetings of the professorial board, a council of which the Principal was the chairman. This duty Shan sometimes found frustrating and it was a comfort to him when he could strike up friendships among its members. One such was with Thurston Dart, the eminent harpsichordist and musical scholar, who had come from Cambridge to run the music department at King's College as the King Edward Professor of Music.

Gough, his predecessor in the post, was also a skilled maker of clavichords and was persuaded to make one for the new Principal, which Margaret was also to play. Both on the piano and on the older-fashioned instrument, Shan's keyboard skills were enthusiastic rather than professional, this despite the many piano lessons he had taken during his sabbatical leave in Graz twenty years earlier. Thurston Dart was a man suitably underawed by military reputations and he did not hesitate to engage in light-hearted banter with his Principal. His premature death in 1971 was a severe blow to both the College and to the Hacketts, who had grown very fond of him.

As could be expected in a man of restless energy, Shan could always find time for outside activities, to each of which, as was his ingrained custom, he gave its due amount of attention and an assiduous application of his knowledge and experience. Occasionally these might stray well outside his official duties at King's College. With his own Irish background, the views he had formed from his experiences as GOC in C in Northern Ireland and his deep concern at what he saw as the catastrophic way in which events were moving there, Shan felt certain that he could make a useful contribution to the deliberations of those charged with the resolution of the problem, if only by providing an extra means of communication with the other side. At perhaps the less significant end of the information chain, the fishermen with whom he and Margaret had made warm friends during holiday visits to the Loughros cottage would be telephoned from time to time and they would chat happily together of how things fell in Donegal Bay. This gave some sort of a localized view of public opinion, but to Shan his main and most important contact on the Republican side was David O'Connell, the chief of staff of the IRA and later vice-president of Sinn Fein, whom Shan had met and talked with from time to time at Killibegs, near Loughros. The two, who addressed each other by their Christian names, maintained contact by telephone while Shan was in London. They would discuss the meaning and importance of events as they occurred, both of them aware that anything of apparent significance either of them might impart to the other would be passed on to a quarter where it might be of use. When Whitehall got to know the extent in what Shan was engaged, they made their deep disapprobation plain and the conversations ceased.

He continued to be active in lecturing and in 1970 gave both the Basil Henriques memorial lecture in London and the Harmon memorial lecture at the US Air Force Academy in Colorado. In the first, under the title of 'Hungry Generations', his long-held views on the common humanity of man and of the individual's obligations to the society in which he lives were persuasively put forward. In the second, he spoke of the military in the service of the state, showing the development after the arrival of Napoleon of professionalism in soldiering and the inexorable progression towards total war between nations. He gave examples of the different attitudes in America and the United Kingdom on the need for there to be a clear political aim when military action was undertaken and drew cautionary tales from the actions of MacArthur in Korea, nudging his audience of future senior military figures towards an acceptance that the United States should look outward and take a broader view of its obligations to the world.

Shan became president of the Classical Association for 1970/71 and gave as his presidential address at its annual conference at Easter 1971, a talk on tactical devices in classical warfare. This took, in an amusing and thoroughly scholarly way, passages from Homer's accounts of the Trojan Wars and set against them their equivalents in modern military thinking, returning in his conclusion to what for him were the eternal moral qualities of the soldier of integrity, fortitude and selflessness.

He was invited in 1971 to become a member of the disciplinary tribunal of the Inns of Court and in 1972 joined the Lord Chancellor's Committee on the reform of the law of contempt. His honorary colonel-cies of 10 Parachute Battalion (Territorial Army) and of the Oxford University Officer Training Corps gave him other points of contact with military affairs, but the office that was to afford him particular pleasure came not long after arriving at King's College, when he had what was for him the great distinction of being made Colonel of the Queen's Royal Irish Hussars. Becoming father of his own regiment placed on him responsibility for advice and counsel on everything connected with it, including endorsing the final recommendations on the list of the officer cadets who hoped to join QRIH on leaving Sandhurst as commissioned officers. The young aspirants all came in their turn to King's College for interview and would as a matter of procedure be given a period of waiting in the outer office. After they had passed through their trial by interview and left, Shan would always call in his young and attractive assistant secretary and ask for her opinion of the impression they made on her of their quality and suitability, not so much as prospective army officers but as human beings.

The fulfilment of another long-held wish was being appointed an honorary fellow of New College, which came in 1973. In June 1963, not long after he had become DCIGS, he had written a somewhat wistful letter to Sir William Hayter, the then Warden of New College, enquiring about the likelihood of a fellowship at his old college and saying that he would rather receive one than be DCIGS or anything else in the Army. What event or circumstance might have inspired such an approach to the Warden at such a time is not made clear in his letter; it may simply have been a welling to the surface of his innermost yearning for an eventual return to academic life or possibly just a bad day at the office. The reply from Sir William dashed Shan's hopes in a kindly way but it was followed by a second and less welcome letter from the newly appointed vice-chancellor of Warwick University, himself a New College man. He seemed to have gained the impression, perhaps from a chance conversation with the Warden, that Shan was seeking employment and pressed him to become the bursar of the new university, something a long way from what the DCIGS had had in mind in making his approach.

Shan gave two more important papers in 1974. The first, again a break with tradition, was an address by the Principal to the whole of the faculty and student body of King's College London. In setting out his views on the nature and purpose of a university education, the achievements of King's College in recent times and his hopes for its progress in future, he was following up the commemoration oration he gave soon after his arrival as Principal in 1968 and providing an account of his stewardship. Having been president of the Classical Association, it seemed natural that he should be offered the same position in the English Association three years later. The style of his second presidential address followed very much that of his first; it was learned rather than didactic but where to the classicists he had been amusing, to the English scholars he showed a warm, almost sentimental humanity. In part a narrative of the events in Holland over the winter of 1944/45, in which he was an active player; escaping from the clutches of the Waffen SS after the battle of Arnhem, being courageously taken in by a Dutch family whose simple faith and self-sacrifice had so moved him, its main theme, given the nature of his audience, was the way in which the books in English the de Nooijs had found for him to read during his convalescence had sustained and uplifted him. He went through the different titles that had been at his bedside and commented on the degrees of importance each had meant to him during his confinement. Using frequent quotation, he spoke of how in his avid reading and re-reading of particularly the Authorized Version of the Bible, of Shakespeare and of a Victorian anthology of poetry, his delight in the power of the English language to liberate the spirit was over and over confirmed. Noting the vast inconsistencies in Shakespeare that reading straight through his entire work revealed, he found his thoughts returning above everything else in his work to the tragedy of Lear and how the impression it left on him was such that it was many years before he could bear to go to see it acted on either the stage or the screen. Of the poetry, he mentions especially among much else, some of the sonnets of Shakespeare and the poems of Wordsworth,

Shelley and Coleridge but his great regret is that his anthology only contained fragments of Paradise Lost. He had had to wait for his return to England before he was able, through a gift from Margaret, to read the whole of it.

These were difficult years for the country and not an easy time to be the principal of a university college. Shan's term had begun in the last two years of the Labour government of Harold Wilson and before it had ended would have seen the crisis of the three-day week and the dismissal of Edward Heath's Conservative administration. Its beginning had coincided with the great student demonstration of October 1968, in which the LSE had played such a prominent part and before it ended, King's College would have made their own protest with a march across Blackfriars Bridge to the Ministry of Education (although Shan said that the undisciplined straggle that took place ought in no circumstances to be dignified with the title of a march). The economic difficulties with which the incoming Tory government struggled in vain led to a number of consequences, one of them incidentally the beginning of the long boom in house prices in this country, which continues to this day. Of more immediate and pressing concern to King's College was the 1972 White Paper published by Margaret Thatcher, then secretary of state for education. The Labour Government had announced in 1969 that it would probably be necessary to look for savings in the cost of higher education and had it won the 1970 general election, would undoubtedly have proposed similar measures to those put forward by Mrs Thatcher. Her intention, which was carried out, was to reduce the financial allocation to universities for the five-year period beginning 1972 by two per cent, at a time of rising inflation and when an increase of between three and five percent had been expected. This brought to an end a postwar quarter-century during which the country's universities had enjoyed regular, if generally modest, increases in financial support by successive governments. One outcome of this cutback was a squeeze on student grants and this became the immediate cause of the decision of the student body of King's College to make a protest. A petition was got up, to be presented to the not-then-the-Iron Lady in her offices after a march by the students across the river to the Ministry of Education. None of the professors or other teaching staff intended to take part, but, in mischievous mood, Shan decided he would march with them. On the chosen day in February 1974, with rolled umbrella on his arm, a Homburg hat on his head (he knew exactly the significance of the difference between wearing a Homburg and wearing a bowler hat) and bearing aloft a placard demanding 'More Pay for Principals', he set off at their head. Prudently he decided that, given the possibility of some sort of incident when the attempt was made to present the petition, he would withdraw before the march got to its end. Arranging for his car and driver to be waiting near the Ministry, he left his fellow-protesters and drove home in comfort, although not before newspaper photographers had managed to record a splendid act of solidarity between a Principal and his student body.

Shepherd and Author

In August 1975 Hackett cleared his desk in the Strand and handed over to the new Principal, Sir Richard Way. It was time for another redirection of his energy and talents. Coberley Mill, a sixteen-acre property in the Cotswolds, had been acquired in 1971 and lived in since that time by daughter Bridget and her husband Tim Hope of 10H, he then being employed in Cirencester as the regular training major of the county's yeomanry regiment, the Royal Gloucestershire Hussars. It was extremely useful for Shan and Margaret, while they were still deeply occupied in London, to have members of their own family taking care of the house and able to oversee the alterations and changes the parents wished to see carried out before they themselves moved in permanently.

The Hacketts had gained much pleasure from the bucolic life while they were at Shrivenham and Shan took with a will to his new role as gentleman sheep farmer in the Cotswolds, acquiring a flock of about eighteen Jacob ewes to add to his other distractions. Charlie Thornton, who lived in the village, provided the outdoor services and he and Shan became shepherd and estate manager, the duties and the titles being interchangeable between them. The mill wheels had been long removed and the Hacketts had the millpond cleaned out and, after taking the precaution of sending a sample of water from the pond to the laboratories of King's College for analysis, stocked with brown trout, ensuring that one of the sports he and Margaret most enjoyed was available to them on their doorstep. Unlike many of his contemporaries and successors, he had no great desire to take up directorships in the City or in the general world of business, although he did gladly accept the offer of becoming an honorary liveryman of the Dyers Company, which he regarded rather as belonging to an excellent and undemanding club. He found the dressing up and the ceremonial which formal City occasions required very agreeable and, with Margaret, took especial pleasure in the Court dinners at Dyers' Hall.

Life was as full as it had ever been and possibly even more varied than when Shan had full-time appointments. He remained, too, much in demand. Edward Heath was unsuccessful in persuading him to stand as a member of the European Parliament and he later withstood considerable pressure on him to become Governor of Western Australia. Satisfying as it would have been to return to his roots and the great honour that the offer of such an appointment represented, the Cotswold mill house had only lately been acquired and the attractions of family life there, to which they had long looked forward, Shan and Margaret decided could not be deferred.

Shan soon saw another advantage that the greater freedom of their new life at Coberley would bring him, a chance to write more. He had, he felt, much to write about and there was one subject that seemed to him of particular interest. During the summer of 1945, while still convalescing from his wounds, he had made careful and copious notes of the circumstances of those last days of the battle of Oosterbeek, of Kessel's life-saving surgery, his time in hiding with the de Nooijs and the winter escape across the great rivers that brought him back into British hands. A draft manuscript was completed from the notes during 1950 but for whatever reason Shan put it aside and over many years did nothing to get it published. This in no way indicated that the recollections of his adventure or of its spiritual legacy, the depth of both his admiration for the Dutch and the gratitude he felt for all that they had done for him, had in any way dimmed or been far from his mind and work. An account of it was frequently the subject, at least in part, of one of his lectures, particularly those given to schools and others where he wished to draw attention to the power of the human spirit in adversity. Doctor Helen Hudson of KCL recalls that when, at her request, Shan spoke about his escape and return to a party of women students at a weekend conference in Windsor Great Park, 'one could have heard a pin drop'. By 1975 other accounts that bore on the events in which he had participated during the last winter of the War seemed to him to have given an incomplete picture of what had taken place and he felt the time had come for the story to appear as a book. The manuscript was brought out and given such polish as it needed, a publisher found and a very suitable title, I was a Stranger, taken from St Matthew's Gospel. It was an instant critical and public success on its publication in 1977 by Chatto & Windus and deservedly retains to this day the reputation of being one of the most sensitive and beautifully written accounts of human endeavour and human decency within the vast literature that the long and bloody Second World War produced.

The life of the world during the decades that followed the war was conditioned by fears that another would erupt between the Soviet empire and the West. Shan's own involvement in the situation had been deep and extensive, given expression most publicly in the arguments laid out in his letter written to The Times in February 1968 while he was still Commander of Northern Army Group, calling for the strengthening of NATO so as to reduce any temptation towards military adventurism on the part of the Soviets. By a chance happening they would become the basis for his next book. William Armstrong of Sidgwick and Jackson, the successful London publisher of military titles, had been inspired by an article in The Times that speculated on the form another war in Europe might take to consider the possibility of publishing a work, of the sort known as 'future history', on the subject of an imaginary invasion of Western Europe by the armies of the Warsaw Pact. Together with Elizabeth Longford, the historian and the wife of his chairman, he happened to attend a lecture at the Staff College, Camberley where Shan was in the chair. Greatly impressed by Shan's handling of the occasion and quickly becoming conscious of his remarkable grasp of military matters, Armstrong knew he had found the ideal person to realize the book he had been contemplating. Over lunch at the Garrick Club, apparently an extended one even by the standards of that establishment, he and Shan came to an agreement to proceed together with the project. A plan was soon drawn up to produce and publish a book under the title of The Third World War, contracts were signed, a team consisting of two senior sailors, an air marshal, two soldiers, a diplomat and an economist assembled and under Shan's direction and editorship went to work, each one contributing from his own particular expertise at the lively editorial meetings. The book, which appeared in 1978, purported to be an authoritative account of a war that had broken out in the Summer of 1985 and an adroit use of contemporary, mainly military, photographs, and appendices filled with seemingly authentic data helped to lend it verisimilitude. It imagined the war beginning with a Soviet incursion into a post-Tito Yugoslavia, followed by a massive invasion of the West by Warsaw Pact forces. The enemy advance was checked and the conflict entered its nuclear phase. After the destruction of, first, the city of Birmingham, followed by retaliatory Polaris rockets that eliminated Minsk, a palace revolution in Moscow brought down the Soviet government and its successors sued for peace. In less than four weeks the Third World War had ended with the Treaty of Helsinki.

Plausibly and persuasively written, the moral of the story was the same as Shan's 1968 letter – that NATO should not let down its guard and, for the preservation of the West, had to look to the state of its forces. In the authors' notes, which were a commentary on the actual state of world affairs in the year of the book's publication, attention was drawn to the extent of a Soviet military build-up far greater than could be justified by self-defence alone and, presciently, talked of the great damage it had to

208

be doing to the Soviet economy. The book was a considerable success critically and commercially, selling in great numbers throughout the world in both hardback and paperback editions and proving particularly popular in Japan and the United States, where it reached almost cult status. Shan and Margaret had the exhausting job of making extended promotional tours in the United States and Australia, which, although rewarding, they described as having been 'pure Hell'.

On the strength of the first book, the team was brought together again to write a sequel, The Third World War; The Untold Story. In the light of actual international developments during the four years since the publication of the earlier volume, this second book looked in more detail at some of the main events imaginatively described in the earlier publication and also recounted the effect of the war on other parts of the world, the 'vital peripheries', as they were termed. In the first book fellow-members of the team of contributors are mentioned by name only in the statutory declaration of copyright on the reverse of the title page, whereas in the second book, although authorship was credited to and copyright vested in Shan alone, he does in his author's notes give generous acknowledgment individually and by name to the contribution made by the other members of his team. The book restates their belief that, to avoid a nuclear war, the West had to be properly prepared to fight a conventional one and stresses the importance of a reduction in the disparity between the military strengths of the Warsaw Pact countries and NATO. They were not to know that in a few years entirely other events would dramatically reverse the imbalance with which they had been so concerned, without thereby necessarily increasing the security of the West.

The important and influential Lees-Knowles lectures that Shan had given in Cambridge in 1962 had been reprinted by The Times and published in booklet form in 1963. From them, Sidgwick and Jackson produced a new edition, larger in format and lavishly illustrated in colour and this appeared in 1983 under the original title of The Profession of Arms.

The publicity given by this string of titles widened Shan's already formidable reputation as an expert in politico-military matters and the number of calls on him to share his knowledge increased still further. One, Shan later recalled vividly, was an invitation to go to Buenos Aires to give a series of lectures, among which was a talk to the senior members of the armed forces of Argentina together with their commander-in-chief, General Galtieri. Shan could not conceal his distaste at the General's opening remarks when the Argentinian explained that, having recently conducted with great success an internal war against terror, it was time for his country's army to return to the study of conventional warfare.

From 1982 until 1989 Shan also became a regular speaker at the large international conferences organized by the group known as Business International Network, where the purpose was to describe to prominent businessmen the nature of current affairs and current crises in various parts of the world and the influence they might have on global trade and investment. This gave more occasions for Shan and Margaret to travel widely and whenever Margaret was unable to go, daughter Susan, leading by this time an independent life, would take her place.

Another agreeable addition to his speaking programme during this period was an invitation to join Swan Hellenic tours as a lecturer. These voyages, in which Margaret invariably took part, gave him enjoyable opportunities to speak on two of his great passions, classical Greece and Crusader castles. An unusual by-product of these was the writing of what seems to be Shan's only attempt at a theatrical work, a play which did not get beyond the stage of a draft, called 'Greek Waters'.

In 1985 he felt greatly honoured to have been chosen as one of the infrequent recipients of the Chesney Gold Medal, an award that carries with it an obligation to give a lecture at the RUSI on a subject having to do with the military science. Shan was always happy to accept such a duty and chose as his subject, 'The Man at Arms in the Nuclear Age'. It was perfect for him. In a disquisition structured with the same care that might be required for a major musical work, he ranged from the nature of man, (much too clever and not good enough), with his aggressive and acquisitive nature, through the development of weaponry from the earliest times and the evolution of soldiery into formed armies as servants of the state, to modern armed forces and their purpose in the light of the existence of nuclear weapons. He spoke with remarkable prescience on the dangers of the rise in Islamic militancy, although this foresight did not extend, nor would it have generally at the time, to predicting the disappearance of the Soviet Union as a superpower. He saw clearly the great dangers in nuclear proliferation and hoped without much hope that an antidote could be found in the withering away of the nation state. After commenting on the moral objections to war, he concluded by dealing with the importance of ethics in military service and drew on what had been fundamental to the conduct of his own life, the appreciation of the values and qualities necessary in the military group in carrying out its obligations to the State.

At Coberley there was always great activity across all of Shan's manifold interests. At one level there was the regular pattern of the farming year to be properly observed; the tupping of the ewes, lambing, sheep shearing and coping with the wide range of diseases and ailments that the ovine breeds seem so readily to attract. There was the Christian year to be observed, devoutly and regularly fulfilling his obligations to his Church and finding, as he had all through his life, much support and comfort from constant reading of the Authorized Version, to him the best of all books. Professor John Barron would regularly bring down a party of history students from KCL to hear a talk from Shan, to enjoy Margaret's warm hospitality and to visit the Roman villa at Chedworth and other remains in and around Cirencester. Often the Ermine Street Guard would be in attendance, a local Roman re-enactment society that Shan had been instrumental in equipping with authentic-looking weapons and uniforms through financial help from a charity with which he was associated. The BBC came down to make use of the grounds at Coberley as the setting for a television production of Coriolanus; there were book reviews to be written and calls from newspapers for comments on some occurrence, for which they would receive suitable and trenchant observations. There were appearances to be made on television or the wireless, on 'Any Questions', on 'Desert Island Discs', there were the anniversaries of Arnhem or some other military or historical commemoration to be attended with faithful regularity. He was made a Deputy-Lieutenant for Gloucestershire and was assiduous in fulfilling the ceremonial obligations of the office; there were his contacts with his regiment, with the airborne forces and with King's College London to be kept in proper order; there was constantly advice and help to be given to a vast number of people on a variety of subjects by letter and by telephone, or face-to-face to a stream of visitors. There was the social life of a social county to be enjoyed and there was very little time to be still and none to be inactive.

Shan took both pride and pleasure in his trusteeship of the Esmé Fairbairn Trust, which played a most important part during the last ten years of his life. After Shan's death, the Trust, wishing to help preserve his memory at King's College London, offered a substantial donation, which in the end it was decided would endow the college library. In November 2002 Her Majesty formally opened the Maugham Library in the old Public Record Office in Chancery Lane, which also included within it the Hackett Post-Graduate Study Centre.

Since the trauma of the winter of 1944/45 and for the near half-century that had elapsed since he had been reunited with Margaret, Shan seemed to live a charmed life. His career and his reputation had flourished, in the Army and out of it, he had the happiest of marriages and a close family he delighted in and who were delighted with him. Any regrets or upsets there might have been were quickly dismissed and pushed aside by new adventures, although there had been the disappointment of Susan's divorce but fortunately there had been no children of the marriage. A cruel blow was about to be struck and Shan and Margaret would lose the only child of their marriage. Just before Christmas 1992 Susan had been staying at Coberley with her parents and was due to return to London. The weather was very bad, with freezing fog, but Susan was anxious to get home and, with great misgivings on the part of Shan and Margaret, set off alone in her car. Somewhere along the M4 motorway a tyre burst and the car skidded and crashed into the side of the carriageway. It was two hours before a motoring organization finally rescued her and she was returned to her flat, seemingly only badly shaken from her accident. Her injuries, caused by her impact with the steering wheel, were unfortunately more severe than she had at first been prepared to admit and she was taken to the Wellington Hospital and then transferred to the Chelsea and Westminster Hospital, where she died on Christmas Day.

Susan embodied many of her father's gifts and qualities. She had a neat and stylish dress sense, a quick and enquiring mind and a ready wit. Her letter to Philip Howard of The Times, drawing attention to the solecism committed in placing a definite article before hoi polloi, gained, as might be expected, Shan's admiration and approval. Very much her own person, she did not find him intimidating and their relationship was an easy one, matching witticisms and repartee on a basis of equals and she was always ready with a small banana skin to be slipped beneath Shan's highly polished shoe at the first sign that pomposity might be creeping in. 'Oh, come off it, Fred,' she would say (he was always 'Fred' on these occasions), and the twinkle in her father's eye would show that they were back together on the same plane. Her memorial service was held in St Faith's Chapel in Westminster Abbey and it would have pleased her to know that Philip Howard was among those present. Her ashes now lie with her father's in the family vault in Perth.

Two years later, during the fiftieth anniversary pilgrimage to Arnhem in September 1994, Shan and Margaret had attended the Sunday service of remembrance at the Airborne cemetery. Their next engagement was to be at the reception given in the presence of HRH the Prince of Wales at the Hartenstein Hotel, General Urquhart's headquarters during the Battle of Arnhem and by then the Airborne Museum. They were being driven, as on all the previous Arnhem pilgrimages, by Chris van Roekel, a much liked retired schoolmaster, and had with them Major Ronnie Boone, late of 10 Para. There had been some delay in getting the Dutch and British Royals away from the cemetery and by the time the small convoy of which Shan's car formed part was able to move off they were concerned that they would be late for the reception. Travelling at a rate of knots along the dual carriageway Amsterdam road, behind a Dutch police car flashing its blue warning lights, they approached the traffic lights at the left turn into the Dreijenscheweg, the side road that led down into Oosterbeek. It was along this road that the German SS *panzer* troops had established the blocking line against which Shan and 10/Para and 156/Para of his 4 Parachute Brigade had dashed themselves in vain, almost exactly fifty years before. At that point the traffic lights turned red but the escorting police car continued without hesitating and to van Roekel that indicated that the convoy had priority and he was entitled to follow. Two elderly Dutch citizens, waiting in their car at the lights to pass over the Amsterdam road, saw them turn green in their favour and set off, and unavoidably the two vehicles collided. Shan, in the front seat, was fortunately wearing his seat belt and this saved him from more serious injury but he sustained a sharp blow to the side of the head and his left ear was badly cut. Van Roekel had cuts and bruises to the face; Margaret was fortunately unscathed but Boone took the full force of the impact and suffered a broken leg at the very crossroads his battalion had at such high cost tried and failed to capture during the battle in 1944. A Parachute Regiment officer in a following car came to the scene, equipped with the right sort of travelling case, from which a bottle of gin was produced. This served Shan both as a restorative and as a disinfectant to swab the cuts he and van Roeckel had suffered. They were all taken to hospital to be treated, everyone except Boone being discharged during the same afternoon, their day disrupted, the royal reception foregone and shaken by the accident but otherwise to the casual observer, relatively unscathed.

Margaret afterwards felt that the trauma suffered by Shan, at the time approaching his eighty-fourth birthday, was greater either than at it first appeared or than Shan was prepared to acknowledge, and that it marked the beginning of a three-year decline in his health. During the winter of 1996/97 he had a heavy fall at night in the lane leading down to the house that left him unable to get to his feet without the help of Bridget, who fortunately was on hand. The consequence was that from that time he could not walk without a stick and he began to have occasional difficulties with his speech and to lack some clarity in putting his thoughts together. It was a sad turn of events to have to see that fine brain falter but through it all his spirit did not waver. Ian Pulford, the local rector, perhaps with the prospect of a fairly early funeral service in his mind, tried in a rather circumlocutory way during one of his calls to discover what hymns his distinguished parishioner might have in mind for such an occasion. Shan saw through the ploy at once and made it plain it was something he was by no means ready to discuss.

Shan Hackett died at his home, Coberley Mill on 9 September 1997, two months short of his eighty-seventh birthday. In the presence of a great congregation, his memorial service was held in the church of St Martin-in-the-Fields on 24 November in the same year. He was cremated and the final journey of his ashes was back to the land of his birth and to the family mausoleum in Perth, Western Australia.

Epilogue

STATEMENT OF ACCOUNT

The church was packed to overflowing for the service to give thanks for the life and work of General Sir John Hackett. Among the gathering, there was a considerable number of the great and the good, come to recognize the service he had given to his country during a long life of achievement. There were also many who were in St Martin's because their lives had at some time been bound up with the man they had come to celebrate and to honour; servicemen and women who had been with him in peace and war, professors, lecturers, students and staff from King's College, Dutch people whose actions, direct and indirect, had sheltered the wounded soldier during a harsh winter of occupation, friends and neighbours from his Cotswold village and those, too, to whom he might have been better known by reputation than acquaintance. They were there to give tribute to a remarkable man who had done remarkable things and who in a greater or lesser way had added zest and lustre to their lives.

They were to hear a masterly eulogy from Sir Michael Howard, that in the way it was constructed and the manner in which it was delivered, would have drawn applause from its subject and could have served as mini-biography. They also heard a moving address from Sophie, the daughter of Kate ter Horst, perhaps the greatest of the great heroines of the battle of Oosterbeek. They would all have recalled from their memories, as the service proceeded, some incident perhaps not always a joyous one, that connected Shan Hackett to them, or it may be they recalled their impressions on first meeting a man whose reputation would certainly have gone before him.

They would have been struck, at this first meeting, by a neatness and elegance of dress that came from a meticulous observance of a freely accepted code of conduct. He was, after all, the product of a time in England when dominance lay on the side of the male, when style was not confused with exhibitionism and when a Norfolk jacket was considered a perfectly suitable garment in which to climb the Himalayas. His dress

215

was the first of his trademarks and may be attributed in part at least to the influence of New College, reinforced by becoming bound by the uniform regulations of a smart British cavalry regiment and re-emphasized later by taking on the dashing and exotic garb of the TJFF. A Dutchman who as a boy of twelve in Arnhem was hurriedly taken home by his father from their Sunday walk as parachutists began to fall around them, later in life gave it as his opinion that all Englishmen were actors and only those who were not good at it had to do it for a living. Perhaps everyone who has to play a role in life, whether or not in uniform, is to some extent an actor and there are those who accuse Shan Hackett, as he deployed the great firepower of his intellect and learning, of being one. Someone who had known him in the Army and who observed his work at King's said that as a soldier he played the brilliant academic while in academic life he was the bluff soldier. This black and white quip gives no credit to Shan for the subtlety of his leadership and his shrewdness in the judgment of others, but there may be some basis for thinking that his archetypal Englishness had something of the thespian in it. If this is indeed so, behind it lie a long Irish lineage and an Australian upbringing that together gave him an objectivity of view denied to the average Englishman with his ingrained habit of instant classification of all those he meets. The twinkle never far from Shan's eye was the outward evidence of it.

A particularly striking aspect of Shan's persona was his use of the spoken word, noticed first through a most attractive speaking voice. His father had also had a reputation for being a fine public speaker and that might in his case have been owed to that by no means rare combination of Irishness and the legal bar. Combined with the voice was an exceptional ability in the use of the English language; someone has remarked that Shan had the ability to speak, extempore, in perfectly constructed paragraphs. This great gift, which extended in equal measure to the written word, was the product of his lifelong love for language, in particular the English language and for what he termed the treasure house of English culture. He set out the root causes of his love affair in a lecture given during the last few years of his life at King's College London, in November 1992.

Its subject was the relevance of a classical education to the contemporary way of life and he began by speaking of the feeling of disquiet in thoughtful people at the manner in which their lives were being taken over by processes that ostensibly were designed to enrich them. To Shan the study of classics was a means to bring some balance back into a turbulent world and to provide a key to unlock the rich treasure house of English language and literature. Turning to its two classical roots, Latin and Greek, he described the first as the language of *gravitas*, forcible, direct and dignified and through its evolution into the modern languages of Italy, France, Spain, Portugal and Latin America, not deserving the description of a dead language. Greek he admired for its flexibility, for the way the direction and value of a sentence could be altered by the insertion of a participle and to him it had no equal as a medium for the expression of pure thought. He was in no doubt about the debt English owed to these two ancient languages and, mongrel as the result might be considered, he was certain that as an all-round instrument of communication, it had no equal in the modern world. While it might lack some of the essential means of philosophical thought, it was most apt for drama, for lyric verse and for narrative prose and poetry. Those to whom English was native, or, in such as Conrad or Stoppard had become natural, had inherited a tremendous empire of the mind but one under constant threat through ignorance, idleness and arrogance. He accepted that English was in a constant state of flux and did not deplore change but was strongly against wanton or unjustified change and the way the misuse of words not properly understood led to the impoverishment of language. To him the overriding purpose of both the spoken and the written word was to transmit thought from one mind to another through the silence that separated them. He rejoiced in the extent and richness of the English vocabulary and contrasted Racine, who had written all his plays using two thousand words, with Shakespeare, who had used twenty thousand. In the year in which he was speaking, he said it might be that the study of computer sciences was beginning to be thought more relevant to modern life than the study of classics, but to direct education down those lines would give the student little or no knowledge either of human values or of himself. Science was to do with what could be measured, but to the classical scholar that was Shan, only those disciplines where measurement was inappropriate could truly be called 'studies'. He closed his case by saying that the hope and glory of the British Empire, whose true greatness would one day be measured, lay in the present universality of the English language.

Shan's deep feelings about the use of language led to occasional bursts of impatience with others less able than he in the art of expression, but these manifestations of irritation were never intended to demean the individuals concerned. They were due rather to being offended at what he judged to be an insufficiency of exactitude in the others' thought processes that his Socratic view of a life of constant enquiry seemed to demand. On the other hand, he was not averse to what a one-time colleague whose admiration for the little man fell somewhere short of idolatry called 'gratuitous displays of intellectual superiority'. Perhaps, with distant echoes of Doctor Jowett, Shan's physical frame was just too small to hold so much learning and these little eruptions served to relieve the pressure. However cutting his reactions might seem to be towards those he deemed to be guilty of sloppy thinking, he never overlooked that they were bound together in common humanity.

Whenever speaking or writing of his military career, Shan always laid great stress on the importance of the regiment and would say that he had never joined the British Army but only the 8th Hussars, which happened to be part of the Army. What he seemed to have recognized is that the instincts of the English people are not tribal but of a village nature, a semi-articulated desire to pass life in groups with distinct identities and a sense of common purpose, within a structure of a size in which they can feel at ease. Hence, as Shan would have seen it, the reason for the existence of regiments, clubs, societies, of the traditional village both country and urban and of all the other multiplicity of ways in which the English band together. It may be argued that this is generally the nature of the human condition in the West but somehow it appears to call out more insistently to the English. Shan somewhere movingly describes being on a night march with his half-squadron of TJFF cavalry, the regular sounds of the horses' hooves on the track, the creak of leather and the murmured commands and above his head, his bright beloved Sirius and thinking to himself in wonderment that he was being paid for doing something so fulfilling. He might equally have written in the same terms of a night march of his own Irish regiment or as he looked around a Dakota filled with comrades of his 4 Parachute Brigade on their way to a parachute drop. Perhaps, even, he could have felt something of the same sentiments in the middle of Blackfriars Bridge, with his raggle-taggle band of students going off to try to put across an expression of their concern to the Minister for Education. A sense of brotherhood with those with whom he was linked in common endeavour and a bond of affectionate loyalty toward them was always with him from the beginning to the end of his life and that is why so many of those in St Martin's on that November morning felt themselves to be his true comrades in arms.

Shan Hackett, captain of his soul and master of his fate and the possessor of a quick analytical brain, must always have been certain of the essential rightness of the decisions that he arrived at through life. If there were doubts and disappointments, they were not paraded in the open for others to see. In his early life, as a boy child following three older sisters, he might have hoped for a brother to share his growing-up with. He recorded that he was aware that his sister Deborah, the youngest of the family, was an attempt to give him a brother, and perhaps one close to him in age might well have brought about a different Shan, but it could not be imagined that it would have been one less gifted and determined. Denied a brother, he seems never to have regretted being surrounded by sisters, all of whom were to go on to pursue worthwhile careers of their own.

At what point the final decision was made to join the regular army is not clear. He has said that there was always at the back of his mind the thought of becoming a soldier and he did take up a supplementary commission in the Bays in 1931, two years before he was due to go down from Oxford but such a military commitment would have been the normal obligation of an undergraduate during the inter-war years. He had done exceptionally well at Geelong and he in no way seems to have felt that he was not up to the challenge of getting a first-class degree, so it may be speculated that, had he done better and a fellowship offered to him, he might well have chosen an academic career. The letter from H A L Fisher, the Master of New College, in which he urges Shan not to be disappointed in his second-class degree and that he would always find his years at Oxford of great value in life seems to place a barrier across the academic path and it was probably at that point in 1933 that he finally decided on soldiering. The 1960s letter to Sir William Hayter when he was Master of New College, in which Shan enquired about the possibilities of a fellowship, might have been stimulated by his growing realization that he would not rise to the top of the military profession, but it underlines how strong his desire in the 1930s to remain at Oxford must have been. The wishes his family had had for him, either that he should become a lawyer or that he should return to Australia and go into the newspaper business that had made his father's fortune, seem never to have been given any really serious consideration.

Shan's decision, after a few years with 8H in Egypt, to apply for a tour of duty with the TJFF was straightforward. He was a regular officer in the British Army who would return to his own regiment after an attachment for a fixed period of years. Shan's latent interest in Arabs and Arabism had been stimulated by the short tour of duty that 8H had carried out in Palestine during the early part of the Arab revolt and after that, the return to the social scene in Cairo could have felt rather mundane. There were also the attractions about which Shan was quite open, of the higher rates of pay the attached officers enjoyed under the regime of the Colonial Office and the relief that would follow in the tiresome matter of his debts at Ladbroke's. He also saw that he would get a lot more riding than with 8H, in course of being mechanized and by being stationed in the very region where the campaigns of Saladin during the Third Crusade had been conducted, which he was writing about, he would be better placed to get on with his BLitt paper. He was furthermore, greatly attracted to the desert, to its rapid sunrise and its short twilights, to the way every aspect of the landscape changed as the sun moved across the sky and to the evidence of ancient civilizations and of other peoples that could be found all around him. In sum, the tour with the TJFF was very rewarding. While doing it he would fight two military campaigns, receive his first wounds in action and gain his first decorations and awards, pass through Staff College, be given his first staff appointment and earn his BLitt. He would also, during the course of it, meet Margaret and, at the end of his tour, marry her and enter into a long and happy life together and a partnership in which the whole would turn out to be even greater than the far from inconsiderable parts.

1944 was a year of crisis when Shan would undergo one of the most testing periods in his entire life, Operation Market Garden and the time in hiding in Holland that followed it. He had been given at a comparatively young age a marvellous opportunity to raise, train and lead into action as its commander a brigade of some of the best troops in the wartime Army. The battle and the events that followed it tested his resolve to the utmost and, as it all developed, he must time and again have wondered why things had gone so disastrously wrong and whether there were things that he might have done to produce a different outcome.

The scale of the failure at Arnhem and the variety of circumstances that brought it about were beyond Shan's own capacity to rectify. The flawed plan with the landings of 1st Airborne Division spread over several days, the distance between the dropping zones and the objectives, the inability, or reluctance, to make full use of the intelligence information on the strength and disposition of German forces, the absence during a crucial period in the battle of the airborne divisional commander and his senior brigade commander, the argument that followed the delayed arrival of 4 Parachute Brigade on the second day about who should take charge of the division and how it should be employed in the situation it found itself, these were only the more obvious obstacles to the achievement of what had been intended to be a decisive action of the Allied campaign in North-West Europe and one that would lead to final victory over Germany.

Setting aside any speculation on how events would have been altered had XXX Corps been able to keep closer to the planned rate of advance up the corridor, could any alternative have been found to the hard pounding that destroyed 4 Parachute Brigade and for a time reduced its commander's role to that of an infantry junior leader?

There is nothing to show that Shan was not totally supportive of his divisional commander in the decisions he took nor are there any post-hoc criticisms by him of Roy Urquhart's conduct of 1st Airborne Division's part in Operation Market Garden. In fact, he later described Urqhuart as the greatest battlefield commander he fought under in all the war years. Perhaps while events were unfolding in the Arnhem battle, the high command was beginning to have second thoughts about the strategic value of even a successful thrust along that route to Germany. General Bradley's remark that Market Garden was a sixty-mile dash up a blind alley is the saddest of commentaries on so much bravery.

However differently things might have turned out, what is beyond any doubt is that he was admired and revered by all those who served under him and generated in the way he exercised command both loyalty and affection, which, in survivors of the Battle of Oosterbeek in particular, remains to this day.

The central fact in Shan's post-war military career is that he never became CGS or CDS. He would seem to have had most of the qualifications needed for these high offices in the circumstances of the Cold War; his strategic thinking was sound, as the observations in his letter to The Times on the role of NATO and in subsequent lectures and articles make clear, and he had powerful diplomatic skills, which were demonstrated in his relationships with NATO commanders and their governments during the time he was commander NORTHAG, when he also showed a marked ability to work in most effective harness with HBM Ambassador in Bonn. Whether he would have been able to work harmoniously with the politicians at home is another matter and some of the things said by Healey in his autobiography, The Time of my Life, would seem to bear that out. In any case it seems to have been generally accepted that with the post-war reorganization of the Ministry of Defence, the qualities needed for the senior military leaders in Whitehall had changed and that the chiefs of staff had become politico-military administrators, an unappealing prospect if correct, for someone to whom command of men was first among all the tasks a soldier could be called upon to perform. Certainly it was as a commander that Shan was happiest and where he felt most fulfilled and, much as he might have liked to be appointed field marshal, it is doubtful that he would have been happy as a chief of staff and those few extra years in uniform might have prevented him being offered the chance of becoming the principal of a university college. Had King's College been deprived of the seven years of his stewardship, it, and academic life in this country generally, would have been the poorer for it.

Changing direction at the age of fifty-seven gave Shan new opportunities to impart his wide knowledge of current affairs and his sound opinions on the course world events were taking and. The demands on him for appearances, lectures and articles never lessened during his post-Army years and he spent a lot of time working with a number of different organizations anxious to make use of his wisdom, from broadcasting on the BBC to speaking across the world to research foundations.

The monument to Shan Hackett's substantial achievements in life is built on the foundations of classicism, the military virtues, a restless urge to enquire and a deep well of learning. Without in any way limiting his flexibility of mind, he saw very clearly the central importance of continuity and his sight lines both to the past and into the future were sharply focused and deep in extent. He was consistent without neglecting the need, where it arose, for reconsideration and he held firmly to his principles in all his actions. He was approachable, hospitable, companionable, humorous and blessed above all with a partner in life who complemented him perfectly and helped the little man to seem even greater in stature than he in fact was.

In the last analysis, Shan Hackett's epitaph resides in the recollections of the many hundreds of thousands of people from countries all over the world whose lives he influenced and enriched. Each person's memory, however brief or prolonged their contact with Shan might have been, will in their own mind be distinct, different and very special and each of them will be right.

The obituary of him written by a friend and another Queen's Royal Hussar, General John Strawson, and published in the regimental journal ends appropriately with some lines of Wordsworth that Shan himself had read during his winter confinement after Arnhem.

'This is the happy Warrior, this is He
That every Man at arms would wish to be.'

The End

222

BIBLIOGRAPHY

Australia and Antecedents

Ireland Wm O'Connor Morris: CUP 1905
Campus at Crawley Fred Alexander: Univ of West Australia 1963
Long Last Summer Michael Cannon: Nelson 1985
Lady Hackett's Household Guide: Robertson & Mullens 1940
The Corian: (obit) Geelong Grammar School 1997

Arabs and the TJFF

Imperial Policing Charles Gwynn: Macmillan 1939
Palestine and the Great Powers Michael Cohen: Princeton University Press 1982
Birth of Israel Simha Flapan: Parthenon Books (NY) 1987
History of the Hashemite Kingdom: Abu Nowar
Arab-Israeli War 1948 Edgar O'Ballance: Faber & Faber 1956

Arnhem

Arnhem Roy Urquhart Cassell 1958
Men at Arnhem Tom Angus: Leo Cooper 1976
The Devil's Birthday Geoffrey Powell: Buchan & Enright 1984
Surgeon at Arms Daniel Paul (Lippman Kessel): Heinemann 1958
Arnhem 1944 Martin Middlebrook: Penguin 1995
Airborne Forces 1939/45 TBH Otway: IWM 1990
Arnhem AD Harvey: Cassell 2001
A Tour of the Arnhem Battlefields John Waddy: Leo Cooper 1999
I was a Stranger Shan Hackett: Chatto & Windus 1977
It never snows in September Robert Kershaw: Ian Allan 1994
Travel by Dark Graeme Warrack: Harvill Press 1963
Urquhart of Arnhem John Baynes: Brassey's 1993

223

Whitehall

Harding of Petherton Michael Carver: Weidenfeld & Nicolson 1978
Out of Step Michael Carver: Hutchinson 1989
Macmillan Alistair Horne: Macmillan 1989
The Time of My Life Dennis Healey: Michael Joseph 1989

1939/1945 War

Second World War JFC Fuller, Eyre & Spottiswoode 1948
Second World War Vols 1–6 Winston Churchill, Cassell 1951
The War 1939/45 Desmond Flower, Cassell 1960
Knight's Cross David Fraser, Harper-Collins 1993
Crusade in Europe Dwight D Eisenhower, Heinemann 1948
Normandy to the Baltic Bernard Montgomery, BAOR 1946
Private Army Vladimir Peniakoff (Popski), Jonathan Cape 1950

INDEX

Abdiel, HMS, 70
Abdullah, Regent of Iraq, 41
Afrika Corps, ix, 42, 48–49, 51,53
Airborne Division, 1st, 57, 65, 68, 71, 76,
 84, 88, 95, 96, 97, 98, 99, 109, 114,
 125
 6th, 74, 79, 81, 95, 118
Airborne Division, American, 17th, 81
 82nd, 76, 96, 97
 101st, 76, 96, 97
Airlanding Brigade (1), 65, 66, 67, 72,
 99, 115
Alam Halfa Ridge, 55–7
Alamein, *v.* El Alamein
Aldeburgh, 101
Alexandria, 24, 26, 50, 53, 54, 55, 58
Allied Commission for Austria, 165
Andrews, District Commissioner, Galilee,
 35–36
Antwerp, 87
Apeldoorn, 125, 139
Arab Legion, 31, 38, 168
Armoured Brigade (4), 44, 50–51, 57
 (20), 173
Armoured Division, 1st, 49, 54
 6th, 165
 7th, 44, 173, 184
 11th, 53
Armstrong, William, 208
Army Corps (British)
 VIII, 90
 XII, 90
 XIII Corps, 67
 XXX Corps, 49, 56, 57, 89, 97, 109, 115
Army Council, duties and officers, 182
Army Emergency Reserve, 184
Army Group (21st), 89, 91, 109
Army Remount Depot, 78
Arnhem, Battle of, vii, viii, ix, 57, 62, 84
 planning for, 92–97
 v. Market Garden, Operation

Attlee, Clement, 165
Auchinleck, General, 49, 55
Aurora, HMS, 70
Australian Division, 42–43

BBC, English broadcasts, 142
Bagdolio, Marshal, 68
Baker, George, (later Field Marshal), 184,
 189
Baldwin, Captain, 52
Baldwin, Hanson, 178
Balfour Declaration, 28, 31
Balkans, 49
Bar, Australian, 3
 English, 2
 Irish, 2
Barber, Geelong teacher, 11
Barbarossa, Operation, 42
Bardia, 54
Barron, Professor John, 211
Basra, 42, 44
'Bat', SOE agent, 137, 139, 149, 162
Bays, The (2nd Dragoon Guards), 21
Beach, Lt Col. Hugh, (later Gen Sir),
 184–185
Beckett Hall, Shrivenham, 173, 175–176
Beersheba, 29
Beirut, 43
Beisan, 37
Bennecke, General, 188
Berlin blockade, 171
Berlin Wall, 187
Beveland, 91
Beveridge Report, 164
Biesbosch marshes, 157–158, 160
Bir Hackeim, 49, 50, 51
Bittrich, General, 117
Bizerta, 70
Boeree family, Colonel & Mrs, 139–140,
 148, 176
Bohemia, King of, 191

Boise, USS, 70
Boone, Maj Ronnie, 212–213
Border Regiment, 114, 118
Bourg-el-Arab, 61
Bradley, General, 221
Bray, Co. Wicklow, 2
Brereton, Lewis, Lt Gen., 88, 95
British Army of the Rhine, 172, 184, 187
British Army Review, 177
British Expeditionary Force, 41
Browning, Lt Gen. 'Boy', 88, 91, 97, 119
Brussels, 87
Buenos Aires, 209
Burgess, Ted, (later General Sir Edward), 191
Burma, 38
Bury, 173
Business International Network, 210
Bussell, Grace, *v.* Drake-Brockman, Grace
Busselton, 5
Butcher, Mollie, 200

Cairo, 15, 23–27, 29, 50, 55, 58, 60, 61
Cairo Cavalry Brigade, 22–25, 60
Canal Zone, 42, 55
Capuzzo, 61
Carver, Maj Gen. Michael, (later Field Marshal Lord), 183, 186
Caspers, *v.* Elsa
Cassells, Jim, (later Field Marshal), 190
Catroux, General, 43
Caucasus, 42, 55
Cavalry Club, 201
Central School of Arts & Crafts, 17
Château Boulain, 17
Chatto & Windus, publishers, 207
Chesney Gold Medal, 210
Chindits, 38
Chobham, 173
Chrystall, Colonel, 34
Churchill, Winston, 41, 85, 164, 182
Classical Association, The, 203, 204
Clogher, Bishop of, 181
Clydesmuir, Lord, 186
Coberley Mill, vii, 206*ff*
Cold War, commencement, 166, 184
Comet, Operation, 83
Cottesmore, 162
Cox, Christopher, 19, 21, 23
Covent Garden, 16
Crankshaw, Tony, 160
Crete, 42, 44
Crouch, Maj Joel, 161–162
Cuthbertson House, Geelong, 11

Cyprus, 64
Cyrenaica, 48–50
Czechoslovakia, 197

Dalyell, Tam, MP, 192
Dart, Thurston, 201
Damascus, 43
Dawson, Maj Bruce, 102, 111
de Gaulle, General, 41, 43,44, 187, 197
de Guingand, Maj Gen. Freddy, 59, 60
de Nooij family, Ann, John and Mary, ix, 130–139, 144–156, 204, 207
de Nooij, Ko and Zwerus, 143, 148
de Nooij, Wim, 147
des Voeux, Lt Col Sir Richard, 105, 110

Deelen airfield, 96
Delegacy (KCL), 195, 199
Dentz, General, 44
Deraa, 42
'Desert Rats', 44, 173
Dill, General, 29
Doorn, 150
Dorset Regiment, 37, 119
Drake-Brockman, Deborah, 5
Drake-Brockman, Frederick, 5
Drake-Brockman, Grace, 5–8, 9–10, 16, 18, 20
Dragoon Guards (2nd), The Bays, 21
Dreijenscheweg, 104, 105
Driel, 115, 118, 119
Dublin, Trinity College, 2, 16
Dunkirk, 41
Dutch Resistance, ix, 122, 126–127, 133, 139, 140, 150–161
Dyers' Company, and Hall, 206

Ede, 129*ff*; liberation of, 162
Egypt, first experiences of, 15
later posting to, 22–24
Eighth Army, 48, 49, 51, 54 , 55, 60, 61, 67
main faults in desert, 54
Eindhoven, 97
Eisenhower, General, 78, 83, 90
El Agheila, 48–49
El Alamein, 54, 55, 58, 59, 60, 61
first battle of, 55–56
second battle of, 61
Elbe, River, 190
Elsa, guide, 153–154, 156
Emmanuel, King of Italy, 68
English Association, 204
Ermine Street Guard, 211
Esmé Fairbairn Trust, 211

226

Esplanade Hotel, Busselton, 5
Evans, Canon Sidney, 195–196

Fethard, 1
First Allied Airborne Army, 88, 91
Fisher, H. A. L., 18–19, 21, 219
Fitzpatrick, General Sir Desmond, 194
flags *vice* radio communication, 51
flying bomb, *v.* V–1 bomb
Foggia, 71
Foreign Legion, 42
Forrest, Sir John, (later Lord), 4, 5
Fort Capuzzo, 49, 53, 61
Free French, 41–43, 50
Frena, Margaret, 4, *v.*Hackett, Lady

GHQ, Middle East, ix, 59, 60, 61
Galtieri, General, 209–210
Garrick Club, 208
Gay Club (KCL), 201
Gaza, 29
Gazala, 49, 50–4, 55, 56, 57, 58
Geelong Grammar School, 10*ff*, 15, 16, 219
General Election, 1945, 164–165
Geneva Convention, 59
Georgette, sailing vessel, 5
German 1st Parachute Division, 71
German weaponry, 47, 52
Gimblett, Lieut, 52
Ginkel Heath, 102, 128
Gioia, airfield, 72
Glider Pilot Regiment, 66, 120
Glubb, Maj, (later Lt Gen Sir John) 31, 168
Grave, 97
Graves, Robert, 15
Graz, 167
    University, 171–172, 202
Greece, 42, 44, 49
Greek Waters, 210
Green Jacket battalion, 50
Green Jackets, 34, 40
Greenwich, Royal Naval College, 172
Grenoble, University, 16
Groot Ammers, 155, 156
GSO1 Raiding Forces, 59–61
Guards Armoured Division, 89
Guards' Chapel, Birdcage Walk, 86

Hackett, Sir John Winthrop, 2–9, 12, 14, 16, 18
Hackett, Lady, vii, x, 40, 44–45, 73–74, 77, 161–162, 164, 167, 171, 175–177, 181, 189, 201, 205, 210–213
Hackett Post-Graduate Study Centre, 211

Hackett, Shan
    appearance, vii
    birth, 6
    death, 214
    education in Australia, 9–12
    honours and awards, 29, 38, 44, 57, 172, 173, 181, 183, 193
    interviews at Imperial War Museum, 82
    languages, ability with, 17, 24, 26–27, 29–30, 171, 216–217
    leadership qualities, ix
    marriage, 40, 44, 77
    Memorial Service, x, 214
    military education, views on, 179, 181
    sisters, 6, 16, 218
    stepdaughters, 164, 175, 181
    wounded in action, 43, 53, 117, 120
Hackett, Susan Veronica, 164, 167, 172, 175, 210, 212
Haifa, 28, 41, 168
Hailsham, Viscount, 165
Haj Amin, Grand Mufti, 28
Haket, William, 1
Hampshire, sailing vessel, 3
Harkess, Colin, 161
Harlow, Padre, 120
Harmon Memorial Lecture, 202
Harper, Rev. Charles, 3–4
Harper, Prescott, 4–5
Hartenstein Hotel, 120, 212
Haselden, Jock, 58
Hastings, 1
Hayter, Sir William, 203–204, 219
Healey, Denis, 172, 183, 184, 185, 186, 192, 196, 221
Heath, Edward, 205, 206
Heathcoat-Amory, Lt Col. Derick, viii, 101, 111
Hely-Hutchinson, Hon. D. E., 17
Henriques, Basil, Lecture, 202
Heveadorp ferry, 118
Hicks, Brigadier 'Pip', 102, 103, 108
High Trees School, Woolacombe, 77
Himeimat Ridge, 59
Hitler, Adolph, 18, 23, 27–28, 187
    attempted assassination, 87
Hogg, Quintin, (later Lord Hailsham), 165
Hooper, Maj Richard, 36,
Hope, Tim and Bridget, 181, 206, 213
Hopkinson, Maj Gen 'Hoppy',71–72
Hore-Ruthven, Pat, 44
Horrocks, General, 56–57, 89, 119, 196
Howard, Maj John, 79
Howard, Professor Sir Michael, 196, 215

Howard, Philip, 212
Hudson, Dr Helen, 207
Hull, Dick, 189
Hussars (4th), 55
  (4th /8th), 55–57
  (8th) King's Royal Irish, 2, 22, 24, 25–27,
    29, 30, 40, 44, 45, 47, 49–54, 57
  change to armoured regiment, 47, 51
  A Squadron, 47, 52, 54
  B Squadron, 47, 52, 54
  C Squadron, 47, 49, 50–54
  (11th), 22, 29
  (13th/18th), 34
  Queen's Royal Irish Hussars, 176, 203
Hussein, King of Jordan, 31
Huth, Captain, 52–53

Imperial Defence College, 172, 177, 180
Imperial General Staff, 182
Imperial War Museum, 82
Indian medical unit, 53
Indian Motor Brigade (3), 51
Indian Parachute Brigade (50), 63
Infantry Brigade, (HQ 39), 180
  (17), 67
Infantry Division, 1st, 29, 37
  43rd, 119
Inns of Court, 203
IRA, 180
Iraq, 27, 30, 32, 38, 41–42, 55
Iron Curtain, 166
Ismay, General Lord, 182
Italian 4th Dragoons, 26–27
Italy, declaration of war by, 41
  surrender, 68–70
  Western Desert, ix, 25–26, 48
I Was A Stranger, 124, 207

Jellicoe, George, 58
Jennings, R. V., 10
jerricans, 48
Jewish Council, 167
Jewish forces, 58
'Johnny' (Jan), 125–126, 127
Jowett, Doctor, 218

Kabrit, 63
Kalpaks, 58
Kars, local Resistance leader, 155, 156
Kendall, Wallis, 16
Kermit Roosevelt Lecture, 190
Kessel, Captain Lipmann, 121, 122, 124,
  125, 126–128, 138, 151, 152, 160,
  161, 207
khamsin, 24, 50

Kilkelly, Lt Col., 51
King Edward Professor of Music (KCL),
  201, 202
King's College, London, ix, 180, 189, 190,
  193, 195–206, 216
King's Own Scottish Borderers, (7th), 102,
  104, 107, 108, 110, 114, 118
Klas, son of Kars, *q.v.*
Koenig, General, 50
Koepel feature, 105
Kraayenbrink, Dr, 131, 148
Kuchelbacker, 190
Kuneitra, 43

Lancers (12th), 22, 50–51, 60
Lathbury, Brigadier Gerald, (later General
  Sir), 102, 126, 129–130, 135, 162,
  181
Lawrence, T. E., 15, 31
League of Nations, 27, 30
leaguers, 49–50
Lebanon, 30, 41–43
Lechlade, school at, 175
Leeper, Alexander, 2–3

Lees-Knowles lectures 1962, 181, 183, 209
Lichtenstein, Prince Constantine von, 18
Liddell Hart, Basil, 177, 178
Liege, 87
Lisburn Cathedral, 181
Little Cotswell Pigeon Fanciers' Guild, 175
London School of Economics, 197, 205
Longford, Elizabeth, 208
Long Range Desert Group, 58, 60
Lonsdale, Maj, 114, 117
Lord Chancellor's Committee, 203
Loughros, Killibegs, Donegal Bay, 181,
  194–195, 202
Lovat, Lord, 18
Lower Rhine, River, 83
Lowland Division, (52nd), 88, 91
Luftwaffe, 41, 49, 54, 56, 57, 144
Lumsden, General, 54
Luxembourg Cathedral, 191

Maarn, 150, 151
Maas, River, 83
McCreery, Dick (General Sir Richard), 60
Mackenzie, Lt. Col., 102, 103
Macmillan, Harold, 182
Madden, Maj Tiny, 117
Malta, 69
Market Garden, Operation, 57, 82–84, 87,
  89, 115, 176, 178, 221

Marseilles, 15, 16
Massu, General, 188
Maugham Library, 211
May, Maj 'Crackers', 63
Melbourne, University, 3
Melbourne, Trinity College, 3
Memmo, SOE agent, 139; and Sam, 140, 141, 145, 146
Mersa Matruh, 23
Messervy, General, 54
Messina, Straits of, 68
Metcalfe (New College scout), 19
Meuse-Escaut canal, 97
Military Commentators' Circle, 177
'Moaning Minnies', 116
Monck-Mason family, 2
Monte Corvino, airfield, 69
Montgomery, General, 55, 56, 59, 61, 78, 83, 90, 161, 199
Mottola, 72
Moulden, Sir Frank, 9-10, 13, 14, 15-17,18, 20
Mountbatten, Lord Louis, 10, 181, 182, 183, 195
Murray, Colonel, 120
Mussolini, dictator, 41, 68

NATO, 172, 179, 187, 192
Napoleon, viii
National Service (conscription), 199
New College, Oxford, vii, 16-19, 162, 194, 203
Nijmegen, 97, 115
Ninth Army, 40, 44
Noble, Sir Peter, 189, 195, 200
Norfolk, Duke of, 185-186
North Irish Horse Regiment, 176
Northern Army Group of NATO, 187
Northolt, airfield, 161

Oakham, Rutland, 77, 164
O'Connell, David, 202
Old Berkshire Hunt, 175
Oosterbeek, 104, 106, 107, 110, 113, 119, 121, 207
Orne, bridges over, 79
Overlord, 73
    equipment used in, 76
    initial plans, 78-79
    preparations for, 75-76
    role of Hackett in training for, 77
Oxfordshire & Buckinghamshire Light Infantry, 79
Oxford University OTC, 20, 203

Packard, Lt. Gen. Sir Douglas, 180
Pakenham-Walsh family, 2
Padua, 165
Palestine, 27-29, 30-31, 35, 36, 38, 39, 40, 41-42, 44-45
    Jewish immigration to, 27-29, 39, 166
    partition, 29, 30, 168
    UK Mandate surrendered, 168
Palestine Police, 29, 38
Panzer Division, 9th SS, 105, 106, 117
Parachute Brigade, (1), 67, 99, 102, 109, 113, 114, 121
    (2), 73, 102, 109, 114, 115
    (4), 61-62, 68, 69, 70, 71, 72, 76-77, 78, 81, 84, 87, 96, 103, 104, 105, 107, 108, 109, 110, 114, 115
Parachute Division, German, (1st), 71
Parachute Field Ambulance, (133), 64, 103,121
Parachute Regiment, 10th Battalion, 64, 70, 71, 72, 103, 104, 105, 106, 107, 108, 110, 114, 116, 118
    10th Battalion (Territorial Army), 203
    11th Battalion, 64, 103, 109, 113, 114, 117
    151st Battalion, 63
    156th Battalion, 63, 64, 70, 71, 72, 103, 104, 105, 108, 110, 116, 118
Pas de Calais, 75
Patton, General, 82
Peake, Colonel, 31, 38
Pearson, Sergeant, 120
Peel Commission, 36
Peenemunde, 87
Pembroke, Earl of, 1
Penelope, HMS, 70
Persian Gulf, 42, 44
Perth, Western Australia, 4, 6
Phillips, Major, 52
Piet, Dutch Resistance, 158-160
Poliakoff, Maj, 60, 71
Polish Independent Parachute Brigade Group, 83, 84, 88, 91, 96, 107, 115, 118, 119
Ponte di Primosole, Catania, 67
Ponte Grande, Syracuse, 66
'Popski's Private Army', 60
Pott, Maj John, 105
Powell, Maj Geoffrey, 104, 112, 118, 119
Prague Spring, 196
Prince of Wales, HRH, 10, 212
'private armies', 57-8
Profession of Arms, The, 209
Pulford, Ian, 213
Punch table, 42

Qattara Depression, 55, 59
Queen's College, Belfast, 183, 194
Queen's Own Highlanders, 195
Queen's Royal Irish Hussars, 176, 203
Queripel, Captain Lionel, 107, 110

Radcliffe Infirmary, Oxford, 162
Radio Orange (BBC), 142
Ragged Robin III, 177
Raiding Forces, 59–60
Ramat David, 63
Rashid, 36–37
Rashid Ali, 41–42
Rathmacarthy, 1
Redman, Theo, 151
Reggio, 68
Renkum, 134, 154
Resistance Groups, 92
Ritson, Maj Teddy, 111
Roberts, Sir Frank, 187, 189–190
Roberts, Col. 'Pip', (later Maj Gen), 53
Rommel, Field Marshal Erwin, 42, 44, 48,
    49–50, 53, 54, 55–56, 58, 59, 61
Royal Air Force, 56, 58
  Amman, 32
  Volunteer Reserve, 20
Royal Air Force Groups, (38, 46), 88
Royal Army Educational Corps, 164
Royal Army Medical Corps, 117, 121, 139
Royal Engineers, 4 Parachute Squadron, 64
Royal Horse Artillery, 50
Royal Naval Hospital, Alexandria, 53, 54
Royal Navy, 57, 58
Royal Sussex Regiment, 2nd Battalion, 64
Royal Tank Regiment (3), 53–54
Royal Ulster Constabulary, 180
Royal Ulster Rifles, 37
Royal United Services Institution, 177
Royal visits to Ireland, 1961–2, 181

SAS, 58, 60, 61, 80, 92
SHAEF, 88, 89, 91
Sacred Squadron, 58
St Elizabeth Hospital, Oosterbeek, 117,
    120–122, 127
St Faith's Chapel, Westminster Abbey, 212
Saladin thesis, 25, 219
Salerno, 69
Sandhurst, 22
Sarona, 40
Scheldt Estuary, 91, 178
Schoenbrunn Palace, Vienna, 166
Schoonhoven, 154
Shepheard's Hotel, Cairo, 24

Shrivenham, Royal Military College of
    Science, (RMCS), 173–179
  educational standards at, 174
Sidgwick & Jackson, publishers, 208
Sidi Barrani, 48
Sikh, HMS, destroyer, 58
Sinai, 29
Sliedrecht, 155, 156, 157, 160
Smyth, Ken, Lt Col., 64, 105, 114, 122,
    128
Somerset House, London, 195
Somerton, Neil, 200
Sosabowski, General, 83, 96, 119
South Staffordshire Regiment, 66, 102, 109
Special Boat Service, 58
Station Road, Ede, 139–140
Stirling, David, 58, 61, 161
Stirling, General Sir William, 187
Stoke-on-Trent, 173
Strawson, Major General John, 222
Suez Canal, 41
Swan Hellenic Tours, 210
Swan River, Western Australia, 3
Sullivan, D.M., 12
Swindon, 173
Sykes-Picot agreement, 31
Syracuse, Sicily, 66

Taranto, 69, 70, 72
ter Horst, Kate and Sophie, 215
Territorial Army, 184
  Council of Territorial and Auxiliary
      Forces Associations, 185–186
Territorial and Army Reserve, 186, 203
Thatcher, Margaret, 205
The Third World War (fiction), 191, 208
The Third World War; The Untold Story, 209
Thomas, General, 119
Thomas, Maj Micky, 64
Thompson, Lt Col., Sheriff, 114, 117
Thornton, Charlie, 206
Tiberias, 32, 40
  Hotel in, 40, 64, 167
  Lake, 64
Time of My Life, The, 221
Times, London, The, 17, 42, 192, 209
Tobruk, 49, 55, 58, 59 ,60
Torenstraat, No. 5, Ede, 131–138
Transfigure, Operation, 81, 82
Trans-Jordan Frontier Force, (TJFF), ix,
    31–44
  compensation for soldiers, 169–170
  disbandment, 169–70
  HQ at Zerka, 32, 34, 41, 167
  transfer to War Office, 32, 168

230

uniform, 32, 35
withdrawal to Jordan, 169
Tipperary, County of, 1
Trinity College, Cambridge, 181
Tripoli, 4–9, 55, 57
Tunis, 60
Tunisia, 42, 67
Tuxedo, Operation, 81
Twenty-first Army Group, 89, 161
Tyre, 42

Ultra (Enigma), 92
Umm-al-Walad, 43
University Grants Committee, 196
University of Western Australia, 6, 8, 12,
    183, 196
Urquhart, Maj Gen Roy, 83, 102, 103, 106,
    108, 114, 117, 120, 212, 221
Urquhart, Maj Brian, 93, 176–177
US Airborne Division, (17th), 88
    (82nd), 65, 68, 83, 91
    (101st), 83, 91
US Air Force Academy, Colorado, 202
US Army (3rd), 82, 83
US Troop Carrier Command, (IX), 88
    7 Squadron, 64
Utrecht, 148

V–1 bomb, 86, 142–143
V–2 rocket, 86–7, 143
van Arnhem, Piet, 126–7, 145, 161
van Roekel, Chris, 212–213
Vandyck, Jan, agent, 146, 147, 151–152,
    162
Vichy Government and forces, ix, 41–44
Vienna, 165–167
Vietnam, 187, 197

von Kielmannsegg, General Graf, 188

Waal, River, 83, 15, 158, 163
Waddy, Maj John, 72, 105
Wafd party, 24
Walcheren, 91
Warrack, Colonel Graeme, 117, 120, 145,
    151, 152, 156, 160
Warrenpoint, 195
Warter, Digby Tatham, 135
Washington, 41
Waterford, 2
Wavell, Gen, viii, 42, 48
Way, Sir Richard, 206
Way, Sam, 189
Weizmann, Dr, 31
West Australian and *Western Mail*, 3, 4
Westerbowing heights, 118, 119
Westminster Hospital, 16
Weygand, General, 42
White House position, 114, 118
William of Normandy, King William I, 1
Wilson, Harold, 196, 205
Wilson, General 'Jumbo', (later Field
    Marshal Lord), 40
Wingate, Orde, 38
Winthrop family, 2
Wolfenden, Sir John, 196
Wolfheze, 106, 108, 110

Yugoslavia under Tito, 166

Zerka, 32, 34, 41, 167
Zionists, 28, 38, 39, 168
Zoo, London, 14
    Perth, 6, 14
Zulu, HMS, destroyer, 58